T0184619

# Lecture Notes in Computer Science 11739

More information about this subseries at http://www.springer.com/series/7410

Thomas Groß · Theo Tryfonas (Eds.)

# Socio-Technical Aspects in Security and Trust

9th International Workshop, STAST 2019
Luxembourg City, Luxembourg, September 26, 2019
Revised Selected Papers

 Springer

*Editors*
Thomas Groß 🆔
Computing
Newcastle University
Newcastle upon Tyne, UK

Theo Tryfonas
Faculty of Engineering
Bristol University
Bristol, UK

ISSN 0302-9743          ISSN 1611-3349   (electronic)
Lecture Notes in Computer Science
ISBN 978-3-030-55957-1          ISBN 978-3-030-55958-8   (eBook)
https://doi.org/10.1007/978-3-030-55958-8

LNCS Sublibrary: SL4 – Security and Cryptology

This Springer imprint is published by the registered company Springer Nature Switzerland AG
The registered company address is: Gewerbestrasse 11, 6330 Cham, Switzerland

# Preface

The 9th International Workshop on Socio-Technical Aspects in Security (STAST 2019) aimed at stimulating research on systems secure in the real work and in the interplay with real users. The term "socio-technical," in this context, meant a reciprocal relationship between technology and people. Inherently, a workshop like this brought together members from different security sub-communities and was multidisciplinary and interdisciplinary by nature.

Indeed, there was a considerable diversity in submissions received, in terms of topics addressed as well as in methodologies employed. There were a number of submissions establishing and reflecting on research methodology. We received 4 systematic analyses of security protocols, partially based on formal methods and partially based on cryptography, as well as an attack paper for a real-world system. There were a range of submissions on human factors, including eye tracking studies, true experiments, as well as field studies. Finally, we received 7 review papers, systematic literature reviews, and surveys. In terms of methodologies, there were 15 submissions with a qualitative approach. Of the other 13 submissions, 4 relied on formal or cryptographic methods to support their argument, while 9 used statistical inference.

The peer-review process was conducted in a double-blind fashion. Each submission received a minimum of three reviews. Papers with diverging opinions were assigned additional reviews and received up to five reviews in total. On average, 3.3 reviews per paper were written. Peer-reviewing for each submission included an active discussion phase facilitated by a designated discussion lead. The discussion lead subsequently summarized the Program Committee members' discussion and conclusions in a meta-review, made available to the authors.

Of the 28 papers submitted to the workshop, we accepted the 10 publications presented in this volume, at an acceptance rate of 36%. We organized these works in three coherent chapters. First, "Methods for Socio-Technical Systems" focused on instruments, frameworks, and reflections on research methodology. Second, "System Security" considered security analyses and attacks on security systems. Finally, "Privacy Control" incorporated works on privacy protection and control as well as human factors in relation to these topics.

We recognized Albëse Demjaha, Simon Parkin, and David Pym with the STAST 2019 Best Paper Award for their paper "You've left me no choices," found on page 65 of this volume.

Overall, we found rewarding the spectrum of topics as well as the quality of accepted papers in this volume. Finally, we would like to thank the authors for their submissions and express our great gratitude to the Program Committee members and reviewers whose diligent work made this volume possible.

April 2020

Thomas Groß
Theo Tryfonas

# Message from the Workshop Organizers

STAST 2019 reaches a culmination both in terms of number of submissions and in terms of research quality. Contributions are illuminating and at the same time ground-breaking. The selection process was tough and proficiently conducted by the program chair – at every single stage. These objective observations make us organizers all the more proud to continue the endeavor of organizing this series of workshops.

It is also clear that the European Symposium on Research in Computer Security (ESORICS)—has given STAST the venue that it truly deserves. ESORICS is the most established European research symposium in the area of cybersecurity, privacy, and trust, and as such offers mutual benefit to an event with the focus of STAST.

After all, the pivotal role of the human users in the face of cybersecurity measures is never overstated. For example, a recent, eminent document by ENISA entitled "Cybersecurity Culture Guidelines: Behavioural Aspects of Cybersecurity" definitively leverages models of cyber-security attitudes and behavior to ground cybersecurity culture precisely in the very users of technology.

Finally, we would like to take this opportunity to thank the program chairs Thomas Groß and Theo Tryfonas for their top-quality, impeccable work, all Program Committee members, contributing authors, as well as ESORICS for the subsidiary organizations. STAST was great this year!

April 2020

Giampaolo Bella
Gabriele Lenzini

# Organization

## General Chairs

| | |
|---|---|
| Giampolo Bella | University of Catania, Italy |
| Gabriele Lenzini | University of Luxembourg, Luxembourg |

## Program Committee Chairs

| | |
|---|---|
| Theo Tryfonas | University of Bristol, UK |
| Thomas Groß | Newcastle University, UK |

## Program Committee

| | |
|---|---|
| Esma Aimeur | University of Montreal, Canada |
| Luca Allodi | TU/e Eindhoven, The Netherlands |
| Kalliopi Anastasopoulou | University of Bristol, UK |
| Panagiotis Andriotis | University of the West of England, UK |
| Karla Badillo-Urquiola | University of Central Florida, USA |
| Peter Bednar | Portsmouth University, UK |
| Zinaida Benenson | University of Erlangen-Nuremberg, Germany |
| Michael Carter | Queen's University, UK |
| Lizzie Coles-Kemp | Royal Holloway University of London, UK |
| Sarah Diesburg | University of Northern Iowa, USA |
| Jaroslav Dockal | Masaryk University, Czech Republic |
| Rosario Giustolisi | IT University of Copenhagen, Denmark |
| Pieter Hartel | University of Twente, The Netherlands |
| Ulrike Hugl | University of Innsbruck, Austria |
| Markus Jakobsson | Amber Solutions, USA |
| Maria Karyda | University of the Aegean, Greece |
| Spyros Kokolakis | University of the Aegean, Greece |
| Stewart Kowalski | Norwegian University of Science and Technology, Norway |
| Kat Krol | Google, UK |
| Shujun Li | University of Kent, UK |
| Jean Martina | Universidade Federal de Santa Catarina, Brazil |
| Maryam Mehrnezhad | Newcastle University, UK |
| Masakatsu Nishigaki | Shizuoka University, Japan |
| Jason Nurse | University of Kent, UK |
| Simon Parkin | University College London, UK |
| Saša Radomirovic | University of Dundee, UK |
| Karen Renaud | Abertay University, UK |
| Peter Y. A. Ryan | University of Luxembourg, Luxembourg |

| | |
|---|---|
| Elizabeth Stobert | Concordia University, Canada |
| Kerry-Lynn Thomson | Nelson Mandela Metropolitan University, South Africa |
| Luca Vigaò | King's College London, UK |
| Melanie Volkamer | Karlsruhe Institute of Technology, Germany |
| Emma Williams | University of Bristol, UK |
| Konrad Wrona | NCI Agency, Military University of Technology in Warsaw, Poland |

## Additional Reviewers

Diego Sempreboni
Itzel Vazquez Sandoval
Marie-Laure Zollinger

## Sponsors

securityandtrust.lu

UNIVERSITÉ DU
LUXEMBOURG

# Contents

# Methods for Socio-Technical Systems

# Fidelity of Statistical Reporting in 10 Years of Cyber Security User Studies

Thomas Groß[✉]

Newcastle University, Newcastle upon Tyne, UK
thomas.gross@newcastle.ac.uk

**Abstract.** Studies in socio-technical aspects of security often rely on user studies and statistical inferences on investigated relations to make their case. They, thereby, enable practitioners and scientists alike to judge on the validity and reliability of the research undertaken.

To ascertain this capacity, we investigated the reporting fidelity of security user studies.

Based on a systematic literature review of 114 user studies in cyber security from selected venues in the 10 years 2006–2016, we evaluated fidelity of the reporting of 1775 statistical inferences using the R package statcheck. We conducted a systematic classification of incomplete reporting, reporting inconsistencies and decision errors, leading to multinomial logistic regression (MLR) on the impact of publication venue/year as well as a comparison to a compatible field of psychology.

We found that half the cyber security user studies considered reported incomplete results, in stark difference to comparable results in a field of psychology. Our MLR on analysis outcomes yielded a slight increase of likelihood of incomplete tests over time, while SOUPS yielded a few percent greater likelihood to report statistics correctly than other venues.

In this study, we offer the first fully quantitative analysis of the state-of-play of socio-technical studies in security. While we highlight the impact and prevalence of incomplete reporting, we also offer fine-grained diagnostics and recommendations on how to respond to the situation.

**Keywords:** User studies · SLR · Cyber security · Statistical reporting

## 1 Introduction

Statistical inference is the predominant method to ascertain that effects observed in socio-technical aspects of security are no mere random flukes, but considered to be "the real McCoy."

In general, statistical inference sets out to evaluate a statistical hypothesis stated *a priori*. It employs observations made in studies to establish the likelihood as extreme as or more extreme than the observations made, assuming the statistical hypothesis not to be true. This likelihood is colloquially referred to as

---

Preregistered at the Open Science Framework: osf.io/549qn/.

© Springer Nature Switzerland AG 2021
T. Groß and T. Tryfonas (Eds.): STAST 2019, LNCS 11739, pp. 3–26, 2021.
https://doi.org/10.1007/978-3-030-55958-8_1

a $p$-value. Alternatively to Null Hypothesis Significance Testing (NHST)—and often used complementarily—studies may estimate the magnitude of effects in reality and confidence intervals thereon [5].

The onus of proof is generally on the authors of a study. There are numerous factors influencing whether a study's results can be trusted—a) sound research questions and hypotheses, b) vetted and reliable constructs and instruments, c) documentation favoring reproducibility, d) sound experiment design, yielding internal and external validity, e) randomization and blinding, f) systematic structured and standardized reporting—in the end, it is the outcomes of the statistical inference that often render a final verdict.

These outcomes do not only indicate whether an effect is likely present in reality or not. They also yield what magnitude the effect is estimated at. Thereby, they are the raw ingredient for (i) establishing whether an effect is practically relevant, (ii) evaluating its potential for reuse, and (iii) including it further quantitative research synthesis.

While there have been a number of publications in socio-technical aspects of security offering guidance to the community to that end [2,4,11,15,17] as well as proposals in other communities [1,10,12], the evidence of the state-of-play of the field has been largely anecdotal [17] or in human-coded analysis [3]. While this field is arguably quite young, we argue that it would benefit greatly from attention to statistical reporting, from attaining fault tolerance through reporting fidelity and from preparing for research synthesis (cf. Sect. 2.1).

In this study, we aim at systematically evaluating the fidelity of statistical reporting in socio-technical aspects of security. We analyze (i) whether statistical inferences are fault-tolerant, in the sense of their internal consistency being publicly verifiable, and (ii) whether the reported $p$-values are correct. Through the semi-automated empirical analysis of 114 publications in the field from 2006–2016, we offer a wealth of information including meta-aspects. We compare statistical reporting fidelity of this field with a related field of psychology as well as analyze the trajectory of the field, that is, the trends found over time. We substantiate the these results with qualitative coding of errors observed to elucidate what to watch out for.

*Contributions.* We are the first to subject our own field to a systematic empirical analysis of statistical reporting fidelity. In that, we offer a well-founded introspection in the field of socio-technical aspects of security that can serve program committees and authors alike to inform their research practice.

## 2 Background

### 2.1 Importance and Impact of Statistical Reporting

Null Hypothesis Significance Testing (NHST) establishes statistical inference by stating *a priori* statistical hypotheses, which are then tested based on observations made in studies. Such statistical inference results in a $p$-value, which gives the conditional probability of finding data as extreme as or more extreme than the observations made, assuming the null hypothesis being true. Many fields combine NHST with point and interval estimation, that is, establishing an estimate of the magnitude of the effect in the population and the confidence interval thereon.

**Table 1.** Degrees of fidelity in statistical reporting for the same two-tailed independent-samples $t$-test on a relation with a large effect size (ES). *Note:* $\bigcirc$ = impossible $\circ\!\!\!\bullet$ = can be estimated $\bullet$ = supported

|  | Incomplete triplet | | Complete triplet | |
|---|---|---|---|---|
|  | Sig. | $p$-Value | ES inferrable | ES explicit |
| Example | $p < .05$ | $p = .019$ | $t(24) = 2.52$ , $p = .019$ | $t(24) = 2.52, p = .019$, Hedges' $g = 0.96$, CI $[0.14, 1.76]$ |
| $p$ quantifiable | $\bigcirc$ | $\bullet$ | $\bullet$ | $\bullet$ |
| Cross-checkable | $\bigcirc$ | $\bigcirc$ | $\bullet$ | $\bullet$ |
| ES quantifiable | $\bigcirc$ | $\bigcirc$ | $\circ\!\!\!\bullet$ | $\bullet$ |
| Synthesizable | $\bigcirc$ | $\bigcirc$ | $\circ\!\!\!\bullet$ | $\bullet$ |

**Reporting Fidelity and Fault Tolerance.** Different reporting practices yield different degrees of information and fidelity. It goes without saying that a simple comparison with the significance level $\alpha$, e.g., by stating that $p < .05$, yields the least information and the least fidelity. Reporting the actual $p$-value observed offers more information as well as a means to quantify the likelihood of the effect.

To gain further reporting fidelity and fault tolerance, one would not only report the exact $p$-value, but also the chosen test parameters (e.g., independent-samples or one-tailed), the test statistic itself (e.g., the $t$-value) and the degrees of freedom ($df$) of the test. We, then, obtain a consistent triplet (test statistic, $df$, $p$-value) along with the test parameters. Table 1 exemplifies degrees of fidelity.

The upshot of a diligent reporting procedure including full triplets is that it enables cross-checks on their internal consistency and, thereby, a degree of fault tolerance. Vice versa, if only the $p$-value or a comparison with a significance level is reported, the capacity to validate inferences is impaired.

**Impact on Research Synthesis.** Published studies usually do not stand on their own. To learn what relations are actually true in reality and to what degree, we commonly need to synthesize the results of multiple studies investigating the same relations. More mature fields (such as evidence-based medicine or psychology) engage in systematic reviews and meta analyses to that end.

For these down-stream analyses to be viable, the original studies need to contain sufficient data for subsequent meta-analyses. If the original studies omit the actual test statistics and degrees of freedom, the synthesis in meta analyses is hamstringed or rendered impossible altogether.

## 2.2  Reporting and Methodology Guidelines

Reporting fidelity is usually one of the goals of reporting standards. Given that the field of socio-technical research in cyber security is a young and does not have its own established reporting standards, it is worthwhile to consider ones of other fields. Psychology seems a sound candidate to consider as a guiding example in this study. Other fields, such as behavioral economics, are equally viable.

The publication guidelines of the American Psychology Association (APA) [1] require that inferences are reported with their full test statistics and degrees of freedom. Exact $p$-values are preferred. The APA guidelines require to report appropriate effect sizes and their confidence intervals.

Of course, there are also methodological guidelines that go far beyond reporting statistical tests. For instance, the CONSORT guidelines [12] cover reporting for randomized trials. Furthermore, recently LeBel et al. [10] proposed a unified framework to quantify and support credibility of scientific findings.

Even though socio-technical aspects of security is a young field, there have been initiatives to advance research methodology, considered in chronological order: (i) In 2007, Peisert and Bishop [15] offered a short position paper scientific design of security experiments. (ii) Maxion [11] focused on making experiments dependable, focusing on the hallmarks of good experiments with an eye on validity. (iii) In 2013, Schechter [17] considered common pitfalls seen in SOUPS submissions and made recommendation on avoiding them, incl. statistical reporting and multiple-comparison corrections. (iv) Coopamootoo and Groß proposed an introduction for evidence-based methods [4], incl. sound statistical inference and structured reporting. (v) The same authors published an experiment design and reporting toolset [2], considering nine areas with reporting considerations, incl. test statistics and effect sizes.

## 2.3  Analysis of Statistical Reporting

We analyze statistical reporting of publications with the R package statcheck [7]. The statcheck tool extracts Strings of the form $ts(df) = x, p$ op $y$, where $ts$ is the test statistic, $df$ the degrees of freedom, and op a infix relation, such as, $<$. It recognizes $t$, $F$, $r$, $\chi^2$, and $z$ as test statistics and recomputes the corresponding $p$-values from them. It, hence, enables a consistency check of reported triplets of test statistic, degrees of freedom and $p$-values.

In this analysis, statcheck recognizes one-tailed tests to some extent from searching keywords and computing if a test were valid if considered one-tailed. It adheres to the rounding guidelines of the American Psychology Association (APA) [1]. Nuijten et al. [13] concede that statcheck does not recognize $p$-values adjusted for multiple-comparison corrections.

While the creators of statcheck have argued for its validity and reliability [13,14], the tool faced scrutiny and controversy [18] over its false positive and false negative rates. Schmidt [18], for example, criticized that statcheck's inability to recognize corrected $p$-values, such as from Greenhouse-Geisser corrections. Lakens [9] found reported errors typically to be minor.

For this study, we prepare to mitigate possible statcheck mis-classifications by manually checking and coding its outcomes.

## 2.4   Related Works

In 2016/17 Coopamootoo and Groß [3] conducted a Systematic Literature Review (SLR) on cyber security user studies published in the years between 2006–2016. This research was first presented at a 2017 community meeting of the UK Research Institute in the Science of Cyber Security (RISCS). Their study contained three parts: (i) the SLR itself, yielding a sample of 146 cyber security papers, (ii) a qualitative coding of nine "completeness indicators," based on an *a priori* codebook. (iii) a quantitative analysis on a sub-sample using parametric tests on differences between means (e.g., $t$-tests).

While this study uses the same set of papers as a sample to enable a comparison of results, this study takes an entirely different approach to the analysis: (i) Instead of manual coding of reporting completeness, we focus on the automated analysis reporting fidelity on extracted $p$-values, (ii) we evaluate quantitative properties on inconsistencies and decision errors of a large part of the sample, and (iii) we obtain a fine-grained understanding of "things going wrong" through grounded coding,

## 3   Aims

We define the classes of statcheck outcomes for test statistics and papers.

### Definition 1 (SC Outcome Categories)

*Individual Tests: SCOutcome has the following cases for individual tests:*

1. *CorrectNHST: The NHST is reported with its test statistic triplet. The given triplet is correct, where "correct" is defined as matching triplet of test statistic, degrees of freedom and corresponding re-computed p-value.*
2. *Inconsistency: The reported triplet (test statistic, df, p-value) is inconsistent.*
3. *DecisionError: The reported triplet (test statistic, df, p-value) is grossly inconsistent, that is, the re-computed p-value leads to a different decision on rejecting the null hypothesis.*
4. *Incomplete: A p-values is reported without sufficient data for an evaluation of the triplet (test statistic, df, p-value).*

*Entire Papers: SCOutcome has the following cases for aggregated over papers:*

1. *CorrectNHST: There exist one or more NHSTs reported with correct test statistic triplets. The given complete triplets are correct throughout, where "correct" is defined as matching triplet of test statistic, degrees of freedom and corresponding re-computed p-value. A paper can be classified as CorrectNHST even if there exist incomplete test statistics.*

2. *Inconsistency: There exists an inconsistent triplet (test statistic, df, p-value).*
3. *DecisionError: There exists a gross inconsistency in any reported triplet (test statistic, df, p-value), in which a re-computed p-value leads to a different decision on rejecting the null hypothesis.*
4. *Incomplete: For all p-values reported, it holds that there is insufficient data for a correct triplet (test statistic, df, p-value). For a paper classified as Incomplete, there is not a single p-value with complete test statistic found.*

*We call Complete the complement of Incomplete.*

**RQ 1 (Prevalence).** *How many papers report on Null Hypothesis Significance Testing (NHST) and fall into one of the defined SC outcome categories according to Definition 1 1. CorrectNHST, 2. Inconsistency, 3. DecisionError, 4. Incomplete. Which papers use 1. multiple-comparison corrections (MCC), 2. effect sizes.*

While we originally investigated the use of Amazon Mechanical Turk (AMT) and similar recruiting services, we have declared this aim out of scope for this publication. MCCs and effect sizes are also relevant in relation to power and Positive Predictive Value (PPV) of the studies in question, however, we will consider these inquiries in future work.

We intend to compare the statcheck results in this field with analyses that have been conducted in other fields that seem related. We are most interested in fields at the intersection of human behavior and technology, such as HCI. Granted that statcheck surveys have not been that widely conducted yet, we consider the *Journal of Media Psychology (JMP)* [6] as a primary candidate. This choice is made because of similarities

(i) media psychology is concerned with human subjects and socio-technical aspects,
(ii) media psychology includes topics that might also have been published in user studies in cyber security, such as adversarial behavior (e.g., violence) vis-à-vis of HCI, cyber bullying, behavior on social media,
(iii) media psychology is a relatively young field, JMP having been founded in 1989 and gained its current name 2008.

The distinct difference we are interested in is that JMP is subject to reporting standards (APA). We note that the selection of JMP as comparison sample may be controversial and that—at the same time—comparisons to further fields are easily done, yet out of the scope for this study.

**RQ 2 (Comparison).** *To what extent do the statcheck SCOutcomes differ between our sample in this field and a comparable field in psychology?*
$H_{c,0}$: *The distribution of the SCOutcomes in cyber security user studies is the same as the distribution in the comparison field.* $H_{c,1}$: *There is a systematic difference of SCOutcome in cyber security user studies to the comparison field.*

**RQ 3 (Influence of Venue and Year).** *Considering outcome categories SCOutcome from Definition 1 as response variable, what is the influence of predictors publication Venue and Year?*

1. $H_{V,0}$: *There is no influence of the publication* **Venue** *on the occurrence of the* **statcheck** *outcome* **SCOutcome.** $H_{V,1}$: *There is a systematic influence of the publication* **Venue** *on the occurrence of the* **statcheck** *outcome* **SCOutcome.**
2. $H_{Y,0}$: *There is no influence of the publication* **Year** *on the occurrence of the* **statcheck** *outcome* **SCOutcome.** $H_{Y,1}$: *There is a systematic influence of the publication* **Year** *on the occurrence of the* **statcheck** *outcome* **SCOutcome.**

As an exploratory inquiry, we employ the statcheck analysis to the submissions of STAST 2019, testing its usefulness in supporting PC members.

## 4 Method

The study has been pre-registered at the Open Science Framework (OSF)[1], which also contains Online Supplementary Materials, such as a summary of the SLR specification and the sample itself. All analyses, graphs and tables are computed directly from the data with the R package knitr, where the statcheck output was cached in csv files.

All statistical tests are computed at a significance level of $\alpha = .05$. The Fisher Exact Tests (FETs) for cases with low expected cell frequency are computed with simulated $p$-values with $10^5$ replicates.

### 4.1 Ethics

This study followed the guidelines of the ethical boards of its institution. While we make the entire list of analyzed papers available for reproducibility, we decided not to single out individual papers. We are aware that the descriptive statistics presented allow making a link to the respective papers; we accept that residual privacy risk. *Full disclosure:* one of the sample's papers belongs to the author of this study; statcheck flagged it.

### 4.2 Sample

The target population of this study was cyber security user studies. The sampling frame for this study is derived from a 2016/17 Systematic Literature Review (SLR) conducted by Coopamootoo and Groß [3] whose results were first published at a 2017 Community Meeting of the Research Institute in the Science of Cyber Security (RISCS). This source SLR's search, inclusion and exclusion criteria are reported in Online Supplementary Materials.

We have chosen this sample to gain comparability to earlier qualitative and quantitative analyses on it [3]. This sample restricts the venues considered to retain statistical power for a regression analysis. We stress that the automated the analysis methodology can be easily applied to other samples.

---

[1] osf.io/549qn/.

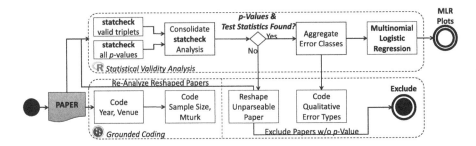

**Fig. 1.** Flow chart of the study's procedure with two interlinked analyses.

## 4.3  Procedure

Our procedure, as depicted in Fig. 1, constituted a mixed-methods approach that fusing two interlinked analysis processes: (i) Statistical Validity Analysis and (ii) Grounded Coding of paper properties and errors detected. Our analysis script received as input the PDFs of studies included from the source SLR.

*Statistical Validity Analysis.* We computed two iterations of statcheck, one only considering statistical statements in standard format and one including all $p$-values found. The statcheck results were subjected to a manual cross-check, possibly resulting the reshaping of papers that statcheck could not parse out of the box. Subsequently, we merged the results of both analyses and aggregated their events (counting number of correct tests, inconsistencies, decision errors and $p$-values without parseable test statistics). We, thereby, established the dependent variable SCOutput per statistical test and per paper.

*Grounded Coding.* We coded paper properties in NVivo. We evaluated the statcheck results in a second lane of grounded coding, classifying errors of statcheck as well as errors committed by authors of the papers.

As a part of this analysis, we "reshape" papers that could not be parsed by statcheck for reasons outside of the research aims of this study. For instance, if a paper embedded statistical tests as image rather than text, we would transcribe the images to text and re-run statcheck on the "reshaped" input.

Once these results are coded, we amend the statcheck outcomes recorded in SCOutcome to ensure that this variable reflects an accurate representation of the sample.

## 4.4  Grounded Coding

Grounded coding refers to the code being grounded in properties found in the data, instead of being based on an *a priori* codebook.

*Paper Properties.* We conducted a systematic coding in NVivo with the purpose to establish overall properties of all papers. We were extracting especially: (i) sample size, (ii) use of multiple-comparison corrections, and (iii) use of dependent-samples tests.

*Analysis Outcomes.* After having run statcheck on the sample, we first conducted a grounded coding of statistical tests marked as inconsistency or decision error. We re-computed the $p$-values from the test statistics ourselves and interpreted the results in the context of the reporting of the paper. We took into account the formulation around the test as well as overall specification of hypotheses, test parameters (e.g., one-tailed) and multiple-comparison corrections. We include the resulting emergent codebook presented in Table 2.

Secondly, we analyzed the outcomes statcheck marked as neither inconsistency nor decision error. For those results, we compared the raw text with statcheck's parsed version as well as recomputed $p$-value. We ignored small rounding differences as statcheck as authors rounding test statistics for reporting will naturally cause small differences. In cases of a mismatch between raw text and interpretation (e.g., in degrees of freedom accounted for), we re-computed the statistics manually.

Finally, we coded whether a mistake by statcheck would be considered a FalsePositive or FalseNegative. After this evaluation, we adjusted the SCOutcome to ensure that the subsequent analysis is based on a correct representation of the sample.

**Table 2.** Codebook of the grounded coding of error types.

| Errors of statcheck | | Errors of authors | |
|---|---|---|---|
| Code | Definition | Code | Definition |
| scParsedOK | parsed the PDF correctly | Typo | Likely mis-typed |
| scCorrect | statcheck result validated | RoundingError | incorrect rounding rules |
| scMisclassified | misclassified test | OneTailedUS | unspecified one-tailed test |
| scMissedMC | missed multiple-comparison corrections specified paper | Miscalculation | miscalculated the statistics, wrong $p$-value for statistic |

## 4.5   Evaluation of statcheck

Appendix A contains the details of the corresponding qualitative coding.

*Reshaping of Unparseable Papers.* There were eight of papers for which statcheck could neither extract $p$-values nor test statistics due to encoding issues (e.g., embedding statistics as images). For all of those, we recorded them as unparseable, yet transformed them into parseable text files for further analysis.

**Table 3.** Confusion matrix for statcheck evaluating tests.

| Predicted | Reference | |
|---|---|---|
| | Positive | Negative |
| Positive | 29 | 5 |
| Negative | 0 | 218 |

Accuracy: .98, 95% CI [.95, .99],
$Acc > NIR(.88), < .001***$,
Sensitivity $= 1.00$, Specificity $=$
.98, PPV $= .85$, $F_1 = .92$

*Errors Committed by statcheck.* Of the total 252 parsed tests, 34 contained an error, 10 of which a decision error. We compared those outcomes against the grounded coding of results and our re-computation of the statistics.

We found that (i) statcheck parsed papers that were correctly reported without fail, (ii) it misclassified two tests, (iii) it detected one-tailed tests largely correctly, (iv) it treated dependent-samples tests correctly, (v) it did not recognize the specified multiple-comparison corrections in three cases. This leaves us with 5 false positives and no false negatives, marked in Sub-Fig. 8a.

*Detection Performance of statcheck.* For the analysis of complete test triplets, we analyzed the confusion matrix of statcheck results vs. our coding (Table 3). The Positive Predictive Value (PPV) of 85.3% indicates a decent likelihood of a positive statcheck report being true.

### 4.6   Multinomial Logistic Regression

We conducted multinomial logistic regressions with the R package nnet [16], relying on Fox's work [8] for visualization. The models were null, year-only, venue-only and year and venue combined. The dependent variables was SCOutput. The independent variables were Year (interval) and Venue (factor).

## 5   Results

### 5.1   Sample

We have refined the inputted sample of 146 publications by excluding publications that do neither contain empirical data nor significance tests ($p$-value), retaining 114 publications for further analysis. We illustrate the sample refinement in Table 4. We include the final sample in the Online Supplementary Materials and outline its distribution by publication venue and year in Table 5. We note that the sample is skewed towards SOUPS and more recent publications. We note that the sample was drawn only from 10 specific venues in an effort to retain power in a logistic regression with venue as a categorical factor.

**Table 4.** Sample refinement and final composition

| Phase | Excluded | Retained sample |
|---|---|---|
| *Source SLR* [3] (Google Scholar) | – | 1157 |
| Inclusion/exclusion | 1011 | 146 |
| *This study* | | |
| Studies with empirical data | 24 | 122 |
| Studies with NHST/*p*-value | 8 | 114 → **Final sample** |

**Table 5.** Sample composition by venue and year.

| | 2006 | 2007 | 2008 | 2009 | 2010 | 2011 | 2012 | 2013 | 2014 | 2015 | 2016 | Sum |
|---|---|---|---|---|---|---|---|---|---|---|---|---|
| SOUPS | 6 | 3 | 4 | 6 | 8 | 4 | 10 | 8 | 13 | 9 | 6 | 77 |
| USEC | 0 | 0 | 0 | 0 | 0 | 0 | 0 | 0 | 4 | 0 | 0 | 4 |
| CCS | 0 | 0 | 0 | 0 | 0 | 0 | 0 | 0 | 4 | 1 | 3 | 8 |
| USENIX | 0 | 0 | 0 | 1 | 0 | 0 | 4 | 1 | 1 | 0 | 0 | 7 |
| PETS | 1 | 0 | 0 | 0 | 0 | 1 | 1 | 0 | 0 | 1 | 2 | 6 |
| TISSEC | 0 | 0 | 0 | 0 | 0 | 1 | 0 | 0 | 0 | 0 | 2 | 3 |
| LASER | 0 | 0 | 0 | 0 | 0 | 0 | 1 | 0 | 0 | 0 | 1 | 2 |
| S&P | 0 | 0 | 0 | 0 | 0 | 0 | 0 | 0 | 1 | 1 | 0 | 2 |
| TDSC | 0 | 1 | 0 | 0 | 0 | 0 | 1 | 0 | 1 | 0 | 1 | 4 |
| WEIS | 0 | 0 | 0 | 0 | 0 | 0 | 0 | 0 | 0 | 1 | 0 | 1 |
| Sum | 7 | 4 | 4 | 7 | 8 | 6 | 17 | 9 | 24 | 13 | 15 | 114 |

## 5.2 Exploration of the Distribution

*Distribution of Qualitative Properties.* We visualize the presence of qualitative properties of papers over time in Fig. 2. We observe (i) Mutliple-Comparison Corrections seeing adoption from 2009 (Fig. 2a), (ii) Effect sizes being on and off over the years (Fig. 2b).

*Distribution of p-Values.* We analyze the distribution of *p*-values per paper. Therein we distinguish incomplete and complete triplets including test statistic and degrees of freedom. In Fig. 3, we depict this *p*-value distribution; Fig. 3a is ordered by number of the tests reported on, distinguishing between complete/incomplete triplets while annotating the presence of multiple comparison corrections (MCC); Fig. 3b is organized by publication year. The included linear regression lines indicate little to no change over time.

## 5.3 Prevalence of Statistical Misreporting

For RQ1, we compare statistical misreporting by venue and year, considering individual tests as well as entire papers (cf. contingency tables in the Online Supplementary Materials).

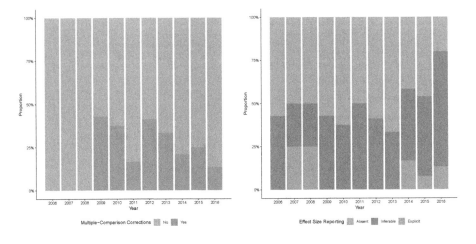

(a) Multiple-comparison corrections (MCC)          (b) Effect size reporting

**Fig. 2.** Properties of SLR papers by year.

*Misreported Tests.* For individual tests, there is a statistically significant association between the statcheck outcomes and the publication venue, FET $p = .034$, as well as the publication year, FET $p < .001$. This offers first evidence to reject the null hypotheses $H_{V,0}$ and $H_{Y,0}$.

Table 6 contains the corresponding contingency table.

**Table 6.** Contingency table of individual test statcheck outcomes by venue, FET $p = .034$.

|              | SOUPS | USEC | CCS | USENIX | PETS | TISSEC | LASER | S&P | TDSC | WEIS |
|--------------|-------|------|-----|--------|------|--------|-------|-----|------|------|
| CorrectNHST  | 170   | 1    | 9   | 4      | 11   | 6      | 5     | 0   | 12   | 0    |
| Inconsistency| 19    | 1    | 3   | 0      | 0    | 0      | 1     | 0   | 0    | 0    |
| DecisionError| 9     | 0    | 0   | 0      | 0    | 0      | 1     | 0   | 0    | 0    |
| Incomplete   | 1028  | 33   | 122 | 100    | 72   | 71     | 19    | 11  | 60   | 7    |

*Papers with Misreporting.* Sub-Figure 6a on p. 15 shows a hierarchical waffle plot of the statcheck outcomes. For aggregated outcomes per paper displayed in Fig. 4, the associations per venue and year are not statistically significant, FET $p = .963$ and FET $p = .455$ respectively. A likely reason for this result is visible in the histograms of Fig. 5: errors are at times clustered, in that, some papers contain multiple errors.

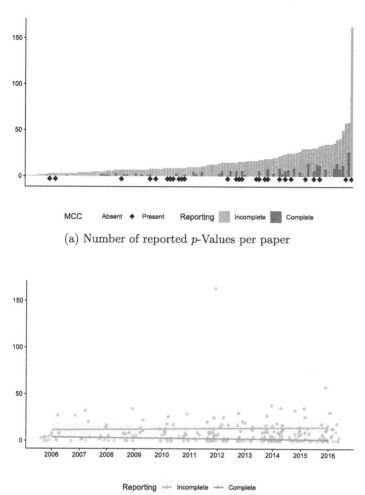

(a) Number of reported $p$-Values per paper

(b) Distribution by Year

**Fig. 3.** Distribution of statistical reporting of papers, that is, how many $p$-values per paper are reported Incomplete or Complete. MCC = Multiple-Comparison Corrections.

## 5.4   Comparison with JMP

With respect to RQ2, the statcheck outcomes of the included SLR and Journal of Media Psychology (JMP) are statistically significantly different, $\chi^2(3) = 88.803, p < .001$. Hence, we reject the null hypothesis $H_{C,0}$ and conclude that there is a systematic difference between fields. We find an effect of Cramér's $V = 0.646$, 95% CI $[0.503, 0.773]$.

If we restrict the analysis to the papers containing Complete tests and, thereby, exclude papers marked Incomplete, we find that the difference between fields is not statistically significant any longer, $\chi^2(2) = 0.197, p = .906$, Cramér's $V = 0.037$, 95% CI $[0, 0.139]$.

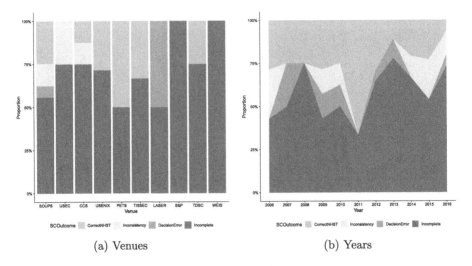

(a) Venues                                    (b) Years

**Fig. 4.** Proportions of per-paper aggregated statcheck outcomes by venue and year. The results by year are shown as area plot to highlight development over time.

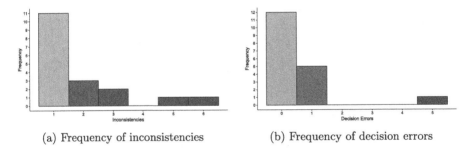

(a) Frequency of inconsistencies          (b) Frequency of decision errors

**Fig. 5.** Number of errors per paper.

## 5.5 Reporting Test Outcomes by Venue and Year

While we analyzed tests and aggregated paper SCOutcome by venue and year, we found that these multinomial logistic regressions were not stable. Even if the models were statistically significant, this missing stability was evidenced in extreme odds-ratios, which was likely rooted in the sparsity of the dataset. (We report all MLR conducted in the Online Supplementary Materials for reference). To overcome the sparsity, we chose to collapse the venue factor into SOUPS and OTHER levels, called venue' (and the corresponding null hypothesis $H_{V',0}$).

A multinomial logistic regression on individual tests with SCOutcome $\sim$ venue'+year with Incomplete as reference level is statistically significant, LR, $\chi^2(6) = 15.417, p = .017$. Because the model explains McFadden $R^2 = .01$ of the variance, we expect little predictive power.

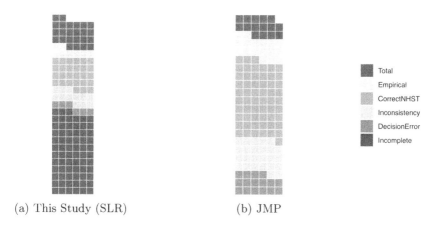

(a) This Study (SLR)                    (b) JMP

**Fig. 6.** Hierarchical Waffle plots comparing user studies (SLR) in cyber security and the Journal of Media Psychology (JMP) (One square represents one paper).

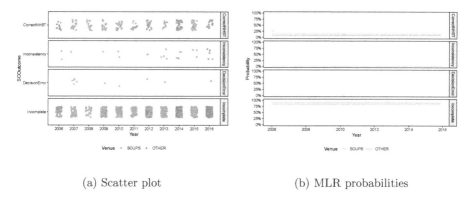

(a) Scatter plot                    (b) MLR probabilities

**Fig. 7.** Per-teststatcheck outcomes by venue and year. *Note:* The multinomial logistic regression (MLR) is statistically significant, LR Test, $\chi^2(6) = 15.417, p = .017$.

The corresponding predictors are statistically significant as well. Hence, we reject the null hypotheses $H_{V',0}$ and $H_{Y,0}$. Figure 7 contains an overview of the scatter plot vs. the predicted probabilities from the MLR.

While we find that there is an effect of year in increasing likelihood of Incomplete outcomes, this only accounts for an increase of 0.2% per year, barely perceptible in the graph. Everything else being equal, a transition from venue SOUPS to OTHER yields an increase of likelihood of the Incomplete outcomes, by a factor of roughly 2. However, these changes are dwarfed by the overall intercept of tests being correct (in comparison to Incomplete).

In absolute terms, the expected likelihood of tests being Incomplete is 80%, with OTHER venues having a few percent greater Incomplete likelihood. SOUPS exhibits an expected likelihood of 13% of being CorrectNHST, while OTHER venues yield a few percent lower likelihood.

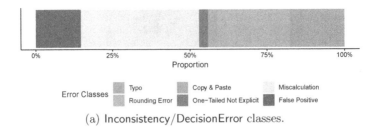

(a) Inconsistency/DecisionError classes.

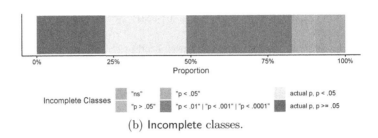

(b) Incomplete classes.

**Fig. 8.** Classification of reported statcheck outcomes.

## 5.6  Qualitative Analysis

We offer a summary of the analysis here, a detailed account is included in Appendix A.

*Composition of Incomplete p-Values.* Sub-Figure 8b contains an overview of the classes of incompletely reported $p$-values. Less than half the cases of incomplete triplets contain an actual $p$-values (half of them, in turn, significant or not significant). 31% of the incomplete cases compared to lower significance bound than $\alpha = .05$. 9% of the tests are simply declared non-significant, another 7% reported as significant wrt. $p < .05$.

*Distribution of p-Values.* Figure 9 shows the difference between reported and computed $p$-values. When comparing reported and re-computed $p$-values, we found that in 22 out of 34 cases, the reported $p$-value was more significant than the computed one (65%).

## 5.7  Significance Detection Performance

We analyzed the decision making of authors on statistical significance of reported results vis-à-vis of recomputed $p$-values (Table 7). We observe a somewhat low specificity of 79.7%. Note that this analysis only refers to a reported significance decision is valid with respect to a corresponding correct $p$-value, and *not* whether a positive reported result is true.

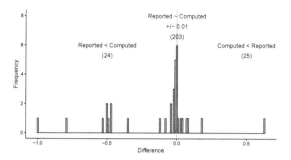

**Fig. 9.** Histogram of difference reported $p$-values minus statcheck-computed $p$-values.

**Table 7.** Confusion matrix for researchers determining significance.

| Predicted | Reference | |
|---|---|---|
| | Significant | NS |
| Significant | 191 | 12 |
| NS | 1 | 47 |

Accuracy: .95, 95% CI [.91, .97],
$Acc > NIR(.76)$, $< .001^{***}$,
Sensitivity $= .99$, Specificity $= .80$,
PPV $= .94$, $F_1 = .97$

## 5.8  Supporting the STAST 2019 PC in Checking Statistics

Aligned with Recommendation 2 in Sect. 7, we offered a statcheck analysis to the STAST PC members to support the workshop's discussion phase. Of 28 submitted papers, 9 papers (32%) included a statistical inference.

Let us consider these 9 papers in detail as an exploratory analysis. One paper contained a major error in terms of statistics being invalid, two papers used the wrong statistical method for the experiment design at hand (e.g., independent-samples statistics in a dependent-samples design). Two of those three papers were also flagged by statcheck. These errors themselves, however, were detected by program committee members, not by the statcheck analysis.

On third of the papers reported statistics in an APA compliant format. 6 papers (66%) reported exact $p$-values, 4 papers (44%) reported effect sizes as required by the STAST submission guidelines. Of the 9 papers, 7 needed multiple-comparison corrections, which only two provided in their initial submission.

In terms of statcheck evaluation with the methodology of this study, we found 5 papers (56%) to be Incomplete, one paper Inconsistent, three papers (33%) CorrectNHST. This distribution is not significantly different from the SLR sample shown in Fig. 6a, $\chi^2(3) = 0.829, p = .843$, Cramér's $V = 0.082$, 95% CI $[0, 0.188]$.

# 6  Discussion

**Incomplete reporting holds back the field.** Nearly two thirds of the papers with $p$-values did not report a single complete test triplet (cf. Fig. 6a). This impairs the ability to cross-check internal consistency of tests and, thereby, undermines fault-tolerance. Hence, such papers have limited credibility and fidelity of statistical information.

The incomplete reporting observed in this study is in stark contrast to the analysis of the Journal of Media Psychology (JMP), in which not a single paper was Incomplete. Hence, we conclude that mandated reporting standards are an effective tool.

It is further troubling that the likelihood of incomplete reporting did not seem to decrease over time (cf. Fig. 7b).

In terms of research reuse and synthesis, the situation is aggravated, because effect sizes are vastly under-reported in this field. Only a small minority reports them explicitly; one third of the papers allows to infer them (cf. Fig. 2b).

There are three consequences to this phenomenon: (i) It is exceedingly difficult for practitioners to ascertain the magnitude of effects and, thereby, their practical significance. (ii) It is near-impossible to compare research results in meta-analyses and to synthesize well-founded summary effects. (iii) Hence, disputes over differences between original studies and replications are hard to settle satisfactorily.

**While some errors are minor, we caution against clustered errors and miscalculations.** Of the 44 papers with complete test statistic triplets analyzed, 60% were deemed correct; more than one quarter had at least one inconsistency; 14% had at least one decision error. Of all tests with complete triplets analyzed 14% were erroneous. Here, the socio-technical security sample showed similar error rates as the psychology sample.

Especially the 26 papers with complete test triplets and correct reporting—one quarter of the sample—stand testament to efforts of authors and program committees "get it right."

The errors observed by statcheck were often minor typos and rounding errors that could have been easily avoided, however nearly 40% seemed to be serious miscalculations. We found that these errors were at times clustered: there are a few papers with a number of errors.

**There is a dark figure of decision errors lurking in the underuse of multiple-comparison corrections.** This study leaves the detailed analysis of power and multiple-comparison corrections (MCCs) to future work. Still, we do not want to withhold insights already apparent from Fig. 3a: There is a Damocles sword hanging over many papers: Multiple-Comparison Corrections (MCCs).

We have seen in Fig. 2a that even though MCCs came in use from year 2009, only about one third of the papers employed them. From Fig. 3a, we observe that there are papers with a considerable number of reported $p$-values without MCCs. Hence, there may well be a sizable dark figure of papers with decision errors in store once adequate MCCs are employed.

These observations inform Recommendation 3 in that observing studies with many comparisons but without corrections can be an indication of the number of comparisons, multiple-comparison corrections as well as the power needed to sustain them only being considered as an afterthought.

**Automated checking of statistical reporting is viable.** The statcheck detection rates were very good and comparable to the rates reported by Nuijten et al. [13]. We note, however, that statcheck did not operate completely autonomously, but was complemented with human coding to overcome parsing issues. We find the approach viable for the use in socio-technical aspects of security.

## 6.1 Limitations

**Generalizability.** The study is based on an existing SLR sample that largely consists of SOUPS publications and only contains few cases for other venues. Dealing with a sparse matrix, the likelihoods computed for non-SOUPS venues as well as overall logistic regressions suffer from more uncertainty.

**Syntactic Validity Checks.** While we have made good experiences with statcheck and only found few false positives and negatives, we observe that statcheck results can suffer from hidden errors. While we complemented the automated analysis with a human review and coding of reported errors, we observe that statcheck could have missed or misinterpreted individual tests. However, based our inspection of the 114 analyzed papers, we expect that the number of statcheck errors is small compared to the 1775 tests analyzed. In the end, an automated tool cannot replace the trained eye of a knowledgable reviewer. However, this study is about the overall distribution of errors, which will be hardly skewed by rare false positives or negatives.

**Deviations from the Pre-registration.** We deviated from the OSF pre-registration by 1. not attempting the exploratory analysis of the impact of authors, 2. not attempting an exploratory logistic regression on completeness indicators, 3. abandoning the planned ordinal logistic regression in favor of the MLR, because SCOutcome did not yield an ordinal scale, 4. merging non-SOUPS venue levels to overcome the sparsity of the dataset, 5. not attempting further cross-validation due to low variance explained.

## 7 Recommendations

The recommendations made here need to be seen as part of a greater paradigm shift. Instead of focusing on single publications, one may consider that a study does not stand on its own. Truly advancing the knowledge of a field calls for creating robust studies that prepare the ground for systematic replications, reuse and research synthesis.

**1. Establish sound reporting standards.** Sound and generally accepted reporting standards could greatly improve the credibility of the field. This could either mean developing systematic reporting standards for socio-technical aspects of security or adopting existing standards.

Developing systematic reporting standards would involve a stable coalition of program committee chairs and members as well as journal editors forming a working group to that effect. Such a working group would likely take into account requirements for this field as well as examples of mature reporting standards from other fields.

Given that considerable thought has gone into APA standards [1] and that these standards apply to human dimensions, they are a viable and sufficiently mature candidate, at least when it comes to statistical reporting. Our analysis showed that the majority of papers reporting complete test statistics triplets were actually compliant to APA requirements.

While not perfect, their recommendations on statistical reporting could have considerable benefits for reporting fidelity, research reusability and synthesis. One option in this context would be to only adopt a subset of recommendations directly benefiting reporting fidelity.

In any case, one would consider sound reporting for test statistics themselves, effect sizes and their confidence intervals, as well as essential information on the sample, design and procedure. Again, this field can well take into account more comprehensive initiatives from other fields [10].

**2. Support PCs in checking statistics.** From our experience researching this study, we can attest that checking statistics can be a tedious affair. Even with all their failings, tools like statcheck can support program committee members in detecting incorrect results. Such an approach certainly requires human mediation to avoid false positives, yet can offer insights at low cost.

As reported in Sect. 5.8, we tested this recommendation on the STAST 2019 program committee. While statcheck correctly identified reporting issues and did not produce a false positive, major errors were discovered by program committee members in the analysis of experiment designs vis-à-vis their statistical inferences. This yields an indication that an automated tool, such as statcheck, will only support but never replace the expert judgment of the reviewers.

There are organizational methods, such as pre-registrations or registered reports, that can support a PC further in ascertaining the integrity of results.

**3. Embrace *a priori* power and multiple-comparison corrections.** We make this recommendation with a grain of salt, as we have not reported on a dedicated study on power, yet. However, even this study on reporting fidelity shows that this consideration would benefit the community.

Low power and missing adequate MCCs can well undermine the results of a good study and increase the likelihood of a positive result being a false positive. We encourage researchers to plan in advance for the power required, accounting for the MCCs necessary for the planned tests.

# 8    Conclusion

This study is the first systematic analysis of a large sample of security user studies with respect to their statistical reporting fidelity. For the first time, we offer a comprehensive, quantitative, and empirical analysis of the state-of-play of the field of socio-technical aspects of security. We offer a wealth of different perspectives on the sample, enabling us to obtain a fine-grained analysis as well as broad recommendations for authors and program committees alike.

We stress that the research and reviewing process for security user studies constitutes a socio-technical system in itself that impacts the decision making in security and privacy. Because scientists and practitioners alike seek to re-use research results, the fidelity or uncertainty of those results—especially their statistical inferences—plays a major role in the credibility of the field and the confidence of its audience. Hence, self-reflection of the field will ultimately impact the decision making by users in security and privacy, as well.

As future work, we consider expanding the sample, including further venues, such as CHI, as well as offering a dedicated analysis of statistical power and Positive Predictive Value (PPV) present in the field.

**Acknowledgment.** We would like to thank Malte Elson for the discussions on statcheck, on the corresponding analyses in psychology, and on general research methodology. We thank the anonymous reviewers of STAST 2019 for their discussion and insightful comments, as well as the volume co-editor Theo Tryfonas for offering additional pages to include the requested changes.

This study was in parts funded by the UK Research Institute in the Science of Cyber Security (RISCS) under a National Cyber Security Centre (NCSC) grant on "Pathways to Enhancing Evidence-Based Research Methods for Cyber Security" (Pathway I led by Thomas Groß). The author was in parts funded by the ERC Starting Grant CASCAde (GA n°716980).

# A    Details on Qualitative Analysis

## A.1    Errors Committed by statcheck

*Parsing Accuracy.* In all 34 error cases, statcheck parsed the PDF file correctly, and its raw test representation corresponded to the PDF. In all but two tests, statcheck recognized the test correctly. In said two cases, it mistook a non-standard-reported Shapiro-Wilk test as $\chi^2$ test, creating two false positives. There was one case in which the statcheck computed $p$-value for an independent-samples $t$-test differed slightly from our own calculation, yet only marginally so, presumably because of a unreported Welch correction.

*One-Tailed Tests.* In seven cases, statcheck recognized one-tailed tests correctly. For three of those tests, the authors framed the hypotheses as one-tailed. In three other tests, the authors used one-tailed test results without declaring their use. There was one additional case in which the authors seemed to have used a one-tailed test, yet the rounding was so far off the one-tailed result that statcheck did not accept it as "valid if one-tailed" any longer. There was one test marked as "one-tail" which statcheck did not recognize as one-tailed, yet that test also suffered from rounding errors.

*Dependent-Samples Tests.* There were 7 papers using dependent-samples methods (such as matched-pair tests or mixed-methods regressions). We found that statcheck treated the corresponding dependent-samples statistics correctly.

*Multiple Comparison Corrections.* In three cases, statcheck did not recognize $p$-values that were correctly Bonferroni-corrected, counting as three false positives. It is an open point, however, how many paper should have employed multiple-comparison corrections, but have not done so, an analysis statcheck does not perform.

## A.2    Errors Committed by Authors

*Typos.* We considered 6 to be typos or transcription errors (18%). Another 1 error seemed to be a copy-paste error (3%)

*Rounding Errors.* Of all 34 reported errors, we found 8 to be rounding errors (24%).

*Miscalculations.* We found 13 cases to be erroneous calculations (38%).

## A.3    Composition of Incomplete $p$-Values

Of 1523 incomplete cases, 134 were declared "non-significant" without giving the actual $p$-value (8.8%). Further, 6 were shown as $p > .05$. (0.394%).

Of the incomplete cases, 102 were reported statistically significant at a .05 significance level (6.7%).

Of the incomplete cases, 477 were reported statistically significant at a lower significance level of .01, .001, or .0001 (31.3%).

Of 1523 incomplete $p$-values, 680 gave an exact $p$-value (44.6%). Of those exactly reported $p$-values, half (367) were claimed statistically significant at a significance level of $\alpha = .05$ (54%). Of those exatly reported $p$-values, 19 claimed an impossible $p$-value of $p = 0$ (2.79%).

## Online Supplementary Materials

We made the materials of the study (specification of the inputted SLR, included sample, contingency tables) publicly available at its Open Science Framework Repository (see Footnote 1).

## References

1. American Psychological Association (ed.): Publication Manual of the American Psychological Association, 6th revised edn. American Psychological Association (2009)
2. Coopamootoo, K.P.L., Groß, T.: Cyber security and privacy experiments: a design and reporting toolkit. In: Hansen, M., Kosta, E., Nai-Fovino, I., Fischer-Hübner, S. (eds.) Privacy and Identity 2017. IAICT, vol. 526, pp. 243–262. Springer, Cham (2018). https://doi.org/10.1007/978-3-319-92925-5_17
3. Coopamootoo, K., Groß, T.: Systematic evaluation for evidence-based methods in cyber security. Technical report TR-1528, Newcastle University (2017)
4. Coopamootoo, K.P.L., Groß, T.: Evidence-based methods for privacy and identity management. In: Lehmann, A., Whitehouse, D., Fischer-Hübner, S., Fritsch, L., Raab, C. (eds.) Privacy and Identity 2016. IAICT, vol. 498, pp. 105–121. Springer, Cham (2016). https://doi.org/10.1007/978-3-319-55783-0_9
5. Cumming, G.: Understanding the New Statistics: Effect Sizes, Confidence Intervals, and Meta-Analysis. Routledge, New York (2013)
6. Elson, M., Przybylski, A.K.: The science of technology and human behavior - standards old and new. J. Media Psychol. 29(1), 1–7 (2017). https://doi.org/10.1027/1864-1105/a000212
7. Epskamp, S., Nuijten, M.B.: statcheck: extract statistics from articles and recompute p values (v1.3.0), May 2018. https://CRAN.R-project.org/package=statcheck
8. Fox, J., Andersen, R.: Effect displays for multinomial and proportional-odds logit models. Sociol. Methodol. 36(1), 225–255 (2006)
9. Lakens, D.: Checking your stats, and some errors we make, October 2015. http://daniellakens.blogspot.com/2015/10/checking-your-stats-and-some-errors-we.html
10. LeBel, E.P., McCarthy, R.J., Earp, B.D., Elson, M., Vanpaemel, W.: A unified framework to quantify the credibility of scientific findings. Adv. Methods Pract. Psychol. Sci. 1(3), 389–402 (2018)
11. Maxion, R.: Making experiments dependable. In: Jones, C.B., Lloyd, J.L. (eds.) Dependable and Historic Computing. LNCS, vol. 6875, pp. 344–357. Springer, Heidelberg (2011). https://doi.org/10.1007/978-3-642-24541-1_26
12. Moher, D., et al.: CONSORT 2010 explanation and elaboration: updated guidelines for reporting parallel group randomised trials. J. Clin. Epidemiol. 63(8), e1–e37 (2010)
13. Nuijten, M.B., van Assen, M.A., Hartgerink, C.H., Epskamp, S., Wicherts, J.: The validity of the tool "statcheck" in discovering statistical reporting inconsistencies (2017). https://psyarxiv.com/tcxaj/
14. Nuijten, M.B., Hartgerink, C.H.J., van Assen, M.A.L.M., Epskamp, S., Wicherts, J.M.: The prevalence of statistical reporting errors in psychology (1985–2013). Behav. Res. Methods 48(4), 1205–1226 (2015). https://doi.org/10.3758/s13428-015-0664-2

15. Peisert, S., Bishop, M.: How to design computer security experiments. In: Futcher, L., Dodge, R. (eds.) WISE 2007. IAICT, vol. 237, pp. 141–148. Springer, New York (2007). https://doi.org/10.1007/978-0-387-73269-5_19

16. Ripley, B., Venables, W.: nnet: feed-forward neural networks and multinomial log-linear models, February 2016. https://CRAN.R-project.org/package=nnet

17. Schechter, S.: Common pitfalls in writing about security and privacy human subjects experiments, and how to avoid them (2013). https://www.microsoft.com/en-us/research/wp-content/uploads/2016/02/commonpitfalls.pdf

18. Schmidt, T.: Sources of false positives and false negatives in the STATCHECK algorithm: reply to Nuijten et al. (2016). https://arxiv.org/abs/1610.01010

# "I Don't Know Too Much About It": On the Security Mindsets of Computer Science Students

Mohammad Tahaei[✉], Adam Jenkins, Kami Vaniea, and Maria Wolters

School of Informatics, University of Edinburgh, Edinburgh, UK
{mohammad.tahaei,adam.jenkins,kami.vaniea,maria.wolters}@ed.ac.uk

**Abstract.** The security attitudes and approaches of software developers have a large impact on the software they produce, yet we know very little about how and when these views are constructed. This paper investigates the security and privacy (S&P) perceptions, experiences, and practices of current Computer Science students at the graduate and undergraduate level using semi-structured interviews. We find that the attitudes of students already match many of those that have been observed in professional level developers. Students have a range of hacker and attack mindsets, lack of experience with security APIs, a mixed view of who is in charge of S&P in the software life cycle, and a tendency to trust other peoples' code as a convenient approach to rapidly build software. We discuss the impact of our results on both curriculum development and support for professional developers.

**Keywords:** Usable security · Secure programming · Computer science students · Software developers · Software development · Education

## 1 Introduction

Software developers can impact millions of lives with seemingly small security decisions that have a large impact on the people using the technologies. One example is the case of the dating site Ashley Madison, where a strong cryptographic algorithm was used to store passwords but was implemented incorrectly [42].

Even for apps where security is not a primary feature, it is a requirement needed for stability and safety of operation. Therefore, software developers need to be keenly aware of the security implications of their design decisions. Ideally, they should have strong support from their tools to avoid security and privacy issues in their resulting code.

Basic tools such as cryptographic libraries (OpenSSL) and federated authentication (OAuth) exist partially to assist developers in integrating common security needs into their projects without needing to know all the complex details. There are also efforts to help raise awareness of common coding and design issues such as the IEEE top ten security flaws [4,5].

© Springer Nature Switzerland AG 2021
T. Groß and T. Tryfonas (Eds.): STAST 2019, LNCS 11739, pp. 27–46, 2021.
https://doi.org/10.1007/978-3-030-55958-8_2

Yet, security remains a pervasive problem in deployed code. In 2013 alone, 88% of apps (out of 11,748) analysed on Google Play had at least one mistake in how the developer used a cryptographic API [19]. Code that they write goes into security-critical applications such as banking software [27] as well as software with less obvious security implications such as Internet connected kettles [46].

Non-usable APIs are a key point of failure for most developers [3,29,35,53, 70]. Providing manuals is not enough. A usability evaluation of programming security in Android found that developers created code with security errors even when they were provided with official documentation [2]. Perhaps more importantly, developer understanding of security is also problematic. Interviews with professional developers show a range of concern about security and privacy knowledge [11]. The situation is exacerbated when developers make non-obvious errors when implementing security which results in believing that code is secure when it is actually not secure [1].

One potential opportunity for changing developers' security attitudes and practices is during their training. In this work, we investigate the security and privacy (S&P) mindsets of a group of twenty graduate and undergraduate computer science (CS) students on a variety of career trajectories, and with a range of exposure to formal security training. Our research questions are:

– What are students' comprehension of S&P related concepts?
– To what extent do students consider S&P while coding applications, and how do they implement it?

Within the context of developer-centred security, our study highlights the extent to which students already have similar mindsets and practices as have been found in professional developers, suggesting that these may form and consolidate early. We conclude that, while early educational intervention would be ideal, we also need to provide developers with usable tools, such as APIs, and easily accessible training, which can be used both by trainees and professionals.

## 2   Related Work

Creating secure software correctly is quite challenging even for professional developers, often resulting in unintended security vulnerabilities [3,29,70]. The OWASP organisation publishes the top ten most critical web application security risks every few years. A review of their last three reports covering seven years terrifyingly that the most common issues are quite stable [51], with common and highly damaging vulnerabilities such as code injection and broken authentication continuously remaining in the top ten.

Arce et al. observed that many of the OWASP vulnerabilities represent unintentional errors or mistakes rather than planned actions and therefore are minimally helpful to someone trying to design a secure system [5]. Instead they propose a set of top ten *security design flaws*, that is security issues that are a planned element of the software. Their list is much higher-level and contains issues such as "earn or give, but never assume, trust" [5, p. 9].

The problem of code vulnerabilities in live software is further exacerbated by the steady reduction of the barriers to entry for new software creators. While generally a good thing, the 'anyone can code' movement has also led to an increase in the number of software creators with minimal formal training in software development and even less training in security. Unsurprisingly, this group also has difficulty creating secure software [50,53].

Neither of these groups is, or should be, expected to be security experts, but the decisions they make can still have serious security impacts. In an effort to better support these software creators, several tools and libraries have been proposed such as OpenSSL, PyCrypto, and cryptography.io which encapsulate many of the security decisions, theoretically making development easier.

Unfortunately, many of these tools still suffer from usability issues, such as confusing API designs [1,19,22,27,34,39,64] or poorly designed documentation [2,47]. Official documentations are often not easy to use, hence developers prefer online resources which may not offer valid and secure solutions. While Stack Overflow, for example, helps with getting code working quickly, the suggested solutions may also result in less secure code [2,23].

Security is also challenging for developers because it causes no obvious visual effect, making it difficult to identify when an unintended state has occurred [21,22]. A common example of invisible security effects is SSL/TLS. When used incorrectly, a connection is still formed, but that connection might not be encrypted, or it might be encrypted, but without certificate validation. This results in a vulnerability to man-in-the-middle (MITM) attacks during connection setup. Fahl et al. observed how challenging this can be for developers to spot. One of their developers even used Wireshark to 'test' the SSL/TLS connection and, because the data was garbled looking, incorrectly concluded things were working even though no certificate checking was happening [22].

Georgiev et al. similarly conducted an analysis of SSL certificate validation in multiple non-browser platforms and showed that many applications on the market are open to a MITM attack where data can be read and modified in transit because developers accidentally or intentionally configure their code to not validate the certificate source [27]. Such problems arise when developers are expected to understand the implications of the different settings of SSL, which is exacerbated by APIs that do not offer a helpful level of abstraction [34].

Security is also not a well-established requirement in the software development workflow. Without a dedicated developer in charge, security becomes a hot potato which is passed between groups because no one wants to deal with it [11,49,54,68]. In interviews with security experts, Thomas et al. found that security auditing is seen as a separate task from software development. While security auditing is performed by the rare breed that are security experts, it is then the developer's job to fix the security issues found [63].

Many future software developers were once Computer Science (CS) students. A survey by Stack Overflow in 2019 showed that 62.4% (75,614 responses) of developers have a degree in CS, computer engineering, or software engineering [60]. Given the importance of this group, many researchers study them to either address gaps between academia and industry [16,37,55,56,61] or to suggest educational tools to improve their skill and abilities [48,62,69]. Research shows that CS students often work under misconceptions which can lead to bad practice. For example, when it comes to software engineering processes and teamwork [61], many think that working alone is a quicker way of working on a software project, which goes against established industry best practice. Here we study the S&P mindsets of CS students with a view to identifying what they know and think about S&P, and what misconceptions exist.

## 3   Methodology

We used semi-structured interviews to explore how a range of students from undergraduate to PhD think about S&P. The semi-structured approach allowed us to probe students' S&P mindsets in detail and investigate how they relate to their own practices as developers.

### 3.1   Interview Design

After informed consent, we explicitly invited participants to talk as much as they wanted on the various topics discussed. The interview began with an open question on academic and professional background and general questions about coding and software development experience. Questions about demographics were asked at the end of the interview in order to minimise stereotype threat. The full interview script is included in the Appendix.

We began the S&P discussion by asking participants to consider creating "a new group discussion app for in-class discussions." They were then asked to free-list the app's features on paper and after they finished they were asked to circle those that were S&P related.

Next, we examined participants' understandings around threats and hackers. We started by asking participants about the hypothetical app: "Who is most likely to try and attack this system? What are they likely going to try and do?" We then moved on to talk about hackers, because work on security folk models has found them to be an important part of how people think about security [67]. We elicited participants' definitions of the term hacker, and their views on hackers' intentions, goals, and background.

We then moved on to considering who was responsible for S&P in software development practice. The discussion was grounded in participants' own experience of writing software, in particular problems with (security) APIs.

Finally, we asked participants about personal security and privacy practices. First, participants were asked to list the words and concepts they associated with 'computer security' on paper. We followed up with questions about good security practices, and their own security practices.

Since prior negative experiences can impact future choices [65], we also asked about prior experiences with compromise, prompting them with examples such as "getting a virus on your computer, losing your password, having an email sent from your account, or loss of data about you" if needed. We explored how the experience was resolved, and what participants learned.

## 3.2   Recruitment

We recruited participants through mailing lists associated with a large Russell Group University in the United Kingdom, Facebook groups, and word of mouth. Advertisements asked for Computer Science students (BSc, MSc and PhD) to participate in an interview about opinions and attitudes around software development, particularly around the handling of requirements prioritisation. All advertisements avoided S&P related words to limit self-selection and priming.

## 3.3   Participants

Our sample, shown in Table 1, includes twenty students (6 BSc, 11 MSc, and 3 PhD students), participants who previously took a computer security course at any University are indicated with 'PS' instead of 'P'. The sample contains five female, and fifteen male students with an average age of 24 years old (range: 20–37, std: 3.8, median: 23). They come from various countries and have diverse CS-related educational backgrounds. Interviews were conducted in English. Our sample reflects both the diversity seen in the tech industry [10,28], and the culturally diverse classrooms found in many computer science departments.

The interviews were advertised to be 60 to 90 min long with a compensation of £10 in cash. In practice, interviews took an average of 68 min (range: 41–108, std: 18.4, median: 65.5) and were completed in July 2018. All interviews were audio recorded with participant consent. The study was conducted in accordance with the Ethics procedures of the School where the students were recruited (cert ID 2870).

We interviewed students over the summer. This meant that the Masters students were in their dissertation phase, and had completed the course work part of their 12-month degree. PhD students in the UK have typically completed a Masters before starting a PhD and are not necessarily required to take courses, pass a qualifying exam, or be a Teaching Assistant, though many choose to take additional courses and tutor. Therefore, beyond teaching and thesis work, PhD students are unlikely to be impacted by security courses taught at the University.

## 3.4   Pilot

We conducted seven pilot interviews with Masters and PhD students, six of which were associated with our research lab but unfamiliar with the work. These interviews were used to iteratively refine the interview script as well as adjust the number and content of questions to keep interviews at about 60 min. The pilot contained some students with no security background to help ensure the phrasing of security questions was clear. Feedback was also sought about the structure, clarity, and accuracy of the interview schedule. Pilot interviewees and interviews were not used in our final analysis.

**Table 1.** Interview study demographics. P = participant without computer security background; PS = participant who self-describes as having taken a computer security course in the past.

| Participant | Gender | Nationality | Age | Expected degree |
|---|---|---|---|---|
| PS01 | M | EU | 29 | PhD |
| P02 | M | EU | 28 | MSc |
| PS03 | F | Asia | 22 | MSc |
| PS04 | M | Asia | 24 | MSc |
| PS05 | M | Asia | 25 | PhD |
| P06 | F | Asia | 23 | MSc |
| P07 | M | Asia | 22 | BSc |
| PS08 | M | UK | 21 | MSc |
| PS09 | M | Asia | 25 | MSc |
| P10 | M | Asia | 21 | BSc |
| P11 | M | EU | 22 | BSc |
| PS12 | M | Asia | 23 | MSc |
| PS13 | M | EU | 21 | BSc |
| P14 | M | EU | 20 | BSc |
| PS15 | M | EU | 25 | PhD |
| PS16 | M | Asia | 37 | MSc |
| P17 | F | EU | 25 | BSc |
| P18 | F | Asia | 23 | MSc |
| P19 | M | UK | 24 | MSc |
| P20 | F | Asia | 20 | MSc |

### 3.5   Interview Analysis

Interview analysis focused on uncovering students' mindsets of S&P as they relate to the software development process. Relevant themes were extracted using a three stage process. First, two researchers listened to the full audio of four interviews which had been selected by the interviewer to cover a wide range of participants, identified relevant parts for more detailed analysis and transcription, and outlined an initial topic guide for coding [45,59]. Audio was used because it provides a richer record of the original interview than a standard transcript. In the second stage, the researchers performed open coding of the transcripts based on the topic guide [45,59].

In the third stage, the open codes were analysed using an affinity diagram [40] to yield a set of seven themes, which are discussed in the Results Sect. 4 below. While some authors suggest reporting how many participants mention each theme [40], we chose to follow standard qualitative research reporting practice and focus on describing and contextualising our themes [57,67].

# 4   Results

All participants all had some form of prior programming experience ranging from classroom projects, internships, and prior employment in industry. Since our participants included a large number of Masters students, they also had classroom experience from prior universities, with several expressing that they had worked in industry either as interns or full time before coming back for a Masters or PhD. Half had taken a computer security course at some point in their education. We did not ask about the details of these courses.

## 4.1   'Computer Security' Word Association Results

Mid-way through the interview participants were asked to free-list words associated with 'computer security'. The words were grouped into topics by the lead researcher with a bottom-up approach. A second researcher then reviewed the groupings and disagreements were resolved through discussion. Table 2 shows the resulting eleven topics.

Participants' understanding of the term 'computer security' was broad, with participants who wrote words providing an average of 9.6 words (range: 2–19, std: 4.2). Listed words included standard security topics such as encryption, attacks, and system security which are readily found in most security text books. Participants also listed company names that are either associated with security (Norton) or that had been discussed recently in the news in relation to security (Facebook [36,66]). Two participants (P02 & P20) were not able to list any words, suggesting uncertainty with the term. "*It is all very flimsy*" (P20), "*To be honest I do not know too much about it*" (P20).

Of the participants who provided words, participants listed words from an average of 4.2 topics (range: 1–7, std: 1.8). The topics cover a wide range, but each individual participant had less range, with at most seven topics mentioned by one participant. Most notable is the lack of a single common topic amongst participants. For example, the most common word 'privacy' was mentioned by only 40% of participants. Common security topics such as passwords, authentication, and encryption also appeared. Some of these topics are similar to what professional developers associate with security, for example, encryption, user control, and user access [30].

## 4.2   Interview Themes

**Security Mindsets.** Participants varied substantially in their understanding of S&P. While some participants had a strong up-front understanding of security which varied minimally during the interview, others had clearly not thought much about the topic before resulting in them re-thinking their opinions mid-interview. This is to be somewhat expected as many people have not previously devoted extensive time to assessing their own understanding of the topic [7].

This theme provides rich additional context to the initial topics identified through free association. Those with a more sophisticated understanding of S&P

**Table 2.** Topics mentioned during free-listing, number of words participants listed associated with that topic, number of unique participants listing at least one word associated with the topic, and a set of sample words representing the range.

| Topic | #Words | #Participants | Example words |
|---|---|---|---|
| Encryption | 28 | 11 | End-to-end, hash, RSA, public/private key, SSL, symmetric |
| Authentication | 28 | 9 | Passwords, permissions, 2FA, tokens, access controls, emails |
| Privacy | 27 | 10 | Anonymity, right to be forgotten, visibility, cookies |
| Attacks | 25 | 8 | Reconnaissance, phishing, buffer overflows, DoS, MITM |
| System security | 13 | 5 | Protocols, database, Unix, system calls, TCP/IPs |
| Social | 13 | 7 | Regulations, roles, responsibilities, public knowledge |
| Finance | 8 | 4 | PayPal, Apple Pay, Bitcoin, online payments |
| Defending | 7 | 5 | Anti-virus/malware, penetration testing, logging, bounties |
| Security holes | 5 | 4 | Failures, physical access, loopholes |
| Companies | 5 | 3 | Facebook, Google, Norton, Red Hat |
| Trade offs | 4 | 3 | Usable security, features vs security, easy to use UX |

tended to use more definitive language, had more stable descriptions of attacker motivations, and were more likely to be sure that their statements were accurate, and to describe less intuitive or extreme scenarios. For example, PS15, a crpytography PhD student, explains that *"in crypto, we assume that the attacker is any code, literally any Turing machine"* (PS15).

Those with an initially less sophisticated understanding of S&P showed signs of forming their opinions as the interview progressed. Often, this would involve contradictions in thoughts as they finally reached a definition for themselves. This was most notable for the hacking theme. Participants with less developed models exhibited less self-assurance around motivations, or definitions of attack scenarios. *"I think [HTTPS] is standard by now, don't they? The more encryption the better? [...] Like exchange of data that's not encrypted at all. I don't think that's happening anymore. I'm not sure but I don't think it is"* (P17).

Similar to non-tech savvy users [67,72], some of our participants think they are not a target for attackers. *"We are just average people. It is ok to have small security measures"* (P11), *"I am also very boring computer user. I just do my courses and I watch movie on Netflix. So I don't really do anything that could put me in front of a virus"* (P20). Conversely, some participants had high awareness of potential attacks, though they still did not perceive themselves as at risk. *"I am running a server at home, which has an SSH access available. There you can see a lot of stuff going on, there are just bots or so whatever trying to get into.*

*That is even a bit scary if you see that happen all the time, but I think my pass has been strong enough to keep them out"* (PS13).

Participants clearly evidenced their own internal struggle over what S&P actually was and when it was or was not needed, which might partially explain its lack of inclusion in initial requirements. *"[My address] is not so important, because every website is required. Maybe because I live in a dormitory, if it is in my home that is different"* (P06).

While participants understood that private data should be protected, they struggled with what 'private data' actually meant. Even when talking about S&P in their private lives, participants had mixed opinions about how problematic it was for data like bank transactions to be leaked. *"So the data [leak] was about the full info about the bank accounts, the transactions, in and out, the current amount in it. For me it was normal [...] to have these transactions. But for some people it was an issue, because they receive money from hidden source, so it was an issue for them"* (PS16).

**Who Are Hackers and What Do They Want?** Some participants' definitions of hackers were well articulated. *"Really theoretical let's say, the adversary we say in crypto is literally anyone that has a computer and some access to your systems"* (PS15). Other participants had a more general understanding. *"The images that you have in your head are from Hollywood. Super smart kids sitting in the corner of a room then CIA calls upon them to solve a problem"* (P02).

We found a wide range of imagined intentions for hacking, such as financial, personal, political, and just for fun. All four types of previously observed models of hackers from Wash's work [67] were mentioned by our participants:

Graffiti, which is a mischief causing attacker with technical background: *"Want to try what they learn from the class. They may write some code to hack some system of the school to show their ability"* (PS12); Burglar, who commits crimes using computers mostly with financial motivations: *"There is nothing but personal interest. Personal gain. Personal satisfaction. And of course they are who just do it for financial gain. Stealing identities, pictures, personal info. Just to sell it afterwards, to like black market"* (PS01); Big fish, who looks only for high valued targets: *"Political incentive that certain countries fund a lot of hacking and cracking to gain power depending how important or how famous you are there might be people who want to get access to your account"* (PS13); and Contractor, a Graffiti hacker with financial/criminal motivations: *"Trained people who are trained to do this kind of stuff. Either by some governments to hack other governments. Or to break the encryption or security mechanism"* (PS05).

**The Role of Security When Planning Software.** When participants were asked about what features they would consider in an in-class discussion app, they commonly mentioned functional requirements including task management, calendar, question/answering, recording classes, and assignment management. Many of these features currently exist in course management software with which the students are familiar, such as Blackboard LEARN and Piazza.

Only four participants (PS08, PS15, PS16, and P19) mentioned S&P in their initial design and feature list, a somewhat small number since ten of our participants had previously taken a security course. Only two of the participants proactively brought up privacy issues. *"First thing that comes to my mind is privacy. Definitely in terms of features. Presumably, the School will wish to host it locally rather than to have some sort of central cloud back service"* (P19), while PS08 noted the connection between privacy and ethics: *"There is some ethical questions involved in the area of student privacy"* (PS08).

Security of the data was also a concern, particularly in terms of information leaks. *"I will make sure of the safety and security because [no one] wants to use the tool if he feel he is vulnerable his info may leak to any unwanted person"* (PS16). PS15 was also able to pull on prior experience and identify specific attacks and solutions that needed to be addressed: *"For sure I put HTTPS and TLS around it. So that would be safe. Because still, I would leave a lot of surface for attacks, because the big applications have more surface for attacks.... All those places where there is user input we basically talk about security, and we have to remember SQL injection and stuff like that"* (PS15).

Some participants turned to more authoritative sources such as laws, regulations, and public policies as a guide for what should and had to be built into the system. *"You have designed an app I guess you also think about security. But you also think about engagement. Does a certain security feature if it is option not legally required, how does it sort of effecting the engagement"* (P02). Some mentioned the EU *General Data Protection Regulation* (GDPR, enforcement date: 25 May 2018) [20], either as a convenience tool for end-users or from a regulation perspective for companies. *"Do we have to be GDPR compliance? Probably, I'm guessing"* (P11) was mentioned by a participant when answering a question about what S&P features his hypothetical classroom app might need.

**Requirements and Responsibilities: Playing Hot Potato.** Several participants recognised security as an *explicit requirement*. They consider the developers' job to be transforming requirements into code. Therefore if security is an explicit requirement, then they have to take it into account during design and development. *"So as a software engineer, if I am already given a certain requirement, I should not care about anything else outside the specs. You are employed as software engineer, you just write your. You are given a list, you just have to code it. Right? Unless you can do that. You are still doing your job"* (PS01).

On the other hand, other participants see security as an *implied requirement* that is always present. *"When the requirement is out but [privacy] has to be taken care of at every single step here. If someone comes to me asking for something then I assume that I do security for all the requirements. Wherever applicable security should be"* (PS04).

Security was also sometimes seen as a problem or requirement that should be solved by a designated entity within their workflow. For some participants, this entity was the *operating system* *"Android, it is responsible. Because Android restricts my way of developing an application. So it should provide sufficient security mechanism for me to rely on"* (PS05), *"Mostly the OS is the one that should provide security"* (PS15). Others considered that a *security team* in the software development workflow should be responsible. *"There should be a security team. Which takes care of that. Just like any other team inside the company. Like UI, testing team"* (PS04).

Many interviewees thought that the *company* as a legal entity is responsible for S&P, and some highlighted the role of legislation and government. *"We are [responsible]. Not me personally but the company that I work for as a legal entity"* (P17). Moreover, a few saw *end-users* having some responsibility as part of the larger S&P ecosystem. *"There should be a certain amount of onus on the user, they should be responsible for like managing their password"* (PS08).

**General Attitudes to APIs.** Participants saw APIs as a useful and handy tool, especially in terms of code re-use *"GUI stuff in python, here you can just call functions without write whole part of code yourself. It's always handy"* (PS03). APIs also allowed them to lean on the knowledge of others and not need to understand all the concepts themselves. *"It is quite useful and simple to import the library from platform. Before I used that library I need to learn each algorithm one by one mathematically. In terms of math the algorithm is quite hard. With library I just can, I import them from Internet. With one or two lines code I can use them. I can focus more on main procedure of neural network and data manipulation, so I can save a lot of time with the library"* (PS12).

Other peoples' code was a large theme when discussing APIs, particularly examples posted online or documentation-like guidance from others. *"Sometimes just some posts either forums or some question and answer community like Stack Overflow. There are people show you how to use in their answers, kind of you can copy paste and modify that to suit your needs"* (PS05). APIs also tended to be designed in such a way that they were easy to start using. *"Maybe it is just experience, that makes it easier, because I was using APIs for so long so it is easy now to just come and start"* (PS01). APIs also made it easy to get code running quickly, especially if the documentation was good and contained examples. *"If you pick a certain thing, you read the documentation, hopefully the documentation is done well, by done well I mean by examples. That you can get something to run as fast as possible because that keeps you motivated"* (PS13).

**Security APIs.** When asked about a 'security API' participants struggled to understand what that could even be, falling back on areas commonly associated with security, like finance. *"What do you mean by security APIs? Something like payment gateway?"* (PS04). Only one participant had a hands on experience with a security API which was problematic. *"There is no feedback [in Android certificate validation]. It is a complete nightmare, various very long complicated classes archaic options that you are supposed to set. All and all was 40–50 lines of code. This was just a block of imperative commands for doing something basic like I'd like to validate against certificate file please. Absolutely crazy"* (P19).

While only observed from one participant, his comments closely match what other researchers have observed from professional developers [6,19,22,27].

P19, who has industry experience both as a developer and an intern, was one of the few people who discussed issues around secure programming, such as buffer overflow and functions with known security issues. *"buffer overflows, system calls are an issue of languages, actually more that anything else. We still use C this is an atrocity, we shouldn't be using C anymore"* (P19). He is referring to common C function calls like `gets` which are impossible to use in a secure way, but are still commonly used due to being part of core C [38].

**Trusting Other Peoples' Code.** Using APIs and examples from the Internet was convenient for our participants, but it also required them to trust people they had never met. Some were concerned about blindly trusting code from unknown sources, but many had no problem instead choosing to trust in collective intelligence. *"If I download, I am often downloading source codes myself from the Internet and then building it. And again I don't have the time or the skill to audit say a code base that has millions of lines. I perhaps trust a little bit too much the crowd of people. If I look at the code base and see something on Github and it has let's say 2000 stars. Few hundred people watching it. The code is all open. I tend to perhaps foolishly I assume that if this many people have looked at it and if there was something up. Surely someone would do have said something. Download the code and build it. So it is possible that I have exposed myself to security issues as a result of that"* (PS08). PS08 is referring to the 'many eyeballs' idea in open source software which is an indicator of security and reliability of code for some developers [32].

Trust is an inherent component of open source, that is code is open for everyone to read. *"As one of the reason I really want an open source app to do this is that this kind of app is allowed to access a lot of info. I don't trust any closed source software. I could use them but I don't trust them. Open source is the only way I could trust software. Although open source you could still add malicious code to open source in hope that people wouldn't discover that. But this is the only way"* (PS05).

Trust in open source reaches to its highest level when people prefer to write less code and reuse others' code instead. *"So my idea is that the least I code the better. As long as [hypothetical app] is still maintained and supported regularly and I do update that regularly. Then I think I will be fine. Because tools that are widely used are very exposed to criticism so their maintainers usually patch up and correct their mistakes as fast as they can. So I'd very aware of what of dangers of the whole thing. And I would be careful to following news. But I'd avoid writing my own code"* (PS15) is a comment on open source software while the participant was discussing her hypothetical classroom app.

# 5 Discussion

**Security Mindsets.** Mindsets are likely to influence actions and decision making [41,43,67]. We found that most students did not have a clearly developed concept of security. In fact, some participants even struggled to come up with words that could be associated with the term 'computer security'. When it comes to threats such as hackers, what they can do, their intentions and capabilities is another point which needs improvements, we observe the similar patterns and folk models in CS students that others have seen in home users [44,67].

Mental models could be partially rooted in media [25]; participants cited media plot elements when describing hackers. End user security has seen success in teaching users to copy existing mental models such as viruses or home safety to better understand and reason about security and privacy [17]. Our results suggest that similar approaches may work in the educational context to improve the mental models of students.

**APIs.** When it comes to APIs, our results closely mirror what related work has shown for professional developers. They often use a combination of online resources to learn and use APIs. They prefer to use easier to use resources, and because official documentation is often not easy to use they tend to go for online resources like Stack Overflow [2]. Professional developers (like our student sample) prefer documentation with examples and matching API scenarios [52,58]. Therefore, API designers are a significant element in secure software development ecosystem particularly industry API designers who have a large impact on developers. By designing usable APIs [29] and easy to understand documentation [58] they can help students and developers learn and use APIs correctly which could result in building secure software.

**Division of Labour.** Who is in charge of doing security at organisations has long been a problem point with different units often thinking that security is the job of another team [5]. A view shared by several of our participants. Though such a tendency is considered to be a "key inhibitor toward secure software development practices" [71, p. 164].

In the work place, security auditors are in charge of checking code for issues which developers are then in charge of fixing [63]. However this system has some downsides. First, auditing takes time during which developers work on other projects and loose the working memory they had about particular code segments. And second, fixing the code requires an understanding of the security issue in order to properly address it, and as has been previously shown, developers have difficulty interacting with security technologies like cryptography libraries due to misunderstandings around how cryptography works [19].

In industry [9] it is necessary to create a security culture where basic security is everyone's responsibility and the security team is a component of that culture rather than the only people who 'do' security. In education such a culture might be facilitated by providing student with code samples that are secure by default and by having them use code checking tools in IDEs that check for problems, such as static analysis tools which teach them not only that they should look for these issues, but also how.

Companies with high security standards make security as a commitment, do not satisfy security because of complexity, and they follow strict formal development and testing processes [31]. Universities can benefit these best practices and tech CS students how to become developers that care about S&P.

**Security as a Requirement.** There are several similarities between the students' views and general industry practices. Student developers' treatment of security as an implied requirement is in line with findings that security is often treated as a non-functional feature in agile methods [13,24], and that the requirement is not explicitly stated [12,15]. When asked to describe the features of the classroom discussion app, which had been intentionally chosen as an example of a task with implicit S&P requirements, many students did not consider S&P as an initial priority. For some students, this might be an artefact of their classroom development experience, where they tend to work on well formed projects that are unlikely to have security as an explicit requirement.

Poor and inconsistent understanding of S&P among CS students is likely to cause conflicts between real and best practices in the software industry. For example, when choosing a framework developers do not consider security as a deciding factor which contradicts secure development best practices [8]. In alignment with other aspects of software development, there is a need to synchronise the development approaches taught in the classroom with those used by industry. That synchronisation needs to occur in both directions such that students are taught industry best standards which they are then able to apply.

**Internships.** Internships are a way to engage students in the topic as well as prepare them for future careers [14,18]. Although they require investments from industry [33] we believe that the shortage of S&P professionals [26] cannot be solved without involving every player. Hence, we encourage industry to offer more internships to CS students in S&P fields to improve the number of students graduating with that type of experience.

## 6   Limitations

Our population includes only students at a single Russell Group university in the UK. Even though our sample was diverse, it was not balanced for gender or security experience. Moreover, only two of our participants were native speakers of English, and we might have obtained more finely differentiated views and opinions if we had been able to interview each participant in their native language. Since we conducted the study during summer vacation time, this resulted in a participant pool biased towards Masters and PhD students, since undergraduate students are not normally present at University in the summer months. Possibly some of our potential participants were in their hometown and could not take part in this study.

# 7 Future Work

We plan to expand our study to other universities with a large scale survey to investigate differences and similarities across curriculum, universities and countries. Extending outcomes of this research to industry and professional developers and comparing results is also a path that could lead to valuable insights. Another interesting avenue for future work is to investigate the impact of open source and code reuse in system security. It also remains to question how developers trust in others' code and import code from different resources without knowing their source and coder.

# 8 Conclusions

In this work we reported on a qualitative analysis of twenty semi-structured interviews with CS students. We find that the attitudes of students match many of those observed by other researchers looking at professional level developers. Students have a range of hacker/attack mindsets, lack of experience with security APIs, a mixed view of who is in charge of S&P in the software life cycle, and a tendency to trust other peoples' code as a convenient approach to rapidly build software. We further give recommendations for both industry and academia to improve software S&P ecosystem.

**Acknowledgements.** Thanks to all participants for their time and everyone associated with the TULiPS Lab at the University of Edinburgh for helpful discussions and feedback. We also thank the anonymous reviewers whose comments helped improve the paper greatly. This work was sponsored in part by Microsoft Research through its PhD Scholarship Programme.

# Appendix: Interview Script

1. Background
   • Can you tell me about yourself? Your academic and professional background? • Can you tell me about your dream job?
2. App scenario
   Let's say you were asked to create a new group discussion app for in-class discussions. • Free list: what features would you consider in this app? • Here is a red pen. Can you circle the features that are security and privacy related? Or where you might have to consider security and privacy when building them? • Why these ones? • Who is most likely to try and attack this system? What are they likely going to try and do?

3. Threats and attacks
   • Can you tell me who hackers are, in your opinion? • Their intentions? • What are hackers trying to get? • Their background?
4. Responsibility attribution
   • Who is responsible for providing security and privacy to end users?
5. Prior coding experiences
   • Tell me about the last piece of software you wrote. • Did you consider security while building your project? If not this one, any other projects? • Can you tell me an example of an API/library? Can you give me some experiences you have had with them? Any experience with security APIs in particular? • What was good about it? Why did you like it? • What was confusing about it?
6. Personal security/privacy practices
   Now we are going to switch to talking about how you handle security and privacy personally as an end user. • Free list: What words and concepts do you associate with computer security? • Can you give me an example of a good computer security practice? What about something you have done yourself? • Have you ever experienced a security or privacy compromise such as getting a virus on your computer, losing your password, having an email sent from your account, or loss of data about you? • How did you find out about the issue? • How did you correct it? • What did you learn from the experience? • Can you tell me some about the experiences you have had with passwords?
7. Background and demographics
   • How old are you? • What is your degree title? • Which year of the program are you in? • What programming languages do you know? • What programming courses have you taken? • What security courses have you taken? • What is your nationality? • Where did you study your undergraduate, Masters, or other degrees?

# References

1. Acar, Y., et al.: Comparing the usability of cryptographic APIs. In: IEEE Symposium on Security and Privacy, pp. 154–171 (2017)
2. Acar, Y., Backes, M., Fahl, S., Kim, D., Mazurek, M.L., Stransky, C.: You get where you're looking for: the impact of information sources on code security. In: 2016 IEEE Symposium on Security and Privacy (SP), pp. 289–305 (2016)
3. Acar, Y., Fahl, S., Mazurek, M.L.: You are not your developer, either: a research agenda for usable security and privacy research beyond end users. In: Cybersecurity Development (SecDev), pp. 3–8. IEEE (2016)
4. Acar, Y., Stransky, C., Wermke, D., Weir, C., Mazurek, M.L., Fahl, S.: Developers need support, too: a survey of security advice for software developers. In: Cybersecurity Development (SecDev), pp. 22–26. IEEE (2017)
5. Arce, I., et al.: Avoiding the Top 10 software security design flaws. Technical report, IEEE Computer Societys Center for Secure Design (CSD) (2014)
6. Arzt, S., Nadi, S., Ali, K., Bodden, E., Erdweg, S., Mezini, M.: Towards secure integration of cryptographic software. In: 2015 ACM International Symposium on New Ideas, New Paradigms, and Reflections on Programming and Software (Onward!), pp. 1–13 (2015)

7. Asgharpour, F., Liu, D., Camp, L.J.: Mental models of security risks. In: Dietrich, S., Dhamija, R. (eds.) FC 2007. LNCS, vol. 4886, pp. 367–377. Springer, Heidelberg (2007). https://doi.org/10.1007/978-3-540-77366-5_34
8. Assal, H., Chiasson, S.: Security in the software development lifecycle. In: Fourteenth Symposium on Usable Privacy and Security (SOUPS) (2018)
9. Assal, H., Chiasson, S.: 'Think secure from the beginning': a survey with software developers. In: Proceedings of the 2019 CHI Conference on Human Factors in Computing Systems (2019)
10. Azhar, M., et al.: Securing the human: broadening diversity in cybersecurity. In: Proceedings of the 2019 ACM Conference on Innovation and Technology in Computer Science Education, pp. 251–252 (2019)
11. Balebako, R., Cranor, L.: Improving app privacy: nudging app developers to protect user privacy. IEEE Secur. Privacy 12(4), 55–58 (2014)
12. Bartsch, S.: Practitioners' perspectives on security in agile development. In: Proceedings of the 2011 Sixth International Conference on Availability, Reliability and Security, pp. 479–484 (2011)
13. Bell, L., Brunton-Spall, M., Smith, R., Bird, J.: Agile Application Security: Enabling Security in a Continuous Delivery Pipeline. O'Reilly Media, Newton (2017)
14. Binder, J.F., Baguley, T., Crook, C., Miller, F.: The academic value of internships: benefits across disciplines and student backgrounds. Contemp. Educ. Psychol. 41, 73–82 (2015)
15. Bowen, J.P., Hinchey, M., Janicke, H., Ward, M.P., Zedan, H.: Formality, agility, security, and evolution in software development. IEEE Comput. 47(10), 86–89 (2014)
16. Cambazoglu, V., Thota, N.: Computer science students' perception of computer network security. In: Learning and Teaching in Computing and Engineering (LaTiCE), pp. 204–207. IEEE (2013)
17. Camp, L.J.: Mental models of privacy and security. IEEE Technol. Soc. Mag. 28(3), 37–46 (2009)
18. Chillas, S., Marks, A., Galloway, L.: Learning to labour: an evaluation of internships and employability in the ICT sector. New Technol. Work Employ. 30(1), 1–15 (2015)
19. Egele, M., Brumley, D., Fratantonio, Y., Kruegel, C.: An empirical study of cryptographic misuse in android applications. In: Proceedings of the 2013 ACM SIGSAC Conference on Computer and Communications Security, pp. 73–84 (2013)
20. The European parliament and the council of the European union: General Data Protection Regulation (GDPR) (2018). https://eur-lex.europa.eu/legal-content/EN/TXT/PDF/?uri=CELEX:32016R0679. Accessed Aug 2019
21. Fahl, S., Harbach, M., Muders, T., Baumgärtner, L., Freisleben, B., Smith, M.: Why eve and Mallory love android: an analysis of android SSL (in) security. In: Proceedings of the 2012 ACM Conference on Computer and Communications Security, pp. 50–61 (2012)
22. Fahl, S., Harbach, M., Perl, H., Koetter, M., Smith, M.: Rethinking SSL development in an appified world. In: Proceedings of the 2013 ACM SIGSAC Conference on Computer & Communications Security, pp. 49–60 (2013)
23. Fischer, F., et al.: Stack overflow considered harmful? The impact of copy paste on android application security. In: 2017 IEEE Symposium on Security and Privacy (SP), pp. 121–136 (2017)
24. Fitzgerald, B., Stol, K.J.: Continuous software engineering: a roadmap and agenda. J. Syst. Softw. 123, 176–189 (2017)

25. Fulton, K.R., Gelles, R., McKay, A., Abdi, Y., Roberts, R., Mazurek, M.L.: The effect of entertainment media on mental models of computer security. In: Fifteenth Symposium on Usable Privacy and Security (SOUPS) (2019)
26. Furnell, S., Fischer, P., Finch, A.: Can't get the staff? the growing need for cybersecurity skills. Comput. Fraud Secur. **2017**(2), 5–10 (2017)
27. Georgiev, M., Iyengar, S., Jana, S., Anubhai, R., Boneh, D., Shmatikov, V.: The most dangerous code in the world: validating SSL certificates in non-browser software. In: Proceedings of the 2012 ACM Conference on Computer and Communications Security, pp. 38–49 (2012)
28. Google: Google diversity annual report (2018). http://diversity.google/annual-report. Accessed Aug 2019
29. Green, M., Smith, M.: Developers are not the enemy!: the need for usable security APIs. IEEE Secur. Priv. **14**(5), 40–46 (2016)
30. Hadar, I., et al.: Privacy by designers: software developers' privacy mindset. Empirical Softw. Eng. **23**(1), 259–289 (2018)
31. Haney, J.M., Theofanos, M., Acar, Y., Prettyman, S.S.: "We make it a big deal in the company": security mindsets in organizations that develop cryptographic products. In: Fourteenth Symposium on Usable Privacy and Security (SOUPS) (2018)
32. Hissam, S.A., Plakosh, D., Weinstock, C.: Trust and vulnerability in open source software. IEE Proc. Softw. **149**(1), 47–51 (2002)
33. Hoffman, L., Burley, D., Toregas, C.: Holistically building the cybersecurity workforce. IEEE Secur. Priv. **10**(2), 33–39 (2012)
34. Iacono, L.L., Gorski, P.L.: I do and I understand. Not yet true for security APIs. So sad. In: Proceedings of the 2nd European Workshop on Usable Security, ser. EuroUSEC (2017)
35. Indela, S., Kulkarni, M., Nayak, K., Dumitras, T.: Toward semantic cryptography APIs. In: Cybersecurity Development (SecDev), pp. 9–14. IEEE (2016)
36. Information Commissioner's Office: Investigation into the use of data analytics in political campaigns (2018). https://ico.org.uk/media/action-weve-taken/2259371/investigation-into-data-analytics-for-political-purposes-update.pdf. Accessed Aug 2019
37. Jones, K., Siami Namin, A., Armstrong, M.: What should cybersecurity students learn in school?: results from interviews with cyber professionals. In: Proceedings of the 2017 ACM SIGCSE Technical Symposium on Computer Science Education, p. 711 (2017)
38. Kernighan, B.W., Ritchie, D.M.: The C Programming Language. Prentice Hall, New Jersey (2006)
39. Lazar, D., Chen, H., Wang, X., Zeldovich, N.: Why does cryptographic software fail?: a case study and open problems. In: Proceedings of 5th Asia-Pacific Workshop on Systems, p. 7. ACM (2014)
40. Lazar, J., Feng, J.H., Hochheiser, H.: Research Methods in Human-Computer Interaction. Morgan Kaufmann, Cambridge (2017)
41. Maier, J., Padmos, A., Bargh, M.S., Wörndl, W.: Influence of mental models on the design of cyber security dashboards. In: Proceedings of the 12th International Joint Conference on Computer Vision, Imaging and Computer Graphics Theory and Applications, IVAPP, (VISIGRAPP), vol. 3, pp. 128–139 (2017)
42. Mansfield-Devine, S.: The Ashley Madison affair. Netw. Secur. **2015**(9), 8–16 (2015)

43. Märki, H., Maas, M., Kauer-Franz, M., Oberle, M.: Increasing software security by using mental models. In: Nicholson, D. (ed.) Advances in Human Factors in Cybersecurity. Advances in Intelligent Systems and Computing, vol. 501, pp. 347–359. Springer, Cham (2016). https://doi.org/10.1007/978-3-319-41932-9_29

44. Mazurek, M.L., et al.: Access control for home data sharing: attitudes, needs and practices. In: Proceedings of the SIGCHI Conference on Human Factors in Computing Systems, pp. 645–654 (2010)

45. Miles, M., Huberman, M.: Qualitative Data Analysis: A Methods Sourcebook. Sage, Los Angeles (1994)

46. Munro, K.: Hacking kettles & extracting plain text WPA PSKs. Yes really! (2015). https://www.pentestpartners.com/security-blog/hacking-kettles-extracting-plain-text-wpa-psks-yes-really. Accessed Aug 2019

47. Nadi, S., Krüger, S., Mezini, M., Bodden, E.: Jumping through hoops: why do java developers struggle with cryptography APIs? In: Proceedings of the 38th International Conference on Software Engineering, pp. 935–946. ACM (2016)

48. Nielson, S.J.: PLAYGROUND: preparing students for the cyber battleground. Comput. Sci. Educ. 26(4), 255–276 (2016)

49. Oliveira, D., Rosenthal, M., Morin, N., Yeh, K.C., Cappos, J., Zhuang, Y.: It's the psychology stupid: how heuristics explain software vulnerabilities and how priming can illuminate developer's blind spots. In: Proceedings of the 30th Annual Computer Security Applications Conference, pp. 296–305 (2014)

50. Oltrogge, M., et al.: The rise of the citizen developer: assessing the security impact of online app generators. In: 2018 IEEE Symposium on Security and Privacy (SP), pp. 634–647 (2018)

51. OWASP: Top 10 Most Critical Web Application Security Risks. Technical report, The OWASP Foundation (2017)

52. Patnaik, N., Hallett, J., Rashid, A.: Usability smells: an analysis of developers' struggle with crypto libraries. In: Fifteenth Symposium on Usable Privacy and Security (SOUPS) (2019)

53. Pieczul, O., Foley, S., Zurko, M.E.: Developer-centered security and the symmetry of ignorance. In: Proceedings of the 2017 New Security Paradigms Workshop, pp. 46–56. ACM (2017)

54. Poller, A., Kocksch, L., Türpe, S., Epp, F.A., Kinder-Kurlanda, K.: Can security become a routine?: a study of organizational change in an agile software development group. In: Proceedings of the 2017 ACM Conference on Computer Supported Cooperative Work and Social Computing, pp. 2489–2503 (2017)

55. Radermacher, A., Walia, G.: Gaps between industry expectations and the abilities of graduates. In: Proceeding of the 44th ACM Technical Symposium on Computer Science Education, pp. 525–530 (2013)

56. Radermacher, A., Walia, G., Knudson, D.: Investigating the skill gap between graduating students and industry expectations. In: Companion Proceedings of the 36th International Conference on Software Engineering, pp. 291–300. ACM (2014)

57. Renaud, K., Volkamer, M., Renkema-Padmos, A.: Why doesn't jane protect her privacy? In: De Cristofaro, E., Murdoch, S.J. (eds.) PETS 2014. LNCS, vol. 8555, pp. 244–262. Springer, Cham (2014). https://doi.org/10.1007/978-3-319-08506-7_13

58. Robillard, M.P., Deline, R.: A field study of API learning obstacles. Empirical Softw. Eng. 16(6), 703–732 (2011)

59. Saldaña, J.: The Coding Manual for Qualitative Researchers. Sage, London (2015)

60. StackOverflow: Developer Survey Results (2019). https://insights.stackoverflow.com/survey/2019. Accessed Aug 2019

61. Sudol, L.A., Jaspan, C.: Analyzing the strength of undergraduate misconceptions about software engineering. In: Proceedings of the Sixth International Workshop on Computing Education Research, pp. 31–40 (2010)
62. Tabassum, M., Watson, S., Chu, B., Lipford, H.R.: Evaluating two methods for integrating secure programming education. In: Proceedings of the 49th ACM Technical Symposium on Computer Science Education, pp. 390–395 (2018)
63. Thomas, T.W., Tabassum, M., Chu, B., Lipford, H.: Security during application development: an application security expert perspective. In: Proceedings of the 2018 CHI Conference on Human Factors in Computing Systems, p. 262 (2018)
64. Ukrop, M., Matyas, V.: Why Johnny the developer can't work with public key certificates. In: Smart, N.P. (ed.) CT-RSA 2018. LNCS, vol. 10808, pp. 45–64. Springer, Cham (2018). https://doi.org/10.1007/978-3-319-76953-0_3
65. Vaniea, K.E., Rader, E., Wash, R.: Betrayed by updates: how negative experiences affect future security. In: Proceedings of the SIGCHI Conference on Human Factors in Computing Systems (2014)
66. Vox: The Cambridge Analytica Facebook scandal (2018). https://www.vox.com/2018/4/10/17207394. Accessed Aug 2019
67. Wash, R.: Folk models of home computer security. In: Proceedings of the Sixth Symposium on Usable Privacy and Security (SOUPS) (2010)
68. Weir, C., Rashid, A., Noble, J.: How to improve the security skills of mobile app developers: comparing and contrasting expert views. In: Twelfth Symposium on Usable Privacy and Security (SOUPS) (2016)
69. Whitney, M., Lipford-Richter, H., Chu, B., Zhu, J.: Embedding secure coding instruction into the IDE: a field study in an advanced CS course. In: Proceedings of the 46th ACM Technical Symposium on Computer Science Education (2015)
70. Wurster, G., van Oorschot, P.C.: The developer is the enemy. In: Proceedings of the 2008 New Security Paradigms Workshop, pp. 89–97. ACM (2009)
71. Xie, J., Lipford, H.R., Chu, B.: Why do programmers make security errors? In: 2011 IEEE Symposium on Visual Languages and Human-Centric Computing (VL/HCC), pp. 161–164 (2011)
72. Zou, Y., Mhaidli, A.H., McCall, A., Schaub, F.: "I've got nothing to lose": consumers risk perceptions and protective actions after the equifax data breach. In: Fourteenth Symposium on Usable Privacy and Security (SOUPS) (2018)

# Data, Data, Everywhere: Quantifying Software Developers' Privacy Attitudes

Dirk van der Linden[1]([✉]), Irit Hadar[3], Matthew Edwards[2], and Awais Rashid[2]

[1] Department of Computer and Information Sciences, Northumbria University,
Newcastle-upon-Tyne, UK
`dirk.vanderlinden@northumbria.ac.uk`
[2] Bristol Cyber Security Group, University of Bristol, Bristol, UK
`{matthew.john.edwards,awais.rashid}@bristol.ac.uk`
[3] Department of Information Systems, University of Haifa, Haifa, Israel
`hadari@is.haifa.ac.il`

**Abstract.** Understanding developers' attitudes towards handling personal data is vital in order to understand whether the software they create handles their users' privacy fairly. We present the results of a study adapting an existing user-focused privacy concern scale to a software development context and running it with a sample of 123 software developers, in order to validate it and develop a model for measuring the extent to which a software developer is (dis)favorable to ensuring their users' privacy. The developed scale exceeds thresholds for internal reliability ($\alpha > .8$), composite reliability ($CR > .8$), and convergent validity ($AVE > .6$). Our findings identified a model consisting of three factors that allows for understanding of developers' attitudes, including: (1) informed consent, (2) data minimization, and (3) data monetization. Through analysis of results from the scale's deployment, we further discuss mismatches between developers' attitudes and their self-perceived extent of properly handling their users' privacy, and the importance of understanding developers' attitudes towards data monetization.

**Keywords:** Developer · Privacy · Attitude · Scale development

## 1 Introduction

Understanding individual developers' attitudes towards privacy – more specifically, their *attitude* towards handling personal data, is an important precursor to understand what drives the formation of their privacy practices while developing software. Attitudes – mental constructs which reveal the extent of positive or negative feelings someone holds towards a particular thing [12] – are an important precursor to behavioral intention. The Theory of Reasoned Action (TRA) posits that behavioral intention via attitude combined with social norms are key

D. van der Linden—This work was authored while the author was at the University of Bristol.

T. Groß and T. Tryfonas (Eds.): STAST 2019, LNCS 11739, pp. 47–65, 2021.
https://doi.org/10.1007/978-3-030-55958-8_3

predictors to whether someone will behave in a particular way [19]. A software developer's attitude towards the handling of personal data is thus an important aspect of understanding how they will handle personal data in reality.

Yet, little work exists to aid in the large-scale measurement of software developers' attitudes towards privacy, or, more practically, their handling of personal data. A scale proposed by Woon and Kankanhalli [29] allows for measurements of developers' attitudes towards incorporating security into application development. But, security is not privacy, and security mindsets have been shown to push developers towards understanding privacy as little more than a *technical* data security issue, discarding the much larger *socio-technical* considerations that properly handling privacy entails [6,15]. More encompassing scales to measure attitudes regarding privacy exist from a consumer's point of view (cf. [7,17,26]). A review of such scales [21] showed that, even in the context of a general population of users, privacy attitudes are elicited in an ad-hoc manner through questionnaires.

To that end, this paper aims to contribute by addressing the lack of systematically developed scales measuring privacy attitude of software developers. To do so, we adapted a widely used and validated scale for internet users' information privacy concerns (IUIPC) [17] to a software development context, empirically testing it among a sample of professional software developers (N = 123), and constructing a software developer-specific model from factors arising out of the data. We make the following major contributions:

- *We present the Software Developers' Privacy Attitude (SDPA) scale for measuring the extent to which a software developer is (dis)favorable to ensuring their users' privacy.* Our analysis identified a three-factor model capturing software developers' attitudes towards handling personal data of users of their software: (1) *informed consent:* the extent to which they ensure their users are given the option and ability to provide informed consent, (2) *data minimization:* the extent to which they minimize the data they collect from users, and (3) *data monetization:* the extent to which they perceive monetizing data as impacting user privacy.
- *We discuss mismatches between developers' attitudes and their self-perceived extent of 'properly' handling their users' privacy.* In particular, our application of the scale showed that developers' attitudes towards data collection reveals they may collect more data than their self-perceived behavior would indicate. More such mismatches may exist depending on the development context and type of personal data handled, which requires more work to point out such potentially dangerous mismatches of attitude and self-perceived behavior.
- *We discuss the importance of understanding developers' attitudes towards the third identified factor of data monetization.* This factor arose out of the data as the most strongly loaded factor, contrasting original work from users' point of view, showing many developers do not look disfavorably on monetizing user data in marketing transactions (through, e.g., advertisement analytics). Because software development is increasingly the domain of solo or small scale developer teams [11,25] who make these monetization decisions, more research is necessary to understand how advertisement-reliant ecosystems

such as mobile and web applications may push developers towards understating the impact their decisions have on their users' privacy.

The rest of this paper proceeds as follows. Section 2 discusses the background and related work. Construction of the scale and its implementation are shown in Sect. 3, and reflections on its further development and use are discussed in Sect. 4. Finally, we conclude in Sect. 5.

## 2 Background and Related Work

### 2.1 Understanding Privacy Attitudes

Senarath and Arachchilage [22] indicate that developers have practical challenges when attempting to embed privacy into their software, in particular relating privacy requirements into engineering techniques, and lack knowledge on privacy concepts. Specific concepts of privacy aware systems such as data minimization were similarly found to be difficult [23].

In order to achieve a fuller picture of software developers' privacy perceptions and overall mindset, Hadar et al. [15] conducted a qualitative investigation using in-depth semi-structured interviews. They found that developers largely approach privacy through a data security lens, focusing on technical aspects and security solutions. They further found that developers' work environment, and in particular the organizational privacy climate, plays an important role in shaping developers' privacy perceptions and attitudes. These findings were qualitatively substantiated; a quantitative scale is required to test correlations between environmental (or other) factors and developers' privacy attitudes.

Ayalon et al. [3] performed an online survey based on example scenarios, to assess software developers' privacy attitudes. They were able to demonstrate evidence possibly suggesting the effect of organizational climate on developers privacy attitudes and behavior. They further found that personal experience as end users affects developers' privacy practices. However, they did not perform a systematic scale development, and the items used to assess personal attitudes had low internal reliability. Our work goes beyond here by showing the systematic adaptation of a scale for quantification of software developers' privacy attitudes, available for other researchers to employ.

### 2.2 Quantifying Privacy Attitudes

In this paper, we adapt the Internet Users Information Privacy Concern (IUIPC) scale [17], which in itself is an adaption and extension of the Concern for Information Privacy (CFIP) scale [26]. As mentioned in the introduction, we use the more general psychological notion of 'attitude', which refers to mental constructs which reveal the extent of positive or negative feelings someone holds towards a particular thing [12]. The IUIPC focuses on consumers' privacy *concerns* – in effect focusing on eliciting specifically the negative feelings, or *attitudes*, that participants hold towards the presented items. We use attitude to allow the scale to clearly capture developers' positive and negative view of data practices, thereby permitting us to contrast how developers may view certain practices positively (e.g., making money by transferring data to third parties) while their users may view them negatively (i.e., by losing control over their data).

The IUIPC is based on the notion of fairness and justice, assuming that the essence of privacy lies in fair and just handling of personal data, from which its three main dimensions flow: personal data is only handled fairly and justly if (1) it is collected appropriately (*collection*), (2) its data subjects are made aware of that collection (*awareness*)), and they are given control over it (*control*). These notions clearly align with the normative context set by regulation such as the GDPR and some of its key articles software has to abide by – including data minimization Art. 5(1)(c); lawfulness, fairness and transparency Art. 12–14; and control: Arts. 15–21.

Malhotra et al. note that with appropriate rewording the scale is expected to reasonably apply to other privacy contexts [17, p. 349] – such as software development. Ensuring an appropriate rewording to this context requires consideration of what just and fair handling of personal data means from a software developers' point of view.

However, developers' attitudes are likely to be more nuanced, reflecting their need to balance the data they collect and the control and awareness they give users over it with their own business demands (e.g., having to incorporate advertisement analytics SDKs to achieve monetization) and legal compliance (e.g., having to comply with relevant data protection acts). Not all developers will have the luxury of delegating business decisions to others, and many have to deal with decisions about how to handle personal data. The extent to which handling of personal data is just, and more importantly, *fair* to developers, will likely incorporate trade-off considerations between what benefits the user, and what benefits the developer or their organization's bottom line. As a result, there may be different attitudes towards, and relations between, the items from the IUIPC. Thus, our paper represents a starting point to explore how developers' privacy attitudes may quantitatively differ from users. To the best of our knowledge, this work is the first to do so in a systematic fashion.

## 3  Development of the SDPA Scale and Model

This section will detail the adaption of the items from the IUIPC to a software development context, through its deployment with a sample of software developers, and the statistical analysis performed to construct the final model.

### 3.1  Adapting the IUIPC Scale to Software Development

Table 1 summarizes the key aspects of the original consumer-focused scale, and how we adapt it to a software development context. We adapted the consumer-focused items developed or adapted by Malhotra et al. [17] to a software development context as per Table 1 (e.g., online companies ⇒ the software I develop; consumer ⇒ my user). Full details are shown in Appendix B. This resulted in items (a)–(i):

**Table 1.** Comparison between IUIPC and SDPA.

|  | IUIPC | SDPA |
|---|---|---|
| Purpose | To reflect Internet users' concerns about Information privacy | To reflect Software developers' attitudes towards handling users' personal data and ensuring privacy |
| Focus | Individuals' perceptions of fairness/justice in the Context of information privacy | Software developers' perception of fairness/justice towards their users in context of personal data handling |
| Context | Mostly online environment | Software development |
| Communication | Mostly two-way communication | *ibid* |
| Dimensions | Collection, control, awareness of privacy practices | Informed consent, data minimization, data monetization |
| Representation | Second-order factor | *ibid* |

(a) It usually bothers me when the software I develop asks my users for personal information.

(b) I sometimes think twice before asking my users for personal information with the software I develop.

(c) It bothers me to collect personal information from so many users with the software I develop.

(d) I'm concerned that the software I develop is collecting too much personal information about my users.

(e) My user's privacy is really a matter of their right to exercise control and autonomy over decisions about how their information is collected, used, and shared by the software I develop.

(f) My users' control of personal information collected by the software I develop lies at the heart of user privacy.

(g) I believe that my users' privacy is invaded when control is lost or unwillingly reduced as a result of a marketing transaction.

(h) The software I develop should disclose the way the data are collected, processed, and used.

(i) A good privacy policy for the software I develop should have a clear and conspicuous disclosure.

(j) It is very important to me that my users are aware and knowledgeable about how their personal information will be used.

Based on the three main factors identified by Malhotra et al. [17] as predictive of behavioral intent for privacy concern, we adapted three questions to assess how software developers perceive themselves to fairly/justly handle personal data in software development. This resulted in items (i)–(iii):

(i) I properly deal with the extent to which my software collects data of its users
(ii) I properly deal with the extent to which my software gives users control over their data
(iii) I properly deal with the extent to which my software informs its users how their data is used

The full questionnaire developed with these items (shown in randomized order to participants) is shown in Appendix A.

## 3.2   Deploying the Adapted Scale

To test the adapted scale, we performed a questionnaire-based study measuring the attitude of software developers towards their users' privacy using the newly adapted SDPA scale. Each item was followed by a 7pt scale anchored with "strongly disagree" and "strongly agree". We obtained approval from our Institutional Review Board (IRB) before any empirical work began. No personal information was captured from any participants.

We used Prolific [1] to recruit participants employed as software developers. In total 123 developers completed the study in the 3-day run-time. Each participant was paid £0.30 for completion of the study. A summary of relevant demographics is shown in Table 2. Note that most covariates (sex, age, etc.) were not explicitly elicited through the questionnaire as Prolific provided these data. Results of the deployment for all items are shown in Figs. 1 and 2.

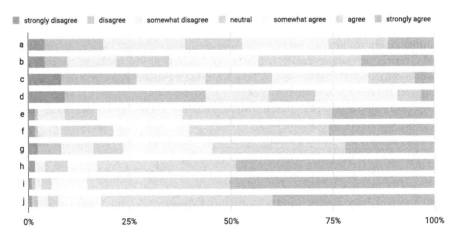

**Fig. 1.** Detailed results for all items (n = 123). Factor 1 includes items e, f, h, i, j; Factor 2 includes items a, b, c, d; Factor 3 includes item g.

**Table 2.** Demographic data of developers (N = 123) from the scale's first deployment.

|  |  | (N = 123) |
| --- | --- | --- |
| Age | 18–24 | 16% |
|  | 25–34 | 59% |
|  | 35–44 | 13% |
|  | >44 | 14% |
| Sex | Male | 79% |
|  | Female | 21% |
| Type of software | Web | 85% |
|  | Desktop | 57% |
|  | Mobile | 51% |
|  | Plugins | 30% |
|  | Embedded | 15% |
|  | OS | 10% |
| Type of employment | Full-time | 81% |
|  | Part-time | 15% |
|  | Other | 4% |
| Place of employment | Europe | 59% |
|  | North America | 37% |
|  | Australasia | 4% |
|  | South America | 1% |

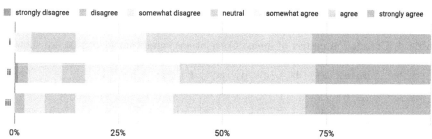

**Fig. 2.** Detailed results for self-perceived proper handling of personal data (n = 123).

### 3.3 Constructing the SDPA Model

Our initial approach to building the SDPA scale for developers adopted the IUIPC's mapping of the 10 items to 3 factors (Collection: a–d, Control: e–g, and Awareness: h–j) for consumers – as indicated by the table segments in Table 3.

To validate this measurement model, we conducted a confirmatory factor analysis (CFA) of goodness-of-fit for the consumer model on our data, evaluated in terms of comparative fit index (CFI), goodness-of-fit index (GFI) and root mean square error of approximation (RMSEA). A model is considered to be satisfactory if CFI $> 0.95$, GFI $> 0.90$ and RMSEA $< 0.06$ [17]. Our adaption of the IUIPC's scale following their consumer-focused model showed acceptable CFI (0.96) and GFI (0.93) but poor RMSEA (0.07).

As such, we explored a better factor loading of the items to account for software developers' context. To do this, we performed a principal component and factor loading analysis (see Table 3). The identified factors are based on item loadings above 0.6 indicating sufficient convergent validity [9]. Subsequently, we calculated a correlation matrix of all items (see Table 4).

**Table 3.** Results from component analysis. All factor loadings above .40 are listed below. Interim reliabilities (Cronbach's $\alpha$): F1, .84; F2, .81; F3 n/a. For comparison, the original model Malhotra et al. defined included three factors: a–d, e–g, and h–j.

| Item | Factor 1 | Factor 2 | Factor 3 |
|------|----------|----------|----------|
| a    |          | .783     |          |
| b    |          | .644     |          |
| c    |          | .886     |          |
| d    |          | .776     |          |
| e    | .759     |          |          |
| f    | .71      |          |          |
| g    |          |          | .902     |
| h    | .786     |          |          |
| i    | .809     |          |          |
| j    | .789     |          |          |

**Table 4.** Correlation matrix of items. Correlations significant at $p < .05$ are shown.

| item | a | b | c | d | e | f | g | h | i | j |
|------|------|------|------|------|------|------|------|------|------|------|
| a | – | | | | | | | | | |
| b | 0.46 | – | | | | | | | | |
| c | 0.69 | 0.47 | – | | | | | | | |
| d | 0.45 | 0.25 | 0.58 | – | | | | | | |
| e | | 0.36 | | | – | | | | | |
| f | 0.23 | 0.28 | | | 0.41 | – | | | | |
| g | 0.33 | 0.22 | | | | 0.31 | – | | | |
| h | | 0.25 | 0.22 | | 0.45 | 0.48 | 0.32 | – | | |
| i | | 0.26 | | | 0.39 | 0.54 | | 0.57 | – | |
| j | 0.24 | 0.27 | | | 0.37 | 0.59 | 0.24 | 0.54 | 0.51 | – |

Table 3 indicates a three-factor model captures developers' attitudes best. These factors measure developers' attitudes towards respectively (1) *informed consent*, (2) *data minimization*, and (3) *data monetization* A two-factor model would have discarded item (g), which loads strongly onto the third factor otherwise – even establishing convergent validity. While this represents a single scale measure, it is in line with other psychological work showing similar validity between single and multiple scale measures [8,28], likely due to its specific focus. Moreover, the importance of including this factor lies also in its unique developer-specific view on handling personal data, giving information not yet provided by other scales.

The revised SDPA model for developers passed all three cut-offs under CFA [CFI = 0.97, GFI = 0.93, RMSEA = 0.06]. The collection factor overlaps with the factor identified by Malhotra et al. for users, but developers' views towards control and awareness diverge, with items spread across two distinct, new factors. Table 5 summarizes the final factors and relevant descriptive statistics. All three factors exhibit convergent validity (CR and AVE above resp. .7 and .5 [4]), and discriminant validity beecause square root of AVE is larger than correlation co-efficients of the factors [10,14]. Additionally, a repeated measures T test confirmed all factors' responses differed significantly (F1–F2: $t(122) = -14.87$, p < 0.01; F1–F3: $t(122) = -4.58$, p < 0.01; F2–F3: $t(122) = 7.55$, p < 0.01).

**Table 5.** Factor summary statistics and estimated correlation matrix

| Factor | Mean | SD | $\alpha$ | $\sigma2$ | CR* | AVE* | Rho (p < 0.05)[†] 1 | 2 | 3 |
|---|---|---|---|---|---|---|---|---|---|
| 1. Informed consent | 5.91 | 1.25 | .84 | 1.55 | .88 | .59 | .77 | | |
| 2. Data minimization | 4.06 | 1.76 | .80 | 3.10 | .86 | .60 | .22 | .78 | |
| 3. Data monetization | 5.26 | 1.57 | n/a | 2.46 | .81 | .81 | .29 | .26 | .90 |

*Internal reliability requires $\alpha > 0.7$, convergent validity requires CR > .7 and AVE > .5

† Data on diagonals indicates squared root of AVE.

## 3.4   Assessing Model–Variable Correlations

We found no indication of an effect of contextual variables or demographic covariates on the SDPA score. Other studies using the original scale we adapted varied in finding some correlations for covariates like age and educational level (cf. [30]), to only finding correlations for educational level and income, with more nuanced differences between age groups (cf. [16]). The lack of correlations to covariates is likely due to high homogeneity in the sample such as most developers being male, similar age ranges, and most having developed web apps likely to elicit more privacy considerations. We did establish a significant correlation between score on the SDPA and self-perceived behavior (Spearman's Rho, $r(121) = 0.30$, p < .05). Exploring this in more detail, relating our factors back to the self-perceived behavior's original factor model reveals only strong correlations between our *informed consent* factor and perceived behavior, as shown in Table 6. Most informative here is the lack of a key correlation: factor 2, *data minimization*, is not significantly correlated to the item measuring self-perceived behavior regarding data minimization (Spearman's Rho, $r(121) = 0.15$, $p > .05$). The detailed results shown in Figs. 1 and 2 visualize this by showing that participants rated their own behavior towards data minimization as highly proper, while their attitude reveals a less fair & just approach.

**Table 6.** Correlation matrix of factors and self-perceived items. Correlations significant at $p < .05$ are shown.

| Item | Factor 1 | Factor 2 | Factor 3 |
|------|----------|----------|----------|
| pCOL | .53 | ! | .22 |
| pCON | .48 | | |
| pAWA | .55 | | |
| pIUIPC | .57 | | |
| SDPA | .65 | .83 | .5 |

### 3.5 Constructing the Final Instrument

The final SDPA instrument as developed here contains three factors measuring developers' attitudes towards key aspects of handling personal data, as defined below. To measure the extent to which a software developer is (dis)favorable to these aspects, the items should be accompanied by a 7pt scale anchored with "strongly disagree" and "strongly agree".

### The SDPA Instrument

Factor 1, *informed consent*: the extent to which developers ensure their users are given the ability and option to provide informed consent.

– My users' privacy is really a matter of their right to exercise control and autonomy over decisions about how their information is collected, used, and shared by the software I develop.
– My users' control of personal information collected by the software I develop lies at the heart of user privacy.
– The software I develop should disclose the way the data are collected, processed, and used.
– A good privacy policy for the software I develop should have a clear and conspicuous disclosure.
– It is very important to me that my users are aware and knowledgeable about how their personal information will be used.

Factor 2, *data minimization*: the extent to which developers minimize the data they collect from their users.

- It usually bothers me when the software I develop asks my users for personal information.
- I sometimes think twice before asking my users for personal information with the software I develop.
- It bothers me to collect personal information from so many users with the software I develop.
- I'm concerned that the software I develop is collecting too much personal information about my users.

Factor 3, *data monetization*: the extent to which developers perceive transferring data to marketing parties as impacting users' privacy.

- I believe that my users' privacy is invaded when control is lost or unwillingly reduced as a result of a marketing transaction.

While the covariates investigated in this work did not yield any significant correlations, further work deploying the scale in specific software development situations may yield meaningful context-specific covariates, and allow for testing of other detailed variables.

### 3.6 Threats to Validity

**Internal Validity.** We adapted validated measures in the study to ensure accurately measuring the needed concepts. All identified factors displayed strong item loading, achieving internal and composite reliability, as well as convergent validity across their items. The data monetization factor so far consists of a single measure, which, while possible to extend to a multi-item measure in future work, is acceptable from a statistical (its convergent validity being well above established thresholds) and psychological (cf. [8,28]) point of view.

**External Validity.** The generalization of these results is limited to some extent by the use of Prolific, which presents a Western bias – most developers, even if spread geographically, worked in Western countries and had English as their first language. However, given the focus of privacy research on this same domain, specifically with European regulations, we accept this as a workable constraint. The identified model presents three key factors identifying developers' attitudes towards handling personal data of their users, but should not be taken as presenting a complete picture of their attitude towards privacy. Further work may expand the model by identifying additional factors, and/or contexts in which factors' salience changes.

## 4    Discussion – Use Cases for the SDPA Scale

This section will explore potential uses of the developed scale, and how the results elicited during our construction of the scale already hint towards interesting points of further application.

### 4.1 Identifying Mismatches Between Attitude and (Self-perceived) Behavior

Figure 1 shows that software developers seem to be comfortable asking for a lot of data from their users. Many disagree with being bothered by collecting personal information from (many) users through the software they develop. Yet, when asked if they deal 'properly' with the extent to which their software collects data of its users, developers predominantly agreed (see Fig. 2, item (i)). This mismatch is further shown by the lack of expected correlation between the model's data collection factor (Spearman's rho, $r = .15, p > .1$), as compared to other correlations shown in Table 6). Thus, there seems to be a difference of opinion between what developers typically think is proper with regards to extent of personal data collection, and what principles like the Fair Information Practice Principles (FIPP) and legislation like the GDPR [20] set as proper data collection behavior. In particular, the FIPP's *collection limitation principle* notes there should be limits to collection of personal data, explicitly worked out in Art. 5(1)(c) of the GDPR:

> "Personal data shall be adequate, relevant and limited to what is necessary in relation to the purposes for which they are processed ('data minimisation')"

Developers' attitudes as measured here show that they are not in line with this notion of data minimization. This is potentially dangerous from a compliance perspective – but more importantly, shows that the social norms surrounding developers in their professional work are not yet where privacy preserving work intends them to be. The application of this scale thus allows for identification of areas where developers need to be made more aware of how they can value and ensure users' privacy.

A similar mismatch exists also between developers' attitudes and how they perceive themselves to properly ensure giving users control over their data. Items e and f in Fig. 1 show that nearly a quarter of developers disagree with the principle that users' right and ability to control their personal information is vital for their privacy. This is in stark contrast to the rights of data subjects (i.e., users) set out in Arts. 12–23 (GDPR), including e.g., right of access, rectification, erasure to data – none of which can happen without a user's adequate ability to control their personal data.

Our query of self-perceived behavior asked developers whether they 'properly' dealt with the various fair and just factors that constitute user concern, but did not specify whether this was to be interpreted morally or legally. Given the above mismatches between developer attitudes and legal specifications, this question could be explored in future work: do developers see themselves as operating to their own (sub-legal) standard, or do they believe they are operating in accordance with relevant laws and regulations which (they believe) are overly sensitive to user concerns?

Further work should also assess other mismatches such as, investigating whether specific types of software (e.g., those working on mobile software) or using specific mechanisms (e.g., those using monetization SDKs) lead to different types of mismatches between developer attitude and regulatory principles set forth in the GDPR.

## 4.2   Investigating Monetization's Effect on Privacy Attitude

In the development of the model, data monetization stood out clearly as a significant component of software developers' privacy attitudes. As Fig. 1 shows in item (g), a quarter of developers do not look disfavorably towards monetizing user data in marketing transactions. Unless communicated clearly, and explicitly establishing a lawful basis for transfering such data (i.e., obtaining explicit consent from the user), such transfers would be not in line with the principle of purpose limitation set out in Art. 5(1)(b) (GDRP). However, often such transfers will happen with the consent of the user even though they are not aware of it as the 'consent' was given in a longer, confusing text, or users simply did not understand the potential impact on their privacy when agreeing.

In this particular case, it is not the legal minutia that is most interesting – it is understanding why software developers would do this. It most obviously links to a need for *monetization* – the increasing pressure for developers to achieve return-on-investment from software they write. Looking at one of the most represented software types, mobile apps, a recent European Parliament briefing shows that the EU app economy is highly successful, accounting for approximately one third of revenues in the global market [18].

To make money with such software, several new revenue models have become widespread over the past decade, such as advertisements, micro-purchases, and so on. But making money with mobile apps is hard, and many developers make very little money indeed [24]. Effectively, advertisements rule the world as a revenue model [27], being used in nearly 40% of all apps. The use of such advertisement libraries brings security and privacy challenges with them, as several malicious advertisement libraries such as Xavier [13] and [5] have been found to put users' privacy at risk by stealing their personal data. Careful selection of which advertisement library to trust is thus a matter of trade-offs between promised revenue, and perceived risk – not of the users' privacy being impacted, but of the developer being held liable for it.

The difficulty of monetizing software in this sector may offer an explanation for the lack of disfavorable attitudes towards monetizing user data in marketing transactions. The European Parliament briefing further noted that many developers have expressed concerns about privacy regulations and further proposals, claiming they would create a disproportionate burden on them [18] – impacting their ability to generate income through revenue models like these.

We would argue this matter needs insight into developers' privacy attitudes, but cannot be approached in isolation – the socio-economic context that shapes their very *need* to trade-off user privacy for achieving some revenue is a complex system of inter-woven personal, economic, and regulatory factors and requires its due attention in further work.

### 4.3 Theory Development Through Combined Application of the Scale

Many other applications exist for the proposed scale in order to further develop theory of software developers' privacy attitudes. Some particular contexts we envision for further work include:

**Determining risk and benefit trade-offs.** The relationship between perceived risk and perceived benefit is well established in psychological literature [2], showing that this relationship is inverse. Further theory development could assess to what extent decisions of developers that may be beneficial to them, such as using advertisement libraries that pose a potential risk for their users' privacy vs. perceived low likelihood of being fined under extant data protection legislation.

**Determining the link between security and privacy in development.** In order to establish software that safeguards its users' privacy, security must be designed into it from the start as well. The extent to which developers' attitudes towards handling personal data and their intention to practice secure application development (cf. [29]) can allow for further insight into when and where security and privacy mindsets are separate or complimentary.

**Determining the impact of developer privacy attitudes on their software.** A reliable quantitative scale for developers' privacy attitude gives us a measure which may be used to quantify the impact of developer attitude and attitudinal/culture interventions on the software they develop for their users. These could be established in terms of user concerns about particular software (i.e., correlation between some users' IUIPC scores for a piece of software, and the SDPA score of its developers) or more direct privacy outcomes such as breaches reported, data items collected, and user awareness.

## 5   Conclusion

In this paper we presented the development of a scale to measure software developers' attitudes towards how they handle personal data in the software they develop, conducted a study with 123 software developers, and discussed points of interest that arose for further research.

We showed that the scale achieved internal and composite reliability and convergent validity over its items. The model that emerged from the developed scale with high goodness-of-fit pinpointed three factors that help to understand software developers' attitudes: (1) informed consent, (2) data minimization, and

(3) data monetization. Through analysis of the scale's first use we showed that there exist mismatches between developers' attitudes on the one hand, and their self-perceived behavior on the other hand. Monetization, in particular, presents such a mismatch where further study in the complex socio-economic reality of software development is needed to understand why developers may wittingly impact their users' privacy through the use of revenue models such as advertisements.

Finally, we proposed a number of further research directions to build out theory of software developers' privacy attitudes, including determining risk and benefit trade-offs, and links between secure development and privacy-minding development.

**Acknowledgments.** This work is partially supported by EPSRC grant EP /P011799/1, Why Johnny doesn't write secure software? Secure software development by the masses, and by the Center for Cyber Law & Policy (CCLP), established by the University of Haifa in collaboration with the Israeli National Cyber Bureau.

# A    Questionnaire

- Participant information sheet and informed consent.
  - ○ I consent to begin the study
- How many years of experience do you have as a software developer?
  - ○ less than 2 years
  - ○ 2 to 4 years
  - ○ 5 or more
- Think about software you have developed. Likely it captures some kind of personal data. This can be, for example, data like names, addresses, identification numbers, location data, usage statistics, or technical data like IP addresses. Here are some statements about personal data of people who use software you develop. From the standpoint of your *role as a software developer*, please indicate the extent to which you **agree** or **disagree** with each statement.
  - (a) It usually bothers me when the software I develop asks my users for personal information.

    Strongly disagree ○ ○ ○ ○ ○ ○ ○ Strongly agree
  - (b) I sometimes think twice before asking my users for personal information with the software I develop.

    Strongly disagree ○ ○ ○ ○ ○ ○ ○ Strongly agree
  - (c) It bothers me to collect personal information from so many users with the software I develop.

    Strongly disagree ○ ○ ○ ○ ○ ○ ○ Strongly agree

(d) I'm concerned that the software I develop is collecting too much personal information about my users.

Strongly disagree ○ ○ ○ ○ ○ ○ ○ Strongly agree

(e) My user's privacy is really a matter of their right to exercise control and autonomy over decisions about how their information is collected, used, and shared by the software I develop.

Strongly disagree ○ ○ ○ ○ ○ ○ ○ Strongly agree

(f) My users' control of personal information collected by the software I develop lies at the heart of user privacy.

Strongly disagree ○ ○ ○ ○ ○ ○ ○ Strongly agree

(g) The software I develop should disclose the way the data are collected, processed, and used.

Strongly disagree ○ ○ ○ ○ ○ ○ ○ Strongly agree

(h) A good privacy policy for the software I develop should have a clear and conspicuous disclosure.

Strongly disagree ○ ○ ○ ○ ○ ○ ○ Strongly agree

(i) It is very important to me that my users are aware and knowledgeable about how their personal information will be used.

Strongly disagree ○ ○ ○ ○ ○ ○ ○ Strongly agree

– Finally, here are some statements about how you consider the extent to which you, as a developer, deal with different aspects of personal data of your software's users. Please indicate the extent to which you **agree** or **disagree** with each statement.

(i) I properly deal with the extent to which my software collects data of its users

Strongly disagree ○ ○ ○ ○ ○ ○ ○ Strongly agree

(ii) I properly deal with the extent to which my software gives users control over their data

Strongly disagree ○ ○ ○ ○ ○ ○ ○ Strongly agree

(iii) I properly deal with the extent to which my software informs its users how their data is used

Strongly disagree ○ ○ ○ ○ ○ ○ ○ Strongly agree

# B    Detailed Item Adaption

| Item | IUIPC | SDPA |
|---|---|---|
| (a) | It usually bothers me when **online companies** ask **me** for personal information. | It usually bothers me when **the software I develop** asks **my users** for personal information. |
| (b) | When **online companies ask me for personal information**, I sometimes think twice before providing it. | I sometimes think twice before **asking my users for personal information with the software I develop**. |
| (c) | It bothers me to **give** personal information to so many **online companies**. | It bothers me to **collect** personal information from so many **users with the software I develop**. |
| (d) | I'm concerned that **online companies** are collecting too much personal information about me. | I'm concerned that **the software I develop** is collecting too much personal information about **my users**. |
| (e) | **Consumer online privacy** is really a matter of **consumer** right to exercise control and autonomy over decisions about how their information is collected, used, and shared. | **My user's privacy** is really a matter of **their** right to exercise control and autonomy over decisions about how their information is collected, used, and shared **by the software I develop**. |
| (f) | **Consumer** control of personal information lies at the heart of consumer privacy. | **My users'** control of personal information **collected by the software I develop** lies at the heart of **user** privacy. |
| (g) | I believe that **online privacy** is invaded when control is lost or unwillingly reduced as a result of a marketing transaction. | I believe that **my users' privacy** is invaded when control is lost or unwillingly reduced as a result of a marketing transaction. |
| (h) | **Companies seeking information online** should disclose the way the data are collected, processed, and used. | **The software I develop** should disclose the way the data are collected, processed, and used. |
| (i) | A good **consumer online privacy policy** should have a clear and conspicuous disclosure. | A good **privacy policy for the software I develop** should have a clear and conspicuous disclosure. |
| (j) | It is very important to **me** that I am aware and knowledgeable about how **my** personal information will be used. | It is very important to me that **my users are** aware and knowledgeable about how **their** personal information will be used. |

# References

1. Prolific (2019). https://www.prolific.ac. Accessed 8 May 2019
2. Alhakami, A.S., Slovic, P.: A psychological study of the inverse relationship between perceived risk and perceived benefit. Risk Anal. **14**(6), 1085–1096 (1994)

3. Ayalon, O., Toch, E., Hadar, I., Birnhack, M.: How developers make design decisions about users' privacy: the place of professional communities and organizational climate. In: Companion of the 2017 ACM Conference on Computer Supported Cooperative Work and Social Computing, pp. 135–138. ACM (2017)
4. Bagozzi, R.P., Yi, Y.: On the evaluation of structural equation models. J. Acad. Mark. Sci. **16**(1), 74–94 (1988)
5. Bauer, A., Hebeisen, B.: Igexin advertising network put user privacy at risk (2017). https://blog.lookout.com/igexin-malicious-sdk. Accessed 20 Oct 2018
6. Birnhack, M., Toch, E., Hadar, I.: Privacy mindset, technological mindset. Jurimetrics **55**, 55 (2014)
7. Buchanan, T., Paine, C., Joinson, A.N., Reips, U.D.: Development of measures of online privacy concern and protection for use on the internet. J. Am. Soc. Inform. Sci. Technol. **58**(2), 157–165 (2007)
8. Cheung, F., Lucas, R.E.: Assessing the validity of single-item life satisfaction measures: results from three large samples. Quality Life Res. **23**(10), 2809–2818 (2014)
9. Chin, W.W., Gopal, A., Salisbury, W.D.: Advancing the theory of adaptive structuration: the development of a scale to measure faithfulness of appropriation. Inf. Syst. Res. **8**(4), 342–367 (1997)
10. Chin, W.W., et al.: The partial least squares approach to structural equation modeling. Modern Methods Bus. Res. **295**(2), 295–336 (1998)
11. Cravens, A.: A demographic and business model analysis of today's app developer. GigaOM Pro (2012)
12. Eagly, A., Chaiken, S.: Attitude Structure and Function, 4th ed. Oxford University Press, Oxford, pp. 269–322 (1998)
13. Xu, E.: (Mobile Threat Response Engineer): Analyzing Xavier: an information-stealing ad library on android (2017). https://blog.trendmicro.com/trendlabs-security-intelligence/analyzing-xavier-information-stealing-ad-library-android/. Accessed 20 Oct 2018
14. Fornell, C., Larcker, D.F.: Evaluating structural equation models with unobservable variables and measurement error. J. Market. Res. **18**(1), 39–50 (1981)
15. Hadar, I., et al.: Privacy by designers: software developers' privacy mindset. Empirical Softw. Eng. **23**(1), 259–289 (2018)
16. Lee, H., Wong, S.F., Chang, Y.: Confirming the effect of demographic characteristics on information privacy concerns. In: PACIS 2016 Proceedings (2016)
17. Malhotra, N.K., Kim, S.S., Agarwal, J.: Internet users' information privacy concerns (IUIPC): the construct, the scale, and a causal model. Inf. Syst. Res. **15**(4), 336–355 (2004)
18. Szczepański, M.: European app economy: state of play, challenges and EU policy (2018). http://www.europarl.europa.eu/RegData/etudes/BRIE/2018/621894/EPRS_BRI(2018)621894_EN.pdf. Accessed 25 June 2019
19. Montano, D.E., Kasprzyk, D.: Theory of reasoned action, theory of planned behavior, and the integrated behavioral model. In: Health Behavior: Theory, Research and Practice, pp. 95–124 (2015)
20. Parliament, E.: Regulation (EU) 2016/679 of the European Parliament and of the Council of 27 April 2016 on the protection of natural persons with regard to the processing of personal data and on the free movement of such data. Official Journal of the European Union (2016). Accessed 24 June 2019
21. Preibusch, S.: Guide to measuring privacy concern: review of survey and observational instruments. Int. J. Hum Comput Stud. **71**(12), 1133–1143 (2013)

22. Senarath, A., Arachchilage, N.A.: Why developers cannot embed privacy into software systems? An empirical investigation. In: Proceedings of the 22nd International Conference on Evaluation and Assessment in Software Engineering 2018, pp. 211–216. ACM (2018)
23. Senarath, A., Arachchilage, N.A.G.: Understanding software developers' approach towards implementing data minimization. arXiv preprint arXiv:1808.01479 (2018)
24. SlashData Developer Economics: Developer Economics: State of the Developer Nation Q1 2015 (2015). https://www.developereconomics.com/reports/developer-economics-state-of-developer-nation-q1-2015. Accessed 25 June 2019
25. SlashData Developer Economics: Developer Economics: State of the Developer Nation Q1 2016 (2016). https://www.developereconomics.com/reports/developer-economics-state-of-developer-nation-q1-2016. Accessed 18 Sept 2017
26. Smith, H.J., Milberg, S.J., Burke, S.J.: Information privacy: measuring individuals' concerns about organizational practices. MIS Q. **20**(2), 167–196 (1996)
27. VisionMobile / SlashData Developer Economics: European App Economy 2015 - Creating Jobs & Driving Economic Growth in Europe (2015). https://www.slashdata.co/free-resources. Accessed 25 Mar 2019
28. Wanous, J.P., Reichers, A.E., Hudy, M.J.: Overall job satisfaction: how good are single-item measures? J. Appl. Psychol. **82**(2), 247 (1997)
29. Woon, I.M., Kankanhalli, A.: Investigation of is professionals' intention to practise secure development of applications. Int. J. Hum. Comput. Stud. **65**(1), 29–41 (2007)
30. Zukowski, T., Brown, I.: Examining the influence of demographic factors on internet users' information privacy concerns. In: Proceedings of the 2007 Annual Research Conference of the South African Institute of Computer Scientists and Information Technologists on IT Research in Developing Countries, pp. 197–204. ACM (2007)

# You've Left Me No Choices: Security Economics to Inform Behaviour Intervention Support in Organizations

Albesë Demjaha[1]([⊠]), Simon Parkin[2], and David Pym[1]

[1] University College London and Alan Turing Institute, London, UK
{albese.demjaha.16,d.pym}@ucl.ac.uk
[2] University College London, London, UK
s.parkin@ucl.ac.uk

**Abstract.** Security policy-makers (influencers) in an organization set security policies that embody intended behaviours for employees (as decision-makers) to follow. Decision-makers then face choices, where this is not simply a binary decision of whether to comply or not, but also *how* to approach compliance and secure working alongside other workplace pressures, and limited resources for identifying optimal security-related choices. Conflict arises due to information asymmetries present in the relationship, where influencers and decision-makers both consider costs, gains, and losses in ways which are not *necessarily* aligned. With the need to promote 'good enough' decisions about security-related behaviours under such constraints, we hypothesize that actions to resolve this misalignment can benefit from constructs from both traditional economics *and* behavioural economics. Here we demonstrate how current approaches to security behaviour provisioning in organizations mirror rational-agent economics, even where behavioural economics is embodied in the promotion of individual security behaviours. We develop and present a framework to accommodate *bounded security decision-making*, within an ongoing programme of behaviours which must be provisioned for and supported. We also point to applications of the framework in negotiating sustainable security behaviours, such as policy concordance and just security cultures.

**Keywords:** Security decision-making · Security economics · Security policy · Security behaviour modelling

## 1 Introduction

Information security in larger organizations is often managed by an information security manager and/or a security team—the *security function* of the organization. The security function is the part of the organization recognised as having the expertise to identify and manage the security technologies and processes

---

A. Demjaha and S. Parkin—Contributed equally.

© Springer Nature Switzerland AG 2021
T. Groß and T. Tryfonas (Eds.): STAST 2019, LNCS 11739, pp. 66–86, 2021.
https://doi.org/10.1007/978-3-030-55958-8_4

necessary to protect the organization from threats that relate to its assets. Outwardly, this is embodied in controls and procedures, often detailed in the organization's security policy (or policies).

Policy may dictate specific *security-related behaviours*, which employees are expected to adopt. There are myriad of ways to promote behaviour change [15], with challenges in guaranteeing that behaviours are changed successfully [55]. Declaring a behaviour in a security policy is then not an assurance that the behaviour will happen. This reality has drawn increasing attention to the need to manage behaviour effectively. Consideration of behaviour change theory and *behavioural economics* [13] is one such approach.

Both research and practice have shown that behaviours may not be adopted in organizations. Employees may not see how policy applies to them, find it difficult to follow, or regard policy expectations as unrealistic [36] (where they may well be [31]). Employees may create their own alternative behaviours [12], sometimes in an effort to approximate secure working, rather than abandoning security [37]. Organizational support can be critical to whether secure practices persist [22], where individuals may assume that others with relevant knowledge and resources will manage the problem for them.

Rational security micro-economics has proved useful for explaining the interaction between organizational security policies and behaviours [8], where security ecosystems are otherwise too complicated to study directly in this way. Similarly, Herley posits that the rejection of advocated security behaviours by citizens exhibits traits of rational economic behaviour [28].

Security managers must have a strategy for how to provision for security, provide workable policy, and support user needs. In early workshops on the Economics of Information Security, Schneier advocated consideration of trade-offs [14, p. 289]; nearing 15 years later, this is not happening sufficiently in organizations. Here we revisit principles of information economics and behavioural economics in tandem, identifying contradictions which point to gaps in support. After reviewing the capacity for economics to explain a range of security-related behaviours (Sect. 2), we demonstrate how current approaches to infrastructure and provisioning of security mirror rational-agent economics, even when behavioural economics is applied to promote individual behaviours (Sect. 3). We show through examples how these contradictions align with regularly cited causes of security non-compliance from the literature.

We present a framework (Sect. 4), based on consolidated economics principles, with the following goal:

> *Better support for 'good enough' security-related decisions, by individuals within an organization, that best approximate secure behaviours under constraints, such as limited time or knowledge.*

This requires us to identify the factors affecting security behaviours, which should be considered by the organization in order to inform policy design, support the identification of provisioning requirements, and describe expectations of users. The framework is intended to underpin provisioning to reach this goal.

We then apply the framework to one of the most widely promoted security behaviours (Sect. 5), the maintenance of up-to-date device software, demonstrating through comparison with independent user studies where the consolidated economics approach – *bounded security decision-making* – can anticipate organizational support requirements. We consider how the framework can be situated to support practitioners (Sect. 6), before concluding with a summary and future work (Sect. 7). A supporting glossary of foundational economics terminology is detailed in the Appendix.

## 2   Related Work

There is a growing body of research advocating the application of economics concepts to security generally, as a means to understand complex challenges. Foundational work by Gordon and Loeb asserted that traditional economics can inform optimal investment in security [26], where here we apply a similar approach to a combination of economic models, to reposition investment challenges related to security behaviour management. Beautement et al. [8] articulate how employees have a restricted 'compliance budget' for security, and will stop complying once they have reached a certain threshold.

Acquisti and Grossklags [2] apply behavioural economics to consumer privacy, to identify ways to support individuals as they engage in privacy-related decision-making. Similarly, Baddeley [6] applies behavioural economics in a management and policy setting, finding for example that loss-aversion can be leveraged in the design of security prompts. Other concepts from behavioural economics have been explored, such as the *endowment effect* [60] and *framing* within the domain of information security and privacy [3,27]. Anderson and Agarwal [3] identify potential in the use of goal-framing to influence security behaviour, where commitment devices have since been explored as a way to influence behaviour change [25]. Verendel [63] applies behavioural economics principles to formalize risk-related decisions toward predicting decision-making problems, positing that aspects of usable security must also be explored.

In addition to understanding security and privacy behaviour through behavioural economics, some have advocated the *influencing* of such behaviour through the application of *nudge theory* [1,61]. Through empirical modelling of behavioural economics, Redmiles et al. [51] effectively advocate for identifying and presenting options which are optimal for the decision-maker, and making the risk, costs, and benefits of each choice transparent. Here we explore where there are 'gaps' in realising these capabilities, which must be closed in order for organizations to support secure behaviours.

In terms of capturing the dynamic between a decision-maker (here, an employee), and the security function – an 'influencer' – Morisset et al. [42] present a model of 'soft enforcement', where the influencer edits the choices available to a decision-maker toward removing bad choices. Here we acknowledge that workarounds and changes in working conditions occur regularly, proposing that the range of behaviour choices is in effect a negotiation between the two parties.

In summary, there is a need to reconcile the advancements in the application of economics to security with how management of behaviour change strategies in organizations is conceptualised. Here we fill in the gaps, where currently there are contradictions and shortcomings which act against both the organization and the individual decision-maker.

# 3   Applying Economics to Organizational Security

Pallas [44] applies institutional economics to revisit information security in organizations, developing a structured explanation of how the centralised security function and decentralized groups of employees interact in an environment of increasingly localised personal computing. Pallas delineates three forms of security apparatus for achieving policy compliance in organizations (as in Table 1): *architectural means* (which prevent bad outcomes by strictly controlling what is possible); *formal rules* (such as policies, defining what is allowed or prohibited for those in the organization); and *informal rules* (primarily security awareness and culture, as well as security behaviours). We demonstrate how a strategic approach is lacking in how to manage the relatively high *marginal costs* of realizing the informal rules which are intended to support formal rules.

**Table 1.** Costs of hierarchical motivation (reproduced from Pallas [44]).

| Meta-measure | Fixed costs | Marginal costs | Enforcement costs (single case) | Residual costs |
|---|---|---|---|---|
| Architectural means | High | Medium | None/negligible | None/negligible |
| Formal rules | Low | Medium | High | Medium |
| Informal rules | Medium | Medium/high | Low | High |

## 3.1   Rational vs. Bounded Decision-Making

In traditional economics, a decision-making structure assumes a rational agent [58,59]. The rational agent is equipped with the capabilities and resources to make the decision which will be most beneficial for them. The agent knows all possible choices, and is assumed to have complete information when evaluating those choices, as well as a detailed analysis of probability, costs, gains, and losses [59]. A rational agent is then capable of making an informed decision that is simultaneously the optimal decision for them.

Behavioural economics, on the other hand, challenges the assumption that agents make fully rational decisions. Instead, the field refers to the concept of *bounded rationality*, which explains that an agent's rationality is bounded due to cognitive limitations and time restrictions. These considerations also challenge the plausibility of complete information, which is practically unrealistic for a bounded agent. According to these restrictions, the bounded agent turns instead

**Table 2.** Rationality vs. bounded rationality in decision-making.

| Traditional economics | Behavioural economics |
|:---:|:---:|
| **RATIONAL AGENT** | **BOUNDED AGENT** |
| - detailed evaluation of costs, gains, and losses | - brief consideration of perceived costs, gains, and losses |
| - complete information | - incomplete information |
| - careful calculation of potential investment | - insufficient skills, knowledge, or time |
| | - quick evaluation of risks driven by loss aversion |
| ↓ | ↓ |
| chosen outcome | decision fatigue |
| ↓ | ↓ |
| optimal decision | satisfactory decision |

to 'rules of thumb' and makes ad hoc decisions based on a quick evaluation of *perceived* probability, costs, gains, and losses [33,58].

Table 2 outlines the differences between the decision-making process of a rational agent and that of a bounded agent. The classical notion of rationality (or, rather, *the neoclassical assumption of rationality* [59]) is quite unachievable outside of its theoretical nature. From the standpoint of traditional rationality, the decision-making agent is assumed to have an objective and completely true view of the world and everything in it. Because of this objective view, and the unlimited computational capabilities of the agent, it is expected that the decision which is taken will be the one which provides maximal utility for the agent.

It is a common misconception that behavioural economics postulates irrationality in people. The difference in viewpoint arises from how rationality was originally defined, rather than from the assumption that people are rational beings. It is agreed upon that people have reasons, motivations, and goals when deciding to do something—whether they do it well or badly, they do engage in thinking and reasoning when making a decision [59]. However, it is important to denote in a more realistic manner how this decision-making process looks for a bounded agent. It is by considering these principles that we explore a more constructive approach to decision-support in organizations.

While an objective view of the world always leads to the optimal decision (Table 2), a bounded agent often settles for a satisfactory decision. Simon [59] argues that people tend to make decisions by *satisficing* [33] rather than optimizing. They use basic decision criteria that lead to a combination of a satisfying and sufficient decision which from their perspective is 'good enough' considering the different constraints. Furthermore, when faced with too many competing decisions, a person's resources become strained and *decision fatigue* [64] often contributes to poor choices. This leads to our goal to: *better support 'good enough' decisions which best approximate secure behaviours under constraints such as limited time or knowledge.*

### 3.2 Why We Are Here, with Too Few Choices

We consider traditional economics and behavioural economics in the context of supporting effective behaviour change. We derived the 'pillars' of behaviour change from the COM-B model [41]: *Capability, Opportunity,* and *Motivation,* which are all required to support a change to a particular *Behaviour.* We discuss how each pillar is represented in the two economic approaches.

**Traditional Economics.** The move from centralized to decentralized computing [44] has resulted in an imposed information asymmetry of having a recognized security function distinct from everyone else in the organization. The security function may declare formal rules and informal rules (training, behaviours), assuming that the decision-maker (individual employee) has the same knowledge that they do. Conversely, the security function does not know about expectations placed on the decision-maker by other functions, assuming they have the capacity to approximate the same knowledge; Capability then cannot be assumed. Motivation comes from formal policies, and architectural means which force certain behaviours; however, if Motivation to follow security rules is not sufficiently related to the assets which the decision-maker cares about, it will not support the recognition of risks which require the behaviour [11] (also impacting Opportunity). As the security function is distinct from the rest of the decentralized 'PC-computing' organization, it is often assumed that information about advocated behaviours has been sufficiently communicated to the decision-maker (where the Opportunity also cannot be assumed, because the 'trigger' does not match the employee's current Ability and Motivation [19,48]).

**Behavioural Economics.** In organizations, capabilities must be supported, but this is often approached in a 'one-size-fits-all' way, such that the decision-maker is forced, through the Motivation of enforced formal rules, to seek out the knowledge to develop the Capabilities they need. however, they may not know if they have the complete and correct knowledge unless someone with that knowledge checks (and closes the information asymmetry). An Opportunity for a new behaviour may be created, through training or shaping of the environment, and assumed to be a nudge toward a behaviour beneficial to the decision-maker [55]. If a behaviour is framed like a 'nudge', but accounts only for what is desirable for the influencer without checking also that it is desirable to the decision-maker, it is a 'prod' which cannot rely on the decision-maker's own resources and willingness to ensure that it works, such that Motivation will fail. If the provisioned choices (the Capability) are no more beneficial than what the decision-maker already has available to them, they may instead adopt 'shadow security' behaviours [37].

## 4    A Framework for Security Choices

### 4.1    Toward a Consistent Strategy

Current approaches to security provisioning in organizations appear as if to support the rational decision-maker, as per traditional economics. We outline the 'contradictions' that currently exist in how the two economic models are being brought together as follows, where examples of 'contradictory' and 'better' approaches to supporting secure behaviours in organizations are illustrated through real-world examples in Table 3.

**Respect Me and My Time, or We are Off to a Bad Start.** Security behaviour provisions tend to imply that the decision-maker has resources available to complete training and policies, but in an organization the decision-maker is busy with their paid job. To avoid 'decision fatigue' and the 'hassle factor' [8] of complying with security, we must consider the *endowment effect* – as also applies to security [35] – and acknowledge that for the busy decision-maker, doing security requires a loss to *something else*. This requires an institutional view to helping the decision-maker to negotiate where that cost will be borne from. The notion of a 'Compliance Budget' [8] suggests to reduce the demands of security expectations, where here we note the need for an upper bound on expectations.

**If This is Guidance, Be the Guide.** The security function must assume that employees are (security) novices. They then will need to be told the cost of security and exactly what the steps are. Otherwise, the novice must guess the duration of an unfamiliar behaviour, and exactly what constitutes the behaviour in its entirety (e.g., knowing where to find personal firewall settings [49]). Unchecked, this leads to satisficing. Current approaches appeal to the skillful user, or assume 'non-divisible' target behaviours [4] (with only one, clear way to do what is being asked).

**Frame a Decision to Make, Not a Decision Made.** Advice is given assuming that what is advised is the best choice, and there is no other choice to be articulated. The advocated choice is rarely, if ever, presented alongside other choices (such as previous sanctioned behaviours, or ad hoc, 'shadow security' behaviours unknown to the security function). We should note also that a choice is often *perceived*, and so elements of a choice can impact the 'gulf of evaluation' [54]. An example is when users form incomplete/incorrect understanding of provisioned two-factor authentication technology options [23].

**Edit Out the Old, Edit in the New.** More security advice is often presumed to be better for security, but is not [29], and can create confusion. Stale advice can persist unless it is curated – an employee may do the wrong thing which is insecure, or the wrong thing which *was* secure but now is not. When policies and technologies change, the decision-maker is often left to do the choice-editing. An example is when old and new security policies are hosted without time-stamps.

**Table 3.** Examples of 'contradictory' and 'better' approaches to supporting secure behaviours in organizations (derived from experiences reported in real-world settings, and relevant studies).

| Behaviour | Contradictory Approach | Failures |
|---|---|---|
| Policy compliance | Publishing policy without communicating location to staff [37] | Assumes knowledge of policy and time to find it |
| Secure passwords | Not communicating the rules for a secure password [45] | Assumes expert knowledge about passwords |
| Authentication choice | Integrating a suite of options into log-on without explaining the options [23] | Lacking support for making reasoned decision |
| Do secure work | Advocating generic security practices [36] | Staff must relate practices to work |
| Security training | Provide training but no time to do it [8] | Staff must negotiate the time themselves |
| Behaviour | Better Approach | Successes |
| Policy compliance | Ensure that the environment naturally supports policy-compliant behaviour [37] | Does not assume any extra effort from staff |
| Secure passwords | Examples of 'strong' passwords (CyberAware UK) | Assumes little-to-no prior knowledge |
| Authentication choice | Communicating the different options in a suite of options at the point of configuration | Puts choices side-by-side |
| Do secure work | Visible board-level support [21], sector-specific tailoring (e.g., differentiated NCSC Guidance for Small Biz. and Small Charities) | Supports interpretation of a perceived choice |
| Security training | Agree a fixed window of paid time to complete training | Cost to (pri. and sec.) tasks negotiated for staff |

## 4.2   Bounded Security Decision-Making

Security research increasingly focuses on organizational security and the interaction between managers, policies, and employees. Principles from economics have been deemed useful in security [14], and concepts from behavioural economics further support understanding of security behaviours in an organizational context [13]. For security policies to be effective, they must align with employees' limited capacity and resources for policy compliance [16].

We use the term *bounded security decision-making*, to move away from any ambiguity that arises when merging concepts from traditional and behavioural economics. This distances from the tendency to apply behavioural intervention concepts to security while assuming the intervention targets to be rational agents. This is in itself a contradiction because a rational agent would by default make the optimal choice and would not require any behavioural aid or intervention (as explored in Sect. 4.1). Similarly, employees cannot possibly dedicate sufficient time or resources for every single task or policy to account for this [16]. This is a consideration that must be acknowledged at the point of security policy design.

To represent these concepts within an information security strategy model, we adapt the security investment model developed by Caulfield and Pym [16], which is constructed within the modelling framework described in [17,18]. This model explicitly considers the decision-point for an agent (the decision-maker), and incorporates elements of the decision-making process (where we reconcile elements of behavioural economics), and available choices provided by the organization (the influencer). We adapt this framework to consider factors which should be considered when provisioning security choices, toward supporting the decision-maker to choose 'good enough' behaviours under constraints on knowledge and resources.

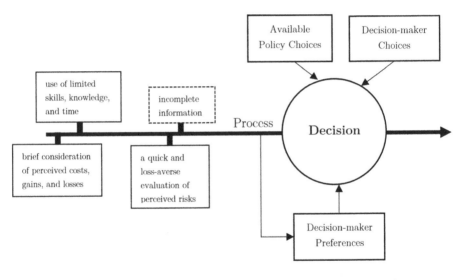

*security vs. competing expectations*

**Fig. 1.** A decision point in a decision-maker's process *bounded security decision-making* (adapting elements from Caulfield and Pym [16]).

Figure 1 illustrates the components and processes which must be considered in policy design. *Influencer* refers to the security policy-maker in the organization, and *decision-maker* (DM) the bounded agent (the employee).

**Process.** On the left-hand side we consolidate factors in decision-making from behavioural economics into the decision-making process that informs a decision (the arrow on the left-hand side). We outline the restrictive factors (limited skills, knowledge, time and incomplete information) which characterize a bounded decision-maker. We acknowledge that the decision-maker is bounded in several ways, from individual skills and knowledge to temporal restrictions set by the organization. Our bounded decision-maker has incomplete information about the world and others, and must make do with information available within their abilities; they can only consider the perceived costs, gains and losses and prioritize subjective interests when faced with a choice.

When evaluating the risks that come with a choice 'losses loom larger than gains' [34, p. 279], and the decision-maker tries harder to avoid losses rather than to encounter gains. This then puts the expectations of the influencer at a loss, as the decision-maker may be more concerned with the loss of productivity than with a potential security gain (where the latter may be all that the influencer – the overseer and expert of security – can see).

**Information Asymmetry.** Information asymmetry regular occurs between the influencer and the decision-maker. In the context of security policies and policy compliance, the following are examples of information asymmetry:

– The recognised differentiation of the influencer being more knowledgeable and capable in security than the decision-maker (as security is arguably the influencer's primary task);
– The influencer's lack of knowledge about the decision-maker's context, and pressures which factor into their choice-making process (resulting in the influencer seeming to perceive the decision-maker as a rational agent with motivation and resources dedicated to security);
– The influencer's lack of awareness about competing company policies with which the decision-maker must *also* comply;
– The decision-maker's lack of information about why security restrictions matter to the organization (overly demanding policies may cause decision-makers to lose sight of why the policies exist in the first place).

Such discrepancies in knowledge and information between the influencer and the decision-maker cause friction and create a power imbalance. Asymmetries should be identified and addressed in order to manage the gap between influencer and decision-maker perceptions (which is engineered by having a distinct, designated security function).

**Decision-Maker Preferences.** The restrictive factors on the left hand side of Fig. 1 influence the decision-maker's preferences. Using these factors as a reference point, the DM may have preferences over complying with one behaviour over another. Advocated security behaviours compete with other behaviours (such as e.g., compliance with HR policies or work deadlines) for the DM's choice of preference, where that preference impacts their final decision. If compliance with e.g., an HR policy requires less technical engagement (and time investment), this will factor into the preferences.

**Choices and Decision.** The two boxes above the Decision circle represent the type of choices available to the decision-maker. Available policy choices consist of the rules listed in the security policy by the influencer, but also any included advice on what to do and solutions provided. In organizations with security policies, the influencer usually assumes that the only choices available to the decision-maker are the ones noted by the policy itself. However, as literature shows, a choice may be to circumvent the policy [12,38], or to attempt to work in a way that best approximates compliance with secure working policies, in the best way the decision-maker knows how to [37]. Though workarounds and circumventions of policy predominantly go unnoticed in organizations, this does not eliminate them from the set of choices available to the decision-maker. Behaviours regarded as choices by the decision-maker – but which are hidden to the influencer – are another information asymmetry (one which introduces risks for the organization [37]). By assuming that the only available choices come from the security policy, the influencer indirectly undermines policy by having less predictable control over policy compliance decisions in the organization.

**Moral Hazard.** When a number of information asymmetries exist in the organization, a moral hazard is likely occurring. A common example of a moral hazard is that of the principal-agent problem, when one person has the ability to make decisions on behalf of another. Here, the person making the decisions (the agent) is the decision-maker, and decisions are being made on behalf of the influencer (the principal) who represents the organization's security function. However, problems between the agent and the principal arise when there are conflicting goals *and* information asymmetry.

If we go back to the decision-maker's perceived risks, we argue that these are not synonymous with the risks that the influencer knows of or is concerned with. Hence, when the decision-maker enacts behaviours, they do so by prioritising their interests and aiming to reduce their perceived risks. Because of the information asymmetry that persists between the decision-maker and the influencer, as well as the decision-maker's hidden choices driven by personal benefit, the influencer cannot always ensure that decisions are being made in their best interest. The moral hazard here is that the decision-maker can take more (security) risks because the cost of those risks will fall on the organization rather than on the decision-maker themselves.

**Choice Architecture.** The circle in Fig. 1 signifies the decision made by the decision-maker. In our framework, we refer to the circle by using the term 'decision' rather than 'choice architecture' for the following reasons: (1) while unusable advocated security behaviours persist, the set of choices is a composite of choices created by both the influencer and the decision-maker, which does not correspond to the accepted nature of a curated choice architecture, and; (2) referring to a choice architecture implies an intention to nudge decision-makers towards a particular choice, which also implies that there exists one optimal choice. As we have mentioned previously, a single optimal choice cannot exist for bounded decision-makers because they have perceived costs, gains, and losses individually; a more helpful approach would be to accommodate a range of choices rather than strictly advocate for one choice which is not being followed.

### 4.3   Framework Implementation

Here we describe steps for applying the framework (as in Fig. 2). We note that smaller organisations may not have the resources to maintain an overview of systems and system usage (more so if elements are outsourced [46]).

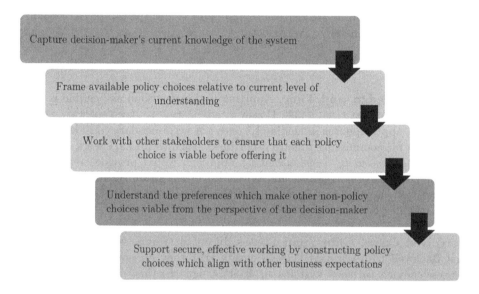

**Fig. 2.** Implementation steps of the *bounded security decision-making* framework.

1. **Capture the *process***: Influencers must understand the decision-maker's process (as defined in Fig. 1) and consider their current knowledge of the system—either as individuals or discernible groups of users. This may also be influenced by any cognitive limitations [9];
2. **Adapt *available policy choices***: Policy choices must be adapted to the decision-maker's current level of understanding and supported with concrete information—working from the decision-maker's current state (of knowledge and resources) rather than the desired security end-state;
3. **Validate *policy choices* with stakeholders**: Collaboration with stakeholders must be established before policy choices are offered, so that the decision-maker is not left responsible for ensuring that it is a possible choice amongst other imperatives;

4. **Acknowledge** *decision-maker preferences* **and choices**: Decision-maker preferences (including their motivations) must be utilized rather than ignored—knowledge of these can aid in aligning policy choices with decision-maker preferences;
5. **Align choices with** *competing expectations*: Influencers must ensure that security policy choices do not interfere with other business expectations.

# 5   Worked Example – Software Security Updates

Here we apply the framework to a pertinent case study – keeping software up-to-date. This is selected from the top online security controls advocated by security experts (as prompted by Reeder et al. [52]). This is also the top piece of advice advocated by e.g., the UK government[1].

## 5.1   Process

**Skills, Knowledge, and Time.** Applying updates as soon as possible is seen as achieving the best results [32]. However, advocating to 'keep software up-to-date' or to 'apply updates immediately' does not accommodate consideration of preferences for committing time to other tasks (such as primary work tasks).

A *bounded security decision-making* approach would provide step-by-step guidance to match skill levels, and potentially the version of software that is currently on a device. Automation could also be considered, if the update process is complex or requires technical skill.

**Perceived Costs, Gains, and Losses.** In organizations, system patches are first deployed to a test-bed [32], to ensure that they do not create problems (losses); advice to 'keep systems up-to-date' ignores this, and also does not declare the cost, in terms of time, for a user to achieve this. This would then be concise, high-level advice which inadvertently assumes that a user knows already how to do this, and how often to do it. An employee may not feel that updates are a concern for them [62], so may not be motivated to do it at all.

A *bounded security decision-making* approach would need to provide an assurance that the latest updates have been tested on a system similar to the one the receiver of the advice is using for their work. This is so that they do not have to establish this for themselves (and to avoid both loss of cognitive automation and a need to rebuild cognitive maps [10]). It would be necessary to convey that an up-to-date system protects specific assets that the decision-maker wants to minimize losses for (where top-management or asset-focused messaging could help).

---

[1] As at the National Cyber Security Centre (NCSC) website.

**Incomplete Information.** The minimal advice does not declare how to check or how often, assuming a rational approach. If an update seems to be taking a long time, a decision-maker may not know if the problem is with the machine (requiring support) or personal expectations (and not being able to troubleshoot problems [65]). There is also an assumption that the user may know the changes that updates will create in advance, when it could impact them in a range of ways [10].

A *bounded security decision-making* approach could involve informing the user of how long each update takes to install [40] (especially if a restart is required), based on testing on a comparable setup (including machine performance, available disk space [40] and provisioned software). It may be that updates can be scheduled centrally [40], for instance to occur when employees are most likely to have their computer on, but not be using it (if the organization has scheduled workplace lunch breaks, for instance). Ultimately, finding a time to install updates and avoid disruption is increasingly difficult to find in a PC-computing work environment.

**Loss-Averse Evaluation of Risks.** A rational approach does not accommodate the chance that the user has had prior bad experiences with updates [62]. It also does not provide assurances that the update will not cause software to cease working properly, and does not declare how much (paid/salaried) time the update will take (assuming this to be none/negligible).

A *bounded security decision-making* approach would provide backups before updates, and point to the existence of the backups (to assuage concerns about losses). A user may simply choose to delay or ignore the installation of an update [62], so there would be a need to convey or imply why this is *not* an appropriate option to consider – this is most readily achieved by presenting the options that the user perceives relative to each other.

## 5.2   Available Policy Choices

Rational advice to keep a system up-to-date does not consider that modern systems may already be doing (some or all of) this, so advice may need to consider specific operating system software (for instance). Unless an OS or application provides separate feature updates and security updates, the value of updates for security may not allow a decision-maker to consider clear choices [43].

A *bounded security decision-making* approach would acknowledge how updates work on the system the decision-maker us using. It would also recognize the other options that are available to the decision-maker, from the perspective of their personal preferences and not solely the one ideal preference of the security function (influencer).

## 5.3   Decision-Maker Choices

Because choices framed for a rational decision-maker are not made explicit and compared meaningfully, the *bounded security* decision-maker may construct the set of choices in an ad hoc fashion, with little to no information about the consequences of taking action or not doing so (the expertise that the security function has which they personally do not have). In an environment of incomplete information, the security function may not know this either (as may be the case with many policy mandates [29]).

## 6    Future Directions

Informed by user-centred security research, we outline directions for how a security manager/function in an organization can consider the proposals we have made (Sect. 4). Security managers cannot be assumed to have in-depth knowledge of the human aspects of security, but may nonetheless value it in security policy decision-making [47], and benefit from methods and tools to do so [53].

### 6.1    A Security Diet

A 'security diet' would document perceived occurrence and costs of advocated behaviours (for instance through a typical working day). Questions can then be asked to reconcile these costs with expected behaviour elsewhere in the organization [35], to determine if time for security tasks is being taken from elsewhere.

If security behaviours add to an already busy schedule, then time constraints, pressure, and stress increase the likelihood of errors [50]. An individual arguably *should not* be expected to commit more than their full working day to all tasks including security. Security is then self-defeating if it leaves the decision-maker to figure out how to make this possible. Consideration of how to manage security with other pressures can reduce this 'gulf of execution' [54].

### 6.2    Just Culture and the Genuine Choice Architecture

If we are to involve the decision-maker in shaping viable options, we would want to find a way to acknowledge the choices employees make which are outside of policy, to include them alongside advocated choices for clear comparison. This does however 'declare' unsecure options, though this aligns with the practice of a 'blame-free', *just culture* [20], toward learning from shortcomings. By defining associated properties of these two sets of choices, support can be negotiated to shape solutions which allow productive and secure working.

### 6.3    Policy Concordance

'Security Dialogues' research [5] promotes a move toward policy concordance—'mutual understanding and agreement' on how the decision-maker will behave. In medicine [30], concordance occurs at the point of consultation, to incorporate the respective views of the decision-maker and influencer.

The definitions of distinct behaviour choices can be considered by both sides when negotiating a solution for security concordance. This then further leverages the co-developed choice architecture. This could 'zoom in' further on decision options, to examine properties of individual choices according to the decision-maker's preferences, comparing to other options which are regarded as viable.

### 6.4   Security Investment Forecasting

Security modelling can begin to forecast the impact of investments in complex environments, before making infrastructure and provisioning changes (e.g., [16]). Security deployed is not security as designed; contact with the complex organizational environment will alter how successful a control is in practice, and how well it fits with other practices in the organization. Incorporating employee perspectives into structured economic models will inform the viability of new controls.

## 7   Conclusion

We have shown how current approaches to security provisioning and infrastructure reflect traditional economics, even when concepts from behavioural economics are applied to 'nudge' individual security behaviours. We have constructed a framework that accommodates a set of security behaviours, as a continuous programme of choices which must be provisioned for to adequately support 'good enough' behaviour decisions. We then apply our framework to one of the most advocated security behaviours—software patching—and demonstrate that the rational-agent view is incompatible with the embrace of isolated behaviour change activities.

Our work identifies considerations for researchers working in organizational security: the importance of capturing where a decision-maker is, alongside where an influencer wants them to be; that a security choice architecture is essentially decentralized and cannot be wholly dictated by any one stakeholder, and; in organizations, security expertise can exist in places recognized by the organization and others not—constructed information asymmetries ought to be accounted for when assessing user behaviours. Future work can involve situated studies in organizations, including participatory design with security managers to develop viable and sustainable security behaviour interventions.

**Acknowledgements.** Demjaha is supported through a Doctoral Studentship granted by the Alan Turing Institute.

**Appendix.** Glossary of terminology, derived from [7, 24, 33, 34, 39, 56, 57, 64].

| Traditional Economics Terminology | |
|---|---|
| Term | Definition |
| Gain | *A gain is an increase in the value of an asset* |
| Loss | *A loss is a decrease in the value of an asset* |
| Cost | *A cost signifies the using up of assets* |
| Investment | *The allocation or use of goods with the expectation of some benefit in the future* |
| Rationality | *The idea that an individual takes into account all information, probability, potential costs, gains or losses in order to take the most beneficial decision* |
| Decision | *The choice that results in the optimal level of benefit for the decision-maker* |
| Rational decision-making | *The process of making a choice that results in the optimal level of benefit for the decision-maker* |
| Information asymmetry | *When one party has more or better information about something than the other party* |
| Moral hazard | *When an individual takes more risks because someone else is responsible for bearing those risks* |
| Principal-agent problem | *When one individual has the ability to make decisions on behalf of another* |
| **Behavioural Economics Terminology** | |
| Term | Definition |
| Perceived gain | *A perceived gain is an increase in the value of an asset that is important and subjective to the decision-maker (as according to limitations of bounded rationality)* |
| Perceived loss | *A perceived loss is a decrease in the value of an asset that is important and subjective to the decision-maker (as according to limitations of bounded rationality)* |
| Perceived cost | *A perceived cost signifies a subjective value of an asset as according to limitations of bounded rationality* |
| Prospect | *The likelihood or possibility of some event occurring in the future* |
| Risk | *The possibility or likelihood of losing something valuable* |
| Co-dependent risks | *When the likelihood of two or more risks are dependent on each other* |
| Loss aversion | *The concept that people are far more psychologically affected by a loss rather than a gain* |
| Bounded rationality | *The idea that an individual's rationality is limited when making a decision because of cognitive limitations and time restriction* |
| Choice architecture | *The practice of influencing an individual's choice by organising the context in which they make decisions* |
| Satisficing | *The act of making a decision which is satisfying and sufficient (given the constraints) rather than optimal* |
| Decision fatigue | *Fatigue caused by the difficulty and effort required to make a choice* |

# References

1. Acquisti, A.: Nudging privacy: the behavioral economics of personal information. IEEE Secur. Priv. **7**(6), 82–85 (2009)
2. Acquisti, A., Grossklags, J.: What can behavioral economics teach us about privacy. Digital Priv. Theory Technol. Practices **18**, 363–377 (2007)
3. Anderson, C.L., Agarwal, R.: Practicing safe computing: a multimedia empirical examination of home computer user security behavioral intentions. MISQ **34**(3), 613–643 (2010)
4. Ashenden, D., Lawrence, D.: Can we sell security like soap?: a new approach to behaviour change. In: Proceedings of the 2013 New Security Paradigms Workshop, pp. 87–94. ACM (2013)
5. Ashenden, D., Lawrence, D.: Security dialogues: building better relationships between security and business. IEEE Secur. Priv. **14**(3), 82–87 (2016)
6. Baddeley, M.: Information security: lessons from behavioural economics. In: Workshop on the Economics of Information Security (2011)
7. Bateman, H., McAdam, K.: Dictionary of Economics. A & C Black Publishers Ltd., London (2003)
8. Beautement, A., Sasse, M.A., Wonham, M.: The compliance budget: managing security behaviour in organisations. In: Proceedings of the 2008 Workshop on New Security Paradigms, pp. 47–58. ACM (2009)
9. Benenson, Z., Lenzini, G., Oliveira, D., Parkin, S., Uebelacker, S.: Maybe poor johnny really cannot encrypt: the case for a complexity theory for usable security. In: Proceedings of the 2015 New Security Paradigms Workshop, pp. 85–99. ACM (2015)
10. Bergman, O., Whittaker, S.: The cognitive costs of upgrades. Interact. Comput. **30**(1), 46–52 (2017)
11. Beris, O., Beautement, A., Sasse, M.A.: Employee rule breakers, excuse makers and security champions: mapping the risk perceptions and emotions that drive security behaviors. In: Proceedings of the 2015 New Security Paradigms Workshop, pp. 73–84. ACM (2015)
12. Blythe, J., Koppel, R., Smith, S.W.: Circumvention of security: good users do bad things. IEEE Secur. Priv. **11**(5), 80–83 (2013)
13. Briggs, P., Jeske, D., Coventry, L.: Behavior change interventions for cybersecurity. In: Behavior Change Interventions for Cybersecurity, pp. 115–136 (2017)
14. Camp, L.J., Lewis, S.: Economics of Information Security, vol. 12. Springer Science & Business Media, Berlin (2006)
15. Caraban, A., Karapanos, E., Gonçalves, D., Campos, P.: 23 ways to nudge: a review of technology-mediated nudging in human-computer interaction (2019)
16. Caulfield, T., Pym, D.: Improving security policy decisions with models. IEEE Secur. Priv. **13**(5), 34–41 (2015)
17. Caulfield, T., Pym, D., Williams, J.: Compositional security modelling. In: Tryfonas, T., Askoxylakis, I. (eds.) HAS 2014. LNCS, vol. 8533, pp. 233–245. Springer, Cham (2014). https://doi.org/10.1007/978-3-319-07620-1_21
18. Collinson, M., Monahan, B., Pym, D.: A Discipline of Mathematical Systems Modelling. College Publications (2012)
19. Das, S., Dabbish, L.A., Hong, J.I.: A typology of perceived triggers for end-user security and privacy behaviors (2019)
20. Dekker, S.: Just Culture: Balancing Safety and Accountability. CRC Press, United States (2016)

21. Demjaha, A., Caulfield, T., Sasse, M.A., Pym, D.: 2 fast 2 secure: a case study of post-breach security changes (2019)
22. Dourish, P., Grinter, E., Delgado De La Flor, J., Joseph, M.: Security in the wild: user strategies for managing security as an everyday, practical problem. Pers. Ubiquit. Comput. **8**(6), 391–401 (2004)
23. Dutson, J., Allen, D., Eggett, D., Seamons, K.: "Don't punish all of us": measuring user attitudes about two-factor authentication. In: EuroUSEC, vol. 2019 (2019)
24. Friedman, J.P.: Dictionary of Business and Economic Terms. Simon and Schuster, New York (2012)
25. Frik, A., Malkin, N., Harbach, M., Peer, E., Egelman, S.: A promise is a promise: the effect of commitment devices on computer security intentions. In: Proceedings of the 2019 CHI Conference on Human Factors in Computing Systems, p. 604. ACM (2019)
26. Gordon, L.A., Loeb, M.P.: The economics of information security investment. ACM Trans. Inf. Syst. Secur. (TISSEC) **5**(4), 438–457 (2002)
27. Grossklags, J., Acquisti, A.: When 25 cents is too much: an experiment on willingness-to-sell and willingness-to-protect personal information. In: WEIS (2007)
28. Herley, C.: So long, and no thanks for the externalities: the rational rejection of security advice by users. In: Proceedings of the 2009 Workshop on New Security Paradigms Workshop, pp. 133–144. ACM (2009)
29. Herley, C.: More is not the answer. IEEE Secur. Priv. **12**(1), 14–19 (2013)
30. Horne, R., et al.: Concordance, adherence and compliance in medicine taking. London: NCCSDO **2005**, 40–6 (2005)
31. Information Security Forum: From promoting awareness to embedding behaviours: Secure by choice, not by chance (2014)
32. Ioannidis, C., Pym, D., Williams, J.: Information security trade-offs and optimal patching policies. Eur. J. Oper. Res. **216**(2), 434–444 (2012)
33. Johnson, E.J., et al.: Beyond nudges: tools of a choice architecture. Market. Lett. **23**(2), 487–504 (2012)
34. Kahneman, D., Tversky, A.: Prospect theory: an analysis of decision under risk. In: Handbook of the Fundamentals of Financial Decision Making: Part I, pp. 99–127. World Scientific (2013)
35. Karlsson, F., Karlsson, M., Åström, J.: Measuring employees' compliance-the importance of value pluralism. Inf. Comput. Secur. **25**(3), 279–299 (2017)
36. Kirlappos, I., Beautement, A., Sasse, M.A.: "Comply or Die" is dead: long live security-aware principal agents. In: Adams, A.A., Brenner, M., Smith, M. (eds.) FC 2013. LNCS, vol. 7862, pp. 70–82. Springer, Heidelberg (2013). https://doi.org/10.1007/978-3-642-41320-9_5
37. Kirlappos, I., Parkin, S., Sasse, M.A.: Learning from "shadow security": why understanding non-compliance provides the basis for effective security. In: Workshop on Usable Security (USEC) 2014 (2014)
38. Koppel, R., Smith, S.W., Blythe, J., Kothari, V.H.: Workarounds to computer access in healthcare organizations: you want my password or a dead patient? ITCH **15**(4), 215–220 (2015)
39. Mankiw, N., Taylor, M.: Microeconomics: thomson learning (2006)
40. Mathur, A., Engel, J., Sobti, S., Chang, V., Chetty, M.: "They keep coming back like zombies": improving software updating interfaces. In: Twelfth Symposium on Usable Privacy and Security (SOUPS 2016), pp. 43–58 (2016)

41. Michie, S., Van Stralen, M.M., West, R.: The behaviour change wheel: a new method for characterising and designing behaviour change interventions. Implementation Sci. **6**(1), 42 (2011)
42. Morisset, C., Yevseyeva, I., Groß, T., van Moorsel, A.: A formal model for soft enforcement: influencing the decision-maker. In: Mauw, S., Jensen, C.D. (eds.) STM 2014. LNCS, vol. 8743, pp. 113–128. Springer, Cham (2014). https://doi.org/10.1007/978-3-319-11851-2_8
43. Morris, J., Becker, I., Parkin, S.: In control with no control: perceptions and reality of windows 10 home edition update features (2019)
44. Pallas, F.: Information security inside organizations-a positive model and some normative arguments based on new institutional economics. TU Berlin - Information Systems Engineering (2009)
45. Parkin, S., Driss, S., Krol, K., Sasse, M.A.: Assessing the user experience of password reset policies in a university. In: Stajano, F., Mjølsnes, S.F., Jenkinson, G., Thorsheim, P. (eds.) PASSWORDS 2015. LNCS, vol. 9551, pp. 21–38. Springer, Cham (2016). https://doi.org/10.1007/978-3-319-29938-9_2
46. Parkin, S., Fielder, A., Ashby, A.: Pragmatic security: modelling it security management responsibilities for SME archetypes. In: Proceedings of the 8th ACM CCS International Workshop on Managing Insider Security Threats, pp. 69–80. ACM (2016)
47. Parkin, S., van Moorsel, A., Inglesant, P., Sasse, M.A.: A stealth approach to usable security: helping it security managers to identify workable security solutions. In: Proceedings of the 2010 New Security Paradigms Workshop. NSPW 2010, pp. 33–50. ACM (2010)
48. Parkin, S., Redmiles, E.M., Coventry, L., Sasse, M.A.: Security when it is welcome: exploring device purchase as an opportune moment for security behavior change. In: Proceedings of the Workshop on Usable Security and Privacy (USEC 2019). Internet Society (2019)
49. Raja, F., Hawkey, K., Jaferian, P., Beznosov, K., Booth, K.S.: It's too complicated, so I turned it off!: expectations, perceptions, and misconceptions of personal firewalls. In: Proceedings of the 3rd ACM Workshop on Assurable and Usable Security Configuration, pp. 53–62. ACM (2010)
50. Reason, J.: Human Error. Cambridge University Press, Cambridge (1990)
51. Redmiles, E.M., Mazurek, M.L., Dickerson, J.P.: Dancing pigs or externalities?: measuring the rationality of security decisions. In: Proceedings of the 2018 ACM Conference on Economics and Computation, pp. 215–232. ACM (2018)
52. Reeder, R., Ion, I., Consolvo, S.: 152 simple steps to stay safe online: security advice for non-tech-savvy users. IEEE Secur. Priv. **15**(5), 55–64 (2017)
53. Reinfelder, L., Landwirth, R., Benenson, Z.: Security managers are not the enemy either. In: Proceedings of the 2019 CHI Conference on Human Factors in Computing Systems, p. 433. ACM (2019)
54. Renaud, K., Goucher, W.: The curious incidence of security breaches by knowledgeable employees and the pivotal role a of security culture. In: Tryfonas, T., Askoxylakis, I. (eds.) HAS 2014. LNCS, vol. 8533, pp. 361–372. Springer, Cham (2014). https://doi.org/10.1007/978-3-319-07620-1_32
55. Renaud, K., Zimmermann, V.: Ethical guidelines for nudging in information security & privacy. Int. J. Hum Comput Stud. **120**, 22–35 (2018)
56. Richard, H., Thaler, C.R.S.: Nudge: improving decisions about health, wealth, and happiness (2008)
57. Shafir, E.: The Behavioral Foundations of Public Policy. Princeton University Press, New Jersey (2013)

58. Simon, H.A.: Rational choice and the structure of the environment. Psychol. Rev. **63**(2), 129 (1956)
59. Simon, H.A.: Models of Bounded Rationality: Empirically Grounded Economic Reason, vol. 3. MIT Press, United States (1997)
60. Thaler, R.: Toward a positive theory of consumer choice. J. Econ. Behav. Organ. **1**(1), 39–60 (1980)
61. Turland, J., Coventry, L., Jeske, D., Briggs, P., van Moorsel, A.: Nudging towards security: developing an application for wireless network selection for android phones. In: Proceedings of the 2015 British HCI Conference, pp. 193–201. ACM (2015)
62. Vaniea, K.E., Rader, E., Wash, R.: Betrayed by updates: how negative experiences affect future security. In: Proceedings of the SIGCHI Conference on Human Factors in Computing Systems, pp. 2671–2674. ACM (2014)
63. Verendel, V.: A Prospect Theory Approach to Security. Chalmers University of Technology, Sweden (2008)
64. Vohs, K.D., Baumeister, R.F., Schmeichel, B.J., Twenge, J.M., Nelson, N.M., Tice, D.M.: Making choices impairs subsequent self-control: a limited-resource account of decision making, self-regulation, and active initiative (2014)
65. Wash, R., Rader, E., Vaniea, K., Rizor, M.: Out of the loop: how automated software updates cause unintended security consequences. In: 10th Symposium On Usable Privacy and Security (SOUPS 2014), pp. 89–104 (2014)

# System Security

# What We Know About Bug Bounty Programs - An Exploratory Systematic Mapping Study

Ana Magazinius$^{(\boxtimes)}$, Niklas Mellegård, and Linda Olsson

RISE ICT Viktoria, Gothenburg, Sweden
{ana.magazinius,niklas.mellegard,linda.olsson}@ri.se
http://www.ri.se

**Abstract.** This paper presents a systematic mapping study of the research on crowdsourced security vulnerability discovery. The aim is to identify aspects of bug bounty program (BBP) research that relate to product owners, the bug-hunting crowd or vulnerability markets. Based on 72 examined papers, we conclude that research has mainly been focused on the organisation of BBPs from the product owner perspective, but that aspects such as mechanisms of the white vulnerability market and incentives for bug hunting have also been addressed. With the increasing importance of cyber security, BBPs need more attention in order to be understood better. In particular, datasets from more diverse types of companies (e.g. safety-critical systems) should be added, as empirical studies are generally based on convenience sampled public data sets. Also, there is a need for more in-depth, qualitative studies in order to understand what drives bug hunters and product owners towards finding constructive ways of working together.

**Keywords:** Bug bounty · Systematic mapping · Literature review

## 1 Introduction

In a digital and connected world, attempts to hack connected units are a problem for companies. Consequences range from economic ones such as patching costs, decreased revenue and plummeting stock prices, to damaged reputation and safety risks [1,63,67]. Meanwhile, what drives hackers to hack ranges from curiosity, to money [31], and reputation [3,4,31,52,57]. This has led companies to engage in constructive collaboration with the hacker community rather than getting into conflict. The earliest example of this type of collaboration was initiated by Hunter & Ready, who in 1983 offered a VW Beetle (Bug!) as a reward for bugs found in their VRTX operating system[1]. Although bug bounty programs (BBP) were not very common at first, with time, Internet giants such as

This research was funded by Swedish funding agency Vinnova, FFI program, HoliSec project (project number 2015-06894).

[1] https://techcrunch.com/2017/01/19/hacking-the-army/.

T. Groß and T. Tryfonas (Eds.): STAST 2019, LNCS 11739, pp. 89–106, 2021.
https://doi.org/10.1007/978-3-030-55958-8_5

Netscape, Google and Facebook initiated BBPs. Government agencies (e.g. the United States Department of Defense) have also initiated BBPs, as have automotive companies such as General Motors and Tesla. The general belief is that BBPs lead to discovery of vulnerabilities not detected in regular penetration testing, because of the size and the skillset of the bug hunter community. Middleman companies, which connect product owners with the bug hunter crowd and manage the bug-hunting process, have become part of the vulnerability discovery ecosystem. iDefense was the first middleman company, followed by many others. Today's white-market middleman companies, such as HackerOne and Bugcrowd, host hundreds of public and private BBPs where the bug-hunting crowd are invited to legally test the security of the involved companies' products.

The research on BBPs reflects this evolution; for the past two decades, researchers have provided theoretical and empirical contributions to the body of knowledge. However, a compilation of these research efforts is lacking. A 2018 search for literature reviews on BBP research only resulted in one minor study, compiling just eleven papers [28]. Hence, there is a need to more extensively map this research area, to illuminate what is known and what remains under-researched. In this paper, we address this by a systematic mapping study which may lay the grounds for future research. The aim of this study is to map the research area and answer the following research questions:

RQ1. What aspects of BBPs that relate to the product owner's perspective have been addressed by research?

RQ2. What aspects of BBPs that relate to the bug-hunting crowd's perspective have been addressed by research?

RQ3. What aspects of BBPs that relate to the mechanisms of vulnerability markets have been addressed by research?

## 2   Methodology

This study is based on the rigorous guidelines for systematic literature reviews (SLR) adapted to suit a mapping study [37,38]. They differ in that SLRs provide in-depth analysis and comparison of different categories of a topic, whereas mapping studies only identify and classify existing research.

A literature search was conducted in late June 2018, on four search engines: Scopus, IEEE Xplore Digital Library, ACM Digital Library and Google Scholar. Search terms were: "bug bounty", "vulnerability reward program" and "vulnerability disclosure". No limit was set for publication date, only material in English was considered. While non-academic reports provide interesting insights, they were excluded due to lack of methodology transparency, and lack of quality ensuring measures such as peer review. The search resulted in 2457 items.

Selection criteria were that the papers should concern 1) mechanisms of crowdsourced vulnerability discovery, or 2) mechanisms of vulnerability disclosure by external bug hunters, or 3) organisations' management of vulnerabilities discovered by external bug hunters. A first selection was made based on title and abstract. To ensure reliability in the selection, all items found in Scopus,

IEEE Xplore and ACM were reviewed independently by two researchers. Items found in Google Scholar (the source of most items), the top 15% were reviewed by two researchers and the remaining 85% by one researcher. This was considered sufficient as a validity check and the first selection resulted in 216 papers. All selected papers were examined by at least one researcher excluding papers which content did not match the selection criteria. The borderline papers were discussed within the research team. This process resulted in the final selection of 72 papers (see Appendix 4), approved by all three researchers. The papers were categorised into one, or more, of three main categories (corresponding to the three research questions); product owner, the bug-hunting crowd and vulnerability market mechanisms. This categorisation was chosen as it puts focus on the two main actors in a BBP and on the relationships between them and other actors. Each researcher was assigned a category to review in depth, after which all categories were discussed within the team. This was the point of departure for the analysis.

## 3   Results

While the research on bug bounties has been ongoing since 2000, there has been a noticeable increase in the number of published papers since 2016. The earliest paper included in this study focused on the product owner category, followed by the first paper on market mechanisms in 2004, and the first paper on crowd related topics in 2007 (see Fig. 1).

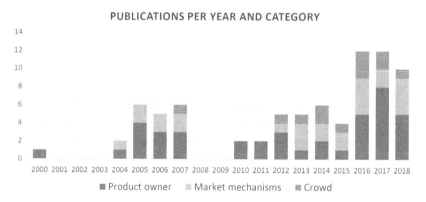

**Fig. 1.** Publications per year and category (one paper can appear in more than one category)

Out of the 72 papers included in this study 44 (61%) are based on empirical evidence, two (3%) are literature reviews, and 26 (36%) are purely theoretical (see Fig. 2). While all three categories used in this paper consist of both empirical and theoretical research, product owner and market mechanisms categories also include literature reviews (see Fig. 2).

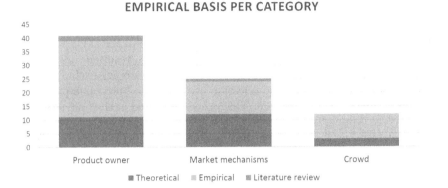

Fig. 2. Empirical basis per category (one paper can appear in more than one category)

Further, an increase in the amount of empirical papers can be observed in the past five years (see Fig. 3). These draw data from 28 different datasets, the top ones being CERT (seven cases), followed by HackerOne (five cases), and Wooyun and NVD (three cases respectively).

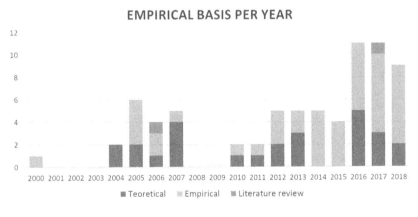

Fig. 3. Empirical basis per year (one paper can appear in more than one category)

## 3.1 Product Owner

Publications in the product owner category consider the perspective of the organiser of a BBP, and/or the owner of the product that is being tested. The category includes 41 papers published between 2000 and 2018 (see Fig. 4), which were classified in subcategories: guidelines, vulnerability life cycle, economic aspects and experience reports (see Fig. 5).

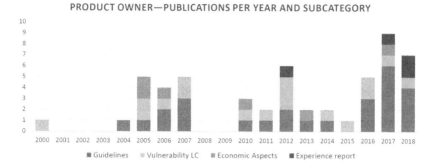

**Fig. 4.** Product owner, publications per year and subcategory (one paper can appear in more than one subcategory)

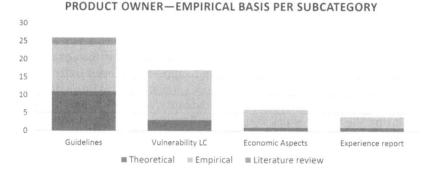

**Fig. 5.** Product owner, empirical basis per subcategory (one paper can appear in more than one subcategory)

**Guidelines.** Papers in this category provide guidelines and recommendations that are relevant to organisers of a bug bounty. [26,71,74] examine historical bug bounties and provide improvement suggestions, and [61] provides a checklist for the organisers. Other papers examine more specific aspects, [17,40,73] investigate how to incentivise a crowd, and [41] how to formulate a BBP announcement. General guidelines for vulnerability disclosure are provided by [7,18,21]. More specific aspects are provided in [30] where disclosure strategies in different domains are examined and mapped to the domain of control engineering. [27] provides a deterrent story about a company going to lengths to try to prevent disclosure rather than to acknowledge and fix vulnerabilities. The paper goes on to present a more efficient strategy applied by another company.

The impact of disclosure on patching practices is investigated in [10], and [14] maps disclosure with number of attacks. One paper examines ethics and moral obligations various actors have with regard to software vulnerabilities [66].

Another perspective is taken in [44] where the rate of discoveries as a BBP progresses is examined and recommendations on adaptation of rewards provided. [24] provides recommendations on how to formulate and communicate terms with a crowd. Some papers focus on risk assessment, [34] proposes a systematic approach to assessing the risk of a vulnerability causing adverse effects, while [63] investigates incidents in other domains and maps those to military systems.

One paper examines the methods of operation when detecting a vulnerability and provides recommendations on how to avoid vulnerabilities and improve security [25]. Another focuses on vulnerability reporting, providing recommendations on how to better manage vulnerability reports [65].

**Vulnerability Life-Cycle.** Papers in this category describe life-cycle models and analyse the dynamics of a vulnerability in its various states of existence. This may provide valuable insights for understanding the dynamics of a vulnerability, such as correlations between disclosure and exploitation or rate of patch uptake. [58] examine whether the delay between disclosure and acknowledgement by the vendor cluster across vendors. [10] explore whether there is a correlation between delay in patching after a disclosure and find no support that instant disclosure means faster patching. They do however find support that open source vendors are quicker to provide patches and that more serious vulnerabilities do seem to receive patches quicker. A somewhat contradictory result was reported in [52]: vendors facing the threat of disclosure, as well as vendors that risk loss of value, tend to provide patches faster. [49] examine whether grace periods between vulnerability discovery and disclosure have an impact on the speed of providing a patch but find no clear relationship. [45] examines whether (and what) publicly available information about a vulnerability has an impact on exploitation, finding that the risk of exploitation increases with increased criticality of the vulnerability and when several vulnerabilities are related to each other. Similarly, [14] finds that zero-day attacks typically last for almost a year before disclosure, but mostly affect few product owners. However, the amount of attacks increases with several orders of magnitude after disclosure. [8,12] analyse the number of attacks over the vulnerability life cycle, and [12] finds that many intrusions occur long after a patch has been released. [46] analyse the time delays between the various stages of the vulnerability life-cycle. [8] present a life-cycle model for a vulnerability and, using empirical data, correlates number of detected attacks to the stages of the life-cycle. [18] provide a theoretical model for the information dissemination of a vulnerability and analyse it from different stakeholders' perspectives.

[6,11] examine factors that affect prioritisation of which vulnerabilities to patch, as well as typical delay between disclosure and the release of a patch. [68] provide a model for patching practices for embedded software industrial control devices which can be used by companies in deciding strategic patching management. Two papers examine patch uptake and explore the rate at which patches are applied by users. [51] examine factors affecting the rate of patch uptake, finding that security experts and developers (and software with automatic updating

mechanisms) have significantly lower median times to patch. [68] examines patch uptake for embedded internet-connected industrial control systems, finding that patch uptake is slow. One paper evaluates CVSS based on severity scoring from a number of public vulnerability reward programs, finding that CVSS can be a useful metric for prioritising patching [70].

**Economic Aspects.** Papers in this category examine economic aspects of vulnerability disclosure, such as the cost of a vulnerability and return on investment for organising a BBP. [26] compare the cost of organising a bug bounty with the results and conclude that the benefits are considerably greater that the cost. [1,67] correlate loss of market value with vulnerability disclosure and conclude that there is usually a brief loss of value. [56] compare the cost of proactively detecting vulnerabilities with the cost of responding to black market exploits and conclude that the reactive approach is more economical.

**Experience Reports.** Two papers describe the Pentagon BBP [19,20] and another one focuses on smart-grid vendors [30]. [2] provides insights into fears experienced prior to BBP and countermeasures taken by the vendors.

### 3.2   Bug Hunter Crowd

The papers in the crowd category provide insight into both the bug-hunting community as a whole and individual bug hunters. Researchers from diverse fields such as information security, software engineering, computer science, information economics and ethics have contributed to this research, which spans over eleven years. Out of twelve papers included in this category four are theoretical and eight are based on empirical evidence collected and analysed using quantitative as well as qualitative research methods (see Fig. 6). The empirical data comes from middleman companies and vulnerability databases. The first publication is from 2007, and the papers have been classified as belonging to one or more of the sub-categories crowd trends, incentives for bug hunting, bug-hunters' skill set and ethics (see Fig. 7).

**Crowd Trends.** Papers in this category describe the bug-hunter community over time. The interest in BBPs has grown over time and both active and the overall crowd are growing [32,71,72], most of which are hunters that are not employed by the companies whose products they test [3,4,33]. The growth in crowd has led to an increase in the number of reported vulnerabilities [32,33,71], in particular ones of medium and critical severity [33,71]. One of the papers suggests a model for organisations' and bug-hunters' utility, concluding that for both parties the utility decreases as more bug hunters join a BBP [74]. This is likely due to the increasing number of reported duplicates, which for product owners means more time spent on reports and for bug hunters means more time spent without reward [74] causing them to switch programs [31,44,71,74].

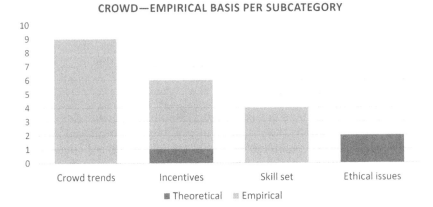

Fig. 6. Bug hunter crowd, empirical basis per subcategory (one paper can appear in more than one subcategory)

The most active bug hunters contribute to a majority of reports [31], in particular more critical ones [72], but still they are a minority of the crowd [31,33,71]. However, having a large crowd might still be preferable for a product owner, since that implies a sizeable contribution [72]. In particular middleman companies might benefit from this, since less active hackers tend to submit bug reports to a larger number of companies [72].

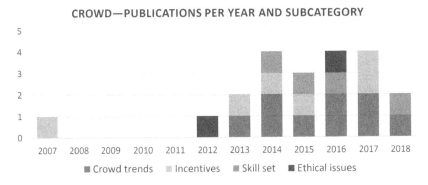

Fig. 7. Bug hunter crowd, publications per year and subcategory (one paper can appear in more than one subcategory)

**Incentives for Bug Hunting.** Papers in this category draw conclusions from both the behaviour of individual bug hunters as well as from the crowd as a whole. Monetary incentives are obviously important [3,4,44,72], particularly for the most active bug hunters [31]. Other incentives are: making products more safe and secure [31,72], building a reputation [72], and curiosity and having fun [3,4]. Further, one paper presents a theoretical model of how loss is reduced for both hunters and product owners [52].

**Bug Hunters' Skill Set.** This category describes the types of vulnerabilities that are addressed by the bug hunters and the skills that bug hunters possess. Most of the bug hunters are reported to have a single skill [33], but on a crowd level the diversity among skills is high [32]. The most commonly reported vulnerability types that bug hunters target are SQL injection, XSS and design flaws [32,33,71,72]. One paper reports that the bug-hunting crowd has a desire to increase their skill set when given the opportunity in form of public vulnerability reports or tutorials [72].

**Ethical Issues.** This category includes papers that provide suggestions on what moral issues to consider as a bug hunter. One paper offers guidelines for bug hunters [22] and the other one states which ethical issues to consider [57]. Both agree that the well-being of humans should be taken into consideration on small scale (e.g. privacy and safety) and large scale (e.g. political outcomes) and urge bug hunters to ensure that their findings are used for good.

### 3.3 Vulnerability Market Mechanisms

This category comprises papers that focus on the buying or selling of vulnerabilities or exploits, or on economic aspects of vulnerabilities. The 25 papers about market mechanisms have been classified as descriptive papers, theoretical models, market trends or ethics papers (see Fig. 8).

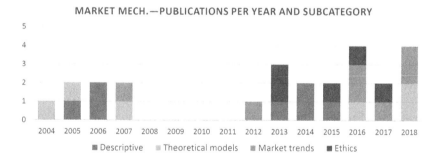

**Fig. 8.** Vulnerability markets, publications per year and subcategory

The research area has evolved since 2004 when the first paper was published. Early papers deal more with theory and descriptions of the area, while later papers examine empirical data and ethical implications. It seems that the area has become more applied with time, although theoretical models still seem to be of interest (see Fig. 9).

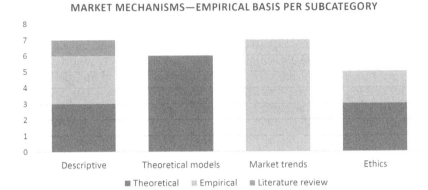

MARKET MECHANISMS—EMPIRICAL BASIS PER SUBCATEGORY

**Fig. 9.** Vulnerability markets, empirical basis per subcategory

**Descriptive Papers.** The papers in this category provide overviews and discussions of the area of vulnerability markets. Several are theoretical and based on economics. For instance, [7] establish that economics of information security is a new and thriving discipline. They apply classical economics theories to vulnerability markets and discuss how this can help understand the market mechanisms. This kind of analysis is also provided by [15,16], who further creates a typology of vulnerability markets: bug challenges, vulnerability brokers, exploit derivatives and cyber-insurance. [53] build on this when investigating the usefulness of different market types: vulnerability brokers, bug challenges, buyer's bug auction and seller's bug auction. [39] use institutional economics theory as a framework to understand vulnerability markets. Black and white markets are described by [9]. A different perspective is given by a discussion on black and white vulnerability markets as a basis for policy recommendations to reduce cybercrime [64].

**Theoretical Models.** These papers are based on mathematical models of market dynamics and agent behaviour. [35,36] use game theory to examine whether market-based mechanisms or a publicly funded intermediary performs better with regard to social welfare, suggesting that a publicly funded intermediary maximises social welfare. Another study models the vulnerability market as an optimisation problem of minimising social cost, attempting to explain why some vendors offer monetary rewards for vulnerabilities while others do not [62]. [54] develop a system dynamics model to describe the growth of a vulnerability black market and suggest that a white market may reduce black market trade. A more recent model covers the choice of selling vulnerabilities to software vendors (white market) or governments (grey market) [29]. [43] use game theory to examine who should foot the bill for information security - software vendors or the government.

**Market Trends.** The majority of these papers are published in recent years, suggesting that vulnerability markets are gaining interest within applied research. [42] analyse the effects of private (as opposed to publicly funded) intermediaries on disclosure and patching time, showing that disclosure time is not affected but time to patch may increase. Another study shows that market-based disclosure is beneficial for security, as it reduces the number of exploitation attempts [55]. [32] show that the more bug hunters that engage in a BBP, the more vulnerabilities are discovered. [50] examine the correlation between CVSS scores and bounties, concluding that the link between CVSS score and bounty is low. [59] examine and discuss exploit pricing, showing that many exploits are sold for a mere $50-100 on the white market. On the black market, exploits are priced equally high or higher [5]. However, [60] show that bug bounty programs can be successful even without monetary rewards.

**Ethics.** The papers in this category concern ethical aspects of vulnerability markets. One paper reports on an expert panel discussion which aimed at increasing awareness of the consequences of vulnerability markets [23]. Questions are raised, such as, can it be considered ethical to trade vulnerabilities in voting systems or in pacemakers? [69] argue that the selling of vulnerabilities may generally be considered ethical but that the selling of zero-day exploits may not. To reduce the market for zero-day exploits, they propose that software vendors should spend their money on in-house vulnerability discovery rather than on BBPs. Two papers concern American law: [13] argues that responsible disclosure infringes on freedom of speech, wherefore full disclosure is preferable, while [47] argues that a framework is needed to discern between criminal acts of disclosure and disclosure for the public good. Finally, one paper points out how society depends on information security and argues that information security should be viewed as a public good [48].

# 4 Discussion and Concluding Remarks

The number of BBPs has grown during the studied period, especially around the time when middleman companies increased their activity on the market. Examination of their public datasets has shown increased number of reported vulnerabilities over time, of medium and critical severity in particular. While the most active hunters tend to find not only more, but also more critical bugs, the contribution of the less active part of the crowd is still sizeable.

**Product Owner.** The increase in research is largest relating to guidelines for and economy of a BBP. It is crucial to know not only the cost of practically organizing a BBP, but also aspects such as: risks in vulnerability disclosure; cost of detecting a vulnerability in-house vs. in a BBP; cost comparisons between a reactive repair due to black market vulnerability discovery and proactive repair based on in-house BBP discovery. While [26] argue that benefits of a BBP greatly overweigh the costs, in purely economic terms the reactive approach might be better as argued by [56], which appears quite cynical.

**Vulnerability Market Mechanisms.** White and black markets are in focus of this category [5,9,16,54,64]. While a white market is shown to be beneficial for establishing the price of vulnerabilities and to manage the "public good" [7,35,36], research also shows that it may be too easy to trade vulnerabilities on the black market instead [15,55,64].

**Bug Hunter Crowd.** While incentives for bug hunting include reputation, learning and fun, the most reported incentive is monetary [4,31,72]. For the most active hackers, monetary incentives are particularly important [31], which makes research on ethical aspects of bug hunting necessary. This type of research is found in all three main categories. Authors urge those selling bugs to consider safety and privacy aspects that otherwise might be in danger as a result of data leakage and vulnerabilities weaponisation [22,48,57].

**Research Gaps.** In order to fill the gaps in current understanding of BBP practice future research should include:

- Diverse data sets: A majority of empirical publications on BBP have used public data sets and open source projects. To our knowledge there are no academic publications examining BBPs for safety critical systems which are experiencing a dramatic increase in connectivity.
- Diverse research methods: Most of the empirical research, in particular that on bug hunters, is quantitative. Qualitative methods would provide more in-depth understanding of bug hunters' mind sets.
- Multidisciplinary research: Most authors have a background in information security or computer science. The literature is complemented by economics, law and philosophy researchers, who often contribute very different perspectives. Implications of BBPs for companies, individuals and states are complex, and multidisciplinary research can provide valuable insights.

Lastly, we believe that the ongoing increase in publications will likely require comprehensive systematic literature review in a few years time when the body of knowledge is substantial enough to draw relevant in-depth conclusions.

## Appendix A

This appendix maps each publication included in the mapping study to the categories it was included in, product owner (PO), crowd (CR), and market mechanisms (MM).

| Ref | Publication | PO | CR | MM |
|---|---|---|---|---|
| 1 | *"Is There a Cost to Privacy Breaches? An Event Study"*, Acquisti, A., Friedman, A., Telang, R | X | | |
| 2 | *"Friendly Hackers to the Rescue: How Organizations Perceive Crowdsourced Vulnerability Discovery"*, Al-Banna, M., Benatallah, B., Schlagwein, D., Bertino, E., Barukh, M.C | X | | |
| 3 | *"Most successful vulnerability discoverers: Motivation and methods"*, Algarni, A.M., Malaiya, Y.K | | X | |
| 4 | *"Software Vulnerability Markets: Discoverers And Buyers*, Algarni, A.M., Malaiya, Y.K | | X | |
| 5 | *"Economic Factors of Vulnerability Trade and Exploitation"*, Allodi, L | | | X |
| 6 | *"Comparing Vulnerability Severity and Exploits Using Case-Control Studies"*, Allodi, L., Massacci, F | X | | |
| 7 | *"The Economics of Information Security"*, Anderson, R., Moore, T | X | | X |
| 8 | *"Windows of vulnerability: a case study analysis"*, Arbaugh, W.A., Fithen, W.L., McHugh, J | X | | |
| 9 | *"0-Day Vulnerabilities and Cybercrime"*, Armin, J., Foti, P. Cremonini, M | | | X |
| 10 | *"Economics of software vulnerability disclosure"*, Arora, A., Telang, R | X | | |
| 11 | *"An Empirical Analysis of Software Vendors' Patch Release Behavior: Impact of Vulnerability Disclosure"*, Arora, A., Krishnan, R., Telang, R., Yang, Y., | X | | |
| 12 | *"Does information security attack frequency increase with vulnerability disclosure? An empirical analysis"*, Arora, A., Nandkumar, A., Telang, R., | X | | |
| 13 | *"A Target to the Heart of the First Amendment: Government Endorsement of Responsible Disclosure as Unconstitutional"*, Bergman, K | | | X |
| 14 | *"Before We Knew It: An Empirical Study of Zero-day Attacks in the Real World"*, Bilge, L., Dumitraş, T | X | | |
| 15 | *"Vulnerability markets"*, Böhme, R | | | X |
| 16 | *"A Comparison of Market Approaches to Software Vulnerability Disclosure"*, Böhme, R | | | X |
| 17 | *"Enter the Hydra: Towards Principled Bug Bounties and Exploit-Resistant Smart Contracts"*, Breindenbach, L., Daian, P., Tramer, F., Juels, A., | X | | |
| 18 | *"Efficiency of Vulnerability Disclosure Mechanisms to Disseminate Vulnerability Knowledge"*, Cavusoglu, H., Cavusoglu, H. Raghunathan, S | X | | |
| 19 | *"Cybersecurity Innovation in Government: A Case Study of U.S. Pentagon's Vulnerability Reward Program"*, Chatfield, A.T., Reddick, C.G | X | | |
| 20 | *"Crowdsourced cybersecurity innovation: The case of the Pentagon's vulnerability reward program"*, Chatfield, A.T., Reddick, C.G | X | | |
| 21 | *"Network Security: Vulnerabilities and Disclosure Policy"*, Choi, Jay Pil; Fershtman, C., Gandal, N | X | | |
| 22 | *"Vulnerabilities and their surrounding ethical questions: a code of ethics for the private sector"*, De Gregorio, A | | X | |
| 23 | *"Markets for zero-day exploits: ethics and implications"*, Egelman, S., Herley, C., van Oorschot, P.C | | | X |
| 24 | *"Private Ordering Shaping Cybersecurity Policy: The Case of Bug Bounties"*, Elazari Bar On, A | X | | |
| 25 | *"To Improve Cybersecurity, Think Like a Hacker"*, Esteves, J., Ramalho, E., De Haro, G | X | | |
| 26 | *"An Empirical Study of Vulnerability Rewards Programs"*, Finifter, M., Akhawe, D., Wagner, D | X | | |
| 27 | *"Vulnerability Disclosure: The Strange Case of Bret McDanel"*, Freeman, E | X | | |
| 28 | *"Web science challenges in researching bug bounties"*, Fryer, H., Simperl, E., Fryer, H., Simperl, E | X | | |
| 29 | *"Revenue Maximizing Markets for Zero-Day Exploits"*, Guo, M., Hata, H., Babar, A | | | X |
| 30 | *"Cyber vulnerability disclosure policies for the smart grid"*, Hahn, A., Govindarasu, M | X | | |
| 31 | *"Understanding the Heterogeneity of Contributors in Bug Bounty Programs"*, Hata, H., Guo, M., Babar, M.A | | X | |
| 32 | *"A study on Web security incidents in China by analyzing vulnerability disclosure platforms"*, Huang, C., Liu, J., Fang, Y., Zuo, Z., | | X | |
| 33 | *"Shifting to Mobile: Network-based Empirical Study of Mobile Vulnerability Market"*, Huang, K., Zhang, J., Tan, W., Feng, Z | | X | X |
| 34 | *"Defining and Assessing Quantitative Security Risk Measures Using Vulnerability Lifecycle and CVSS Metrics"*, Joh, H., Malaiya, Y.K | | X | |
| 35 | *"Economic analysis of the market for software vulnerability disclosure"*, Kannan, K., Telang R | | | X |
| 36 | *"Market for Software Vulnerabilities? Think Again"*, Kannan, K., Telang, R | | | X |
| 39 | *"Shifts in the Cybersecurity Paradigm: Zero-Day Exploits, Discourse, and Emerging Institutions"*, Kuehn, A., Mueller, M | | | X |
| 40 | *"Banishing Misaligned Incentives for Validating Reports in Bug-Bounty Platforms"*, Laszka, A., Zhao, M., Grossklags, J | X | | |
| 41 | *"The Rules of Engagement for Bug Bounty Programs"*, Laszka, A., Zhao, M., Malbari, A., Grossklags, J | X | | |
| 42 | *"An examination of private intermediaries' roles in software vulnerabilities disclosure"*, Li, P., Rao, H.R | | | X |
| 43 | *"Economic solutions to improve cybersecurity of governments and smart cities via vulnerability markets"*, Li, Z., Liao, Q | | | X |

(continued)

| Ref | Publication | PO | CR | MM |
|-----|-------------|----|----|----|
| 44 | "Given enough eyeballs, all bugs are shallow? Revisiting Eric Raymond with bug bounty programs", Maillart, T., Zhao, M., Grossklags, J., Chuang, J | X | X | |
| 45 | "Software Vulnerability Disclosure and its Impact on Exploitation: An Empirical Study", Mangalaraj, G.A., Raja, M.K | X | | |
| 46 | "Security-related vulnerability life cycle analysis", Marconato, G. V., Nicomette, V., Kaâniche, M | X | | |
| 47 | "Hacking Speech: Informational Speech and the First Amendment", Matwyshyn, A.M | | | X |
| 48 | "Stockpiling Zero-Day Exploits: The Next International Weapons Taboo", Maxwell, P | | | X |
| 49 | "Are Vulnerability Disclosure Deadlines Justified?", McQueen, M., Wright, J. L., Wellman, L | X | | |
| 50 | "Vulnerability Severity Scoring and Bounties: Why the Disconnect?", Munaiah, N., Meneely, A | | | X |
| 51 | "The Attack of the Clones: A Study of the Impact of Shared Code on Vulnerability Patching", Nappa, A., Johnson, R., Bilge, L., Caballero, J., Dumitras, T | X | | |
| 52 | "To disclose or not? An analysis of software user behavior", Nizovtsev, D., Thursby, M., | X | X | |
| 53 | "An Assessment of Market Methods for Information Security Risk Management", Pandey, P., Snekkenes, E.A | | | X |
| 54 | "Understanding Hidden Information Security Threats: The Vulnerability Black Market", Radianti, J., Gonzalez, J.J | | | X |
| 55 | "Are Markets for Vulnerabilities Effective?", Ransbotham, S., Mitra, S., Ramsey, J | | | X |
| 56 | "Is finding security holes a good idea?", Rescorla, E | X | | |
| 57 | "Ethical Issues in E-Voting Security Analysis", Robinson, D.G., Halderman, J.A | | X | |
| 58 | "Exploring the clustering of software vulnerability disclosure notifications across software vendors", Ruohonen, J., Holvitie, J., Hyrynsalmi, S., Leppänen, V | X | | |
| 59 | "Trading exploits online: A preliminary case study", Ruohonen, J., Hyrynsalmi, S., Leppänen, V | | | X |
| 60 | "A Bug Bounty Perspective on the Disclosure of Web Vulnerabilities", Ruohonen, J., Allodi, L | | | X |
| 61 | "Current data security issues for financial services firms", Sipes, E.K., James, J., Zetoony, D | X | | |
| 62 | "Economic Motivations for Software Bug Bounties", Sprague, C., Wagner, J | | | X |
| 63 | "Identifying self-inflicted vulnerabilities: The operational implications of technology within U.S. combat systems", Stevens, R | X | | |
| 64 | "Curbing the Market for Cyber Weapons", Stockton, P.N.; Golabek-Goldman, M | | | X |
| 65 | "Doing What Is Right with Coordinated Vulnerability Disclosure", Suárez, R.A., Scott, D | X | | |
| 66 | "Agents of responsibility in software vulnerability processes", Takanen, A., Vuorijärvi, P., Laakso, M., Röning, J | X | | |
| 67 | "Impact of Software Vulnerability Announcements on the Market Value of Software Vendors - an Empirical Investigation", Telang, R., Wattal, S | X | | |
| 68 | "Characterizing and Modeling Patching Practices of Industrial Control Systems", Wang, B., Li, X., de Aguiar, L.P., Menasche, D.S., Shafiq, Z | X | | |
| 69 | "Ethics of the software vulnerabilities and exploits market", Wolf, M.J., Fresco, N | | | X |
| 70 | "Evaluating CVSS Base Score Using Vulnerability Rewards Programs", Younis, A., Malaiya, Y., Ray, I | X | | |
| 71 | "An Exploratory Study of White Hat Behaviors in a Web Vulnerability Disclosure Program", Zhao, M., Grossklags, J., Chen, K | X | X | |
| 72 | "An Empirical Study of Web Vulnerability Discovery Ecosystems", Zhao, M., Grossklags, J., Liu, P | X | | |
| 73 | "Devising Effective Policies for Bug-Bounty Platforms and Security Vulnerability Discovery", Zhao, M., Laszka, A., Grossklags, J | X | | |
| 74 | "Crowdsourced Security Vulnerability Discovery: Modeling and Organizing Bug-Bounty Programs", Zhao, M., Laszka, A., Maillart, T., Grossklags, J | X | X | |

# References

1. Acquisti, A., Friedman, A., Telang, R.: Is there a cost to privacy breaches? An event study. In: Proceedings of International Conference on Information Systems, p. 19 (2006)
2. Al-Banna, M., Benatallah, B., Schlagwein, D., Bertino, E., Barukh, M.C.: Friendly hackers to the rescue: how organizations perceive crowdsourced vulnerability discovery. In: Proceedings of the Pacific Asia Conference on Information Systems, p. 15 (2018)

3. Algarni, A.M., Malaiya, Y.K.: Most successful vulnerability discoverers: motivation and methods. In: Proceedings of the International Conference on Security and Management (SAM), p. 1. The Steering Committee of The World Congress in Computer Science, Computer Engineering and Applied Computing (WorldComp) (2013)
4. Algarni, A.M., Malaiya, Y.K.: Software vulnerability markets: discoverers and buyers. Int. J. Comput. Inf. Sci. Eng. **8**, 71–81 (2014). Zenodo
5. Allodi, L.: Economic factors of vulnerability trade and exploitation. In: Proceedings of the 2017 ACM SIGSAC Conference on Computer and Communications Security - CCS 2017, pp. 1483–1499 (2017)
6. Allodi, L., Massacci, F.: Comparing vulnerability severity and exploits using case-control studies. ACM Trans. Inf. Syst. Secur. **17**(1), 1:1–1:20 (2014)
7. Anderson, R., Moore, T.: The economics of information security. Science **314**(5799), 610–613 (2006)
8. Arbaugh, W.A., Fithen, W.L., McHugh, J.: Windows of vulnerability: a case study analysis. Computer **33**(12), 52–59 (2000)
9. Armin, J., Foti, P., Cremonini, M.: 0-day vulnerabilities and cybercrime. In: 10th International Conference on Availability, Reliability and Security, pp. 711–718 (2015)
10. Arora, A., Telang, R.: Economics of software vulnerability disclosure. IEEE Secur. Priv. **3**(1), 20–25 (2005)
11. Arora, A., Krishnan, R., Telang, R., Yang, Y.: An empirical analysis of software vendors' patch release behavior: impact of vulnerability disclosure. Inf. Syst. Res. **21**(1), 115–132 (2010)
12. Arora, A., Nandkumar, A., Telang, R.: Does information security attack frequency increase with vulnerability disclosure? An empirical analysis. Inf. Syst. Front. **8**(5), 350–362 (2006). https://doi.org/10.1007/s10796-006-9012-5
13. Bergman, K.M.: A target to the heart of the first amendment: government endorsement of responsible disclosure as unconstitutional. Northwest. J. Technol. Intellect. Property **13**, 38 (2015)
14. Bilge, L., Dumitraş, T.: Before we knew it: an empirical study of zero-day attacks in the real world. In: Proceedings of the 2012 ACM Conference on Computer and Communications Security, CCS 2012, pp. 833–844. ACM, New York (2012)
15. Böhme, R.: Vulnerability markets. Proc. 22C3 **27**, 30 (2005)
16. Böhme, R.: A comparison of market approaches to software vulnerability disclosure. In: Müller, G. (ed.) ETRICS 2006. LNCS, vol. 3995, pp. 298–311. Springer, Heidelberg (2006). https://doi.org/10.1007/11766155_21
17. Breindenbach, L., Daian, P., Tramer, F., Juels, A.: Enter the hydra: towards principled bug bounties and exploit-resistant smart contracts. In: 27th USENIX Security Symposium, pp. 1335–1352 (2018)
18. Cavusoglu, H., Cavusoglu, H., Raghunathan, S.: Efficiency of vulnerability disclosure mechanisms to disseminate vulnerability knowledge. IEEE Trans. Softw. Eng. **33**(3), 171–185 (2007)
19. Chatfield, A.T., Reddick, C.G.: Cybersecurity innovation in government: a case study of U.S. Pentagon's vulnerability reward program. In: Proceedings of the 18th Annual International Conference on Digital Government Research - DGO 2017, Staten Island, NY, USA, pp. 64–73. ACM Press (2017)
20. Chatfield, A.T., Reddick, C.G.: Crowdsourced cybersecurity innovation: the case of the Pentagon's vulnerability reward program. Inf. Polity **23**(2), 177–194 (2018)
21. Choi, J.P., Fershtman, C., Gandal, N.: Network security: vulnerabilities and disclosure policy*. J. Ind. Econ. **58**(4), 868–894 (2010)

22. De Gregorio, A.: Vulnerabilities and their surrounding ethical questions: a code of ethics for the private sector. In: 2016 International Conference on Cyber Conflict (CyCon U.S.), pp. 1–4 (2016)
23. Egelman, S., Herley, C., van Oorschot, P.C.: Markets for zero-day exploits: ethics and implications. In: Proceedings of the 2013 Workshop on New Security Paradigms Workshop - NSPW 2013, Banff, Alberta, Canada, pp. 41–46. ACM Press (2013)
24. Elazari Bar On, A.: Private ordering shaping cybersecurity policy: the case of bug bounties. SSRN Scholarly Paper ID 3161758, Social Science Research Network, Rochester, NY (2018)
25. Esteves, J., Ramalho, E., Haro, G.D.: To improve cybersecurity, think like a hacker. MIT Sloan Manage. Rev. **58**(3), 71 (2017)
26. Finifter, M., Akhawe, D., Wagner, D.: An empirical study of vulnerability rewards programs. In: 22nd USENIX Security Symposium, pp. 273–288 (2013)
27. Freeman, E.: Vulnerability disclosure: the strange case of Bret McDanel. Inf. Syst. Secur. **16**(2), 127–131 (2007)
28. Fryer, H., Simperl, E.: Web science challenges in researching bug bounties. In: Proceedings of the 9th ACM Conference on Web Science, WebSci 2017, pp. 273–277. ACM (2017)
29. Guo, M., Hata, H., Babar, A.: Revenue maximizing markets for zero-day exploits. In: Baldoni, M., Chopra, A.K., Son, T.C., Hirayama, K., Torroni, P. (eds.) PRIMA 2016. LNCS (LNAI), vol. 9862, pp. 247–260. Springer, Cham (2016). https://doi.org/10.1007/978-3-319-44832-9_15
30. Hahn, A., Govindarasu, M.: Cyber vulnerability disclosure policies for the smart grid. In: 2012 IEEE Power and Energy Society General Meeting, pp. 1–5 (2012)
31. Hata, H., Guo, M., Babar, M.A.: Understanding the heterogeneity of contributors in bug bounty programs. In: 2017 ACM/IEEE International Symposium on Empirical Software Engineering and Measurement (ESEM), pp. 223–228 (2017)
32. Huang, C., Liu, J., Fang, Y., Zuo, Z.: A study on Web security incidents in China by analyzing vulnerability disclosure platforms. Comput. Secur. **58**, 47–62 (2016)
33. Huang, K., Zhang, J., Tan, W., Feng, Z.: Shifting to mobile: network-based empirical study of mobile vulnerability market. IEEE Trans. Serv. Comput. **13**(1), 144–157 (2018)
34. Joh, H., Malaiya, Y.K.: Defining and assessing quantitative security risk measures using vulnerability lifecycle and CVSS metrics. In: Proceedings of the International Conference on Security and Management, p. 7 (2011)
35. Kannan, K., Telang, R., Xu, H.: Economic analysis of the market for software vulnerability disclosure. In: Proceedings of the 37th Annual Hawaii International Conference on System Sciences, p. 8 (2004)
36. Kannan, K., Telang, R.: Market for software vulnerabilities? Think again. Manage. Sci. **51**(5), 726–740 (2005). https://www.jstor.org/stable/20110369
37. Kitchenham, B., Charters, S.: Guidelines for performing systematic literature reviews in software engineering. EBSE Technical report (2007)
38. Kitchenham, B.A., Budgen, D., Brereton, O.P.: Using mapping studies as the basis for further research - a participant-observer case study. Inf. Softw. Technol. **53**(6), 638–651 (2011). Special Section: Best papers from the APSEC
39. Kuehn, A., Mueller, M.: Shifts in the cybersecurity paradigm: zero-day exploits, discourse, and emerging institutions. In: Proceedings of the 2014 New Security Paradigms Workshop, pp. 63–68. ACM, New York (2014)

40. Laszka, A., Zhao, M., Grossklags, J.: Banishing misaligned incentives for validating reports in bug-bounty platforms. In: Askoxylakis, I., Ioannidis, S., Katsikas, S., Meadows, C. (eds.) ESORICS 2016. LNCS, vol. 9879, pp. 161–178. Springer, Cham (2016). https://doi.org/10.1007/978-3-319-45741-3_9

41. Laszka, A., Zhao, M., Malbari, A., Grossklags, J.: The rules of engagement for bug bounty programs. In: Meiklejohn, S., Sako, K. (eds.) FC 2018. LNCS, vol. 10957, pp. 138–159. Springer, Heidelberg (2018). https://doi.org/10.1007/978-3-662-58387-6_8

42. Li, P., Rao, H.R.: An examination of private intermediaries' roles in software vulnerabilities disclosure. Inf. Syst. Front. **9**(5), 531–539 (2007). https://doi.org/10.1007/s10796-007-9047-2

43. Li, Z., Liao, Q.: Economic solutions to improve cybersecurity of governments and smart cities via vulnerability markets. Gov. Inf. Q. **35**(1), 151–160 (2018)

44. Maillart, T., Zhao, M., Grossklags, J., Chuang, J.: Given enough eyeballs, all bugs are shallow? Revisiting Eric Raymond with bug bounty programs. J. Cybersecur. **3**(2), 81–90 (2017)

45. Mangalaraj, G.A., Raja, M.K.: Software vulnerability disclosure and its impact on exploitation: an empirical study. In: Proceedings of AMCIS 2005, p. 9 (2005)

46. Marconato, G.V., Nicomette, V., Kaâniche, M.: Security-related vulnerability life cycle analysis. In: 2012 7th International Conference on Risks and Security of Internet and Systems (CRiSIS), pp. 1–8 (2012)

47. Matwyshyn, A.M.: Hacking speech: informational speech and the first amendment. Northwestern University Law Review, p. 52 (2013)

48. Maxwell, P.: Stockpiling zero-day exploits: the next international weapons taboo. In: Proceedings of 5th International Conference on Management Leadership and Governance, p. 8 (2017)

49. McQueen, M., Wright, J.L., Wellman, L.: Are vulnerability disclosure deadlines justified? In: 2011 Third International Workshop on Security Measurements and Metrics, pp. 96–101 (2011)

50. Munaiah, N., Meneely, A.: Vulnerability severity scoring and bounties: why the disconnect? In: Proceedings of the 2nd International Workshop on Software Analytics, SWAN, Seattle, WA, USA, pp. 8–14. ACM, New York (2016)

51. Nappa, A., Johnson, R., Bilge, L., Caballero, J., Dumitras, T.: The attack of the clones: a study of the impact of shared code on vulnerability patching. In: 2015 IEEE Symposium on Security and Privacy, pp. 692–708 (2015)

52. Nizovtsev, D., Thursby, M.: To disclose or not? An analysis of software user behavior. Inf. Econ. Policy **19**(1), 43–64 (2007)

53. Pandey, P., Snekkenes, E.A.: An assessment of market methods for information security risk management. In: Proceedings of 16th IEEE International Conference on High Performance and Communications (2014)

54. Radianti, J., Gonzalez, J.J.: Understanding hidden information security threats: the vulnerability black market. In: 2007 40th Annual Hawaii International Conference on System Sciences (HICSS'07), p. 156c (2007)

55. Ransbotham, S., Mitra, S., Ramsey, J.: Are Markets for Vulnerabilities Effective? MIS Q. **36**(1), 43–64 (2012)

56. Rescorla, E.: Is finding security holes a good idea? IEEE Secur. Priv. Mag. **3**(1), 14–19 (2005)

57. Robinson, D.G., Halderman, J.A.: Ethical issues in e-voting security analysis. In: Danezis, G., Dietrich, S., Sako, K. (eds.) FC 2011. LNCS, vol. 7126, pp. 119–130. Springer, Heidelberg (2012). https://doi.org/10.1007/978-3-642-29889-9_10

58. Ruohonen, J., Holvitie, J., Hyrynsalmi, S., Leppänen, V.: Exploring the clustering of software vulnerability disclosure notifications across software vendors. In: 2016 IEEE/ACS 13th International Conference of Computer Systems and Applications (AICCSA), pp. 1–8 (2016)
59. Ruohonen, J., Hyrynsalmi, S., Leppănen, V.: Trading exploits online: a preliminary case study. In: 2016 IEEE Tenth International Conference on Research Challenges in Information Science (RCIS), pp. 1–12 (2016)
60. Ruohonen, J., Allodi, L.: A bug bounty perspective on the disclosure of web vulnerabilities. In: Proceedings of 17th Annual Workshop on the Economics of Information Security (2018)
61. Sipes, E.K., James, J., Zetoony, D.: Current data security issues for financial services firms. J. Invest. Compliance **17**(3), 55–59 (2016)
62. Sprague, C., Wagner, J.: Economic motivations for software bug bounties. Econ. Bull. **38**(1), 550–557 (2018)
63. Stevens, R.: Identifying self-inflicted vulnerabilities: the operational implications of technology within U.S. combat systems. In: 2017 International Conference on Cyber Conflict (CyCon U.S.), pp. 112–118 (2017)
64. Stockton, P.N., Golabek-Goldman, M.: Curbing the market for cyber weapons. Policy Rev. **32**, 29 (2013)
65. Suárez, R.A., Scott, D.: Doing what is right with coordinated vulnerability disclosure. Biomed. Instrum. Technol. **51**(s6), 42–45 (2017)
66. Takanen, A., Vuorijärvi, P., Laakso, M., Röning, J.: Agents of responsibility in software vulnerability processes. Ethics Inf. Technol. **6**(2), 93–110 (2004). https://doi.org/10.1007/s10676-004-1266-3
67. Telang, R., Wattal, S.: Impact of software vulnerability announcements on the market value of software vendors - an empirical investigation. SSRN Scholarly Paper, Social Science Research Network (2005)
68. Wang, B., Li, X., de Aguiar, L.P., Menasche, D.S., Shafiq, Z.: Characterizing and modeling patching practices of industrial control systems. In: Proceedings of the 2017 ACM SIGMETRICS/International Conference on Measurement and Modeling of Computer Systems, p. 9. ACM, New York (2017)
69. Wolf, M.J., Fresco, N.: Ethics of the software vulnerabilities and exploits market. Inf. Soc. **32**(4), 269–279 (2016)
70. Younis, A., Malaiya, Y.K., Ray, I.: Evaluating CVSS base score using vulnerability rewards programs. In: Hoepman, J.-H., Katzenbeisser, S. (eds.) SEC 2016. IAICT, vol. 471, pp. 62–75. Springer, Cham (2016). https://doi.org/10.1007/978-3-319-33630-5_5
71. Zhao, M., Grossklags, J., Chen, K.: An exploratory study of white hat behaviors in a web vulnerability disclosure program. In: Proceedings of the 2014 ACM Workshop on Security Information Workers, pp. 51–58. ACM, New York (2014)
72. Zhao, M., Grossklags, J., Liu, P.: An empirical study of web vulnerability discovery ecosystems. In: Proceedings of the 22nd ACM SIGSAC Conference on Computer and Communications Security, pp. 1105–1117. ACM (2015)
73. Zhao, M., Laszka, A., Grossklags, J.: Devising effective policies for bug-bounty platforms and security vulnerability discovery. J. Inf. Policy **7**, 372–418 (2017)
74. Zhao, M., Laszka, A., Maillart, T., Grossklags, J.: Crowdsourced security vulnerability discovery: modeling and organizing bug-bounty programs. In: The HCOMP Workshop on Mathematical Foundations of Human Computation, Austin (2016)

# Association Attacks in IEEE 802.11: Exploiting WiFi Usability Features

George Chatzisofroniou$^{(\boxtimes)}$ and Panayiotis Kotzanikolaou$^{(\boxtimes)}$

SecLab, Department of Informatics, University of Piraeus, Pireas, Greece
sophron@latthi.com, pkotzani@unipi.gr

**Abstract.** Association attacks in IEEE 802.11 aim to manipulate wireless clients into associating with a malicious access point, usually by exploiting usability features that are implemented on the network managers of modern operating systems. In this paper we review known association attacks in IEEE 802.11 and we provide a taxonomy to classify them according to the network manager features that each attack exploits. In addition, we analyze the current applicability status of association attacks, by implementing them using the well-known Wifiphisher tool and we review the security posture of modern network managers against known association attacks and their variations. Our results show that association attacks still pose an active threat. In particular, we analyze various strategies that may be implemented by an adversary in order to increase the success rate of association attacks, and we show that even though network managers have hampered the effectiveness of some known attacks (e.g. KARMA), other techniques (e.g. Known Beacons) are still an active threat.

## 1 Introduction

WiFi, or IEEE 802.11 wireless networking, is probably the most popular type of network for wireless home networking, as well as for network sharing of public or guest networks. Most people expect a standard degree of connectivity wherever they go, while organizations rely on WiFi and other wireless protocols to maintain their productivity. However, since its existence WiFi has been subject to various attacks [5, 26, 28].

*Association attacks* are an instance of a man-in-the-middle attacks in WiFi networks. Essentially, they exploit vulnerabilities in the access point selection phase of IEEE 802.11, since the loose definition of this phase leaves room to the vendors for different stack behavior. And since many vendors prioritize usability instead of security, several user-friendly functionalities implemented in most Operating System (OS) network managers, may allow an attacker to fool a client into connecting (associating) with a rogue access point. As vendors are implementing usability features to make the WiFi experience smoother for the end-user, new attacks are keep coming to the surface by exploiting vulnerabilities of the newly added user functionality features.

© Springer Nature Switzerland AG 2021
T. Groß and T. Tryfonas (Eds.): STAST 2019, LNCS 11739, pp. 107–123, 2021.
https://doi.org/10.1007/978-3-030-55958-8_6

Since a wide range of software has inadequate protection against man-in-the-middle attacks, the exposure against such attacks is high. After successfully associating with a victim device, an attacker will be able to intercept part of, or all its network traffic or even leverage this position to exploit device-specific vulnerabilities. Sophisticated phishing attacks may lead to the capture of credentials (e.g. from third party login pages or WPA/WPA2 Pre-Shared Keys) [11]. Note that association attacks may be part of attacks with wider scale. For example, an adversary may be able to expose the real MAC addresses of connected mobile devices bypassing any privacy controls, such as MAC address randomization (e.g. by exploiting Hotspot 2.0 capabilities [9]), and track the location of the victim users.

Several approaches that detect association attacks in IEEE 802.11 have been proposed. Most of them work by collecting the attributes of the nearby networks (including the radio frequency airwaves) and comparing them with a known authorized list. Other user oriented approaches are identifying differences in the number of wireless hops. These techniques are implemented in Wireless Intrusion and Detection Systems (WIDS) that are deployed in Enterprise environments [27] [18]. However, as already stated, WiFi association attacks are not targeting a particular network, but rather on the client devices and the users themselves; hence they can be applied in WiFi environments where WIDS are not available, by exploiting vulnerable usability features implemented at the client side.

*Motivation and Contribution.* In this paper we provide a thorough analysis and classification of WiFi association attacks. We analyze their differences and examine the situations in which these attacks may be active. We show that although modern network managers are assumed to provide adequate protection against known association attacks, new variations can still be an active threat, mainly due to the prioritization given by OS vendors to the usability, instead to the security features, of network management software. To demonstrate the applicability of such attacks, we have incorporated most of them in Wifiphisher [12], a well-known open source WiFi security testing tool. Finally, we analyze the differences of modern Operating Systems and discuss their exposure to each WiFi association attack.

*Paper Structure.* The rest of this paper is structured as follows. In Sect. 2 we provide the necessary background information, including both protocol and implementation details, that is necessary for understanding the internals of the various association attacks. In Sect. 3 we provide a taxonomy of known association attacks, based on the usability features that each attack exploits. To the best of our knowledge this is the first taxonomy of IEEE 802.11 association attacks. In Sect. 4 we review the different implementations of network managers across the modern operating systems and we examine how they react to association attacks. Finally Sect. 5 concludes this paper.

## 2  Background Information: AP Selection Phase and Related Functionality in IEEE 802.11

As explained in Sect. 1 association attacks take advantage of usability features of OS network managers, that usually aim to enhance user-friendliness by automating the access point selection phase. Therefore, in order to understand the origin of such attacks, we will describe the relevant protocol and implementation details. First we review the Access Point Selection process in IEEE 802.11. Then we review the related usability features implemented in the network managers of the most popular OS.

### 2.1  Access Point Selection in 802.11

In the IEEE 802.11 specification [16], two basic entities are defined. First, there is the station (STA), a device that has the capability to use the 802.11 protocol (e.g. a laptop, a desktop, smart phone or any other WiFi enabled device). Then there is the access point (AP), a network device that allows stations to connect to a wired network. The access point typically connects to a router via a wired connection as a standalone device and then provides wireless connections using the WiFi technology.

The first step for a station to associate successfully with an access point is to populate a list of nearby WiFi networks. This list is called the *Available Networks List* (ANL) and each wireless network stored in it is resembled by its logical name, the *Service Set Identifier* (SSID), along with its encryption type. For each stored network in the ANL, the station also stores the identifier of the access point, the *Basic Service Set Identifier* (BSSID), which is a 48-bit label. If more than one BSSIDs correspond to the same SSID, then the BSSID of the AP with the strongest signal is stored in the ANL.

The station can construct the ANL using two different scanning methods (see Fig. 1): a) *passive scanning*, where the station detects special frames called beacon frames that are periodically sent from the access points to announce the presence of a wireless network, or b) *active scanning*, where the station sends a probe message, called null probe request frame, which asks all access points within the wireless range to respond directly with the necessary information required to establish a connection.

After the ANL is populated (i.e. contains at least one nearby network), the station decides if it will attempt connection to one of the networks stored in it. This decision can be made either automatically, by the OS utilizing usability features discussed in the next section, or manually by the end-user who may select one of the networks in the ANL via a user interface. When a wireless network is selected, the station will pick the associated BSSID from the ANL and send a directed probe request to the corresponding access point to ensure that it is within the area. The access point will respond with a probe response. After this process, both endpoints are ready to proceed to the Authentication and Association Process.

During the Authentication and Association Process, each side needs to prove the knowledge of some credentials. Notably in "Open Authentication", as its name implies, there are no credentials and any wireless device can 'authenticate' (connect) to the access point. Once authentication is complete, mobile devices can finally associate with the access point. The association process will allow to the access point to record each station in order to send and transmit data frames to it.

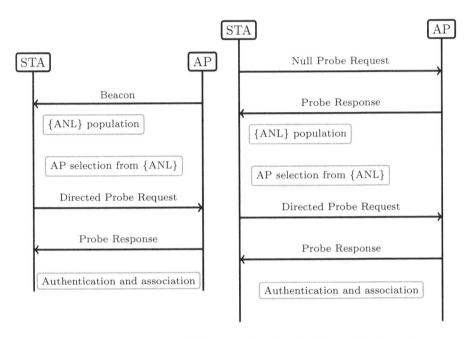

**Fig. 1.** ANL Population using: (a) Passive Scanning (left) and (b) Active Scanning (right)

## 2.2   Usability Features Related to AP Selection

Software vendors have introduced a number of features to automate the process of AP selection without requiring user interaction. In this section we explain in detail these features and discuss their underlying logic.

**Network Manager Implementation Features.** The features that are related with the AP selection phase, usually make use of a special list, called the *Preferred Network List* (PNL). In contrast to the ANL that contains all nearby WiFi networks along with the BSSID of the strongest access point, the PNL contains only networks (SSID and encryption type) that the wireless station will prefer to associate, if they exist within the wireless range. As soon as the ANL is populated and during the AP selection phase, the station will automatically connect to the strongest access point in the intersection of the ANL and the

PNL. If there are no networks around that are also stored in the PNL (i.e. if the intersection of the ANL and the PNL is empty), the station will remain unauthenticated and unassociated until the user manually selects a network.

$$ANL = [wlan_1 : bssid_1, wlan_2 : bssid_2, ..., wlan_n : bssid_n] \tag{1}$$

$$PNL = [wlan_1, wlan_2, ..., wlan_n] \tag{2}$$

$$wlan = [ssid, encryption\ type] \tag{3}$$

The *"auto-reconnect"* feature automatically adds the attributes (SSID and encryption type) of a network to the PNL upon the first connection. The network is usually stored in the PNL until the user manually 'forgets' it. In most operating systems, the default behavior of the auto-reconnect feature differs on the encryption type of the network that the station connects to.

The *"available to all system users"* feature is an extension of the auto-reconnect feature and exists only to multi-user operating systems where each system user has its own version of a PNL. When this feature is enabled, the PNL becomes global across users. For example, if a user adds a network to the PNL, e.g. due to the 'auto-reconnect' feature, then that network will also exist to the PNL of all other users due to the 'available to all users' feature.

The *"active scanning for networks in the PNL"* is another usability feature where the station sends directed probe request frames for networks the stations have associated with in the past (i.e. they exist in the PNL) even if these networks are not around (i.e. they are not in the ANL).

The *"automatically connect to high-quality open networks"* feature allows certain devices to automatically connect to specific high and reliable open networks according to a specific vendor. An example of this feature is the "WiFi Sense" that was introduced by Microsoft in 2016 and it allowed a Windows10 or Windows Phone 8.1 device to automatically connect to suggested open hotspots (WiFi Sense networks). The WiFi Sense feature was removed by Microsoft shortly after the associated risk that we discuss later in this paper was revealed. However, a similar feature was introduced by Google, called WiFi assistant. This feature can be found on Pixel and Nexus devices using Android 5.1 and up in selected countries and it allows automatic connection to open WiFi networks that Google verify as reliable.

Finally, the *"turn on WiFi automatically"* feature will turn the WiFi connection back on when the device is near a network that exists in the PNL of the device.

**802.11 Protocol Features: WiFi Roaming and WiFi Direct.** According to the WiFi specification, an *Extended Service Set* (ESS) may be formed by deploying multiple access points that are configured with the same SSID and security settings. *WiFi roaming* is an operation where the station decides that is time to drop one AP and move to another (in the same ESS). The operation is completely dependent on the client device; as we have discovered after testing, in modern operating systems a WiFi client device will typically attempt to maintain a connection with the access point that can provide the strongest signal within a service set.

*WiFi Protected Setup Push Button Configuration* (WPS-PBC) [3] is an operation where the user presses a (virtual) button on the wireless station and a physical button on the router within 120 s in order for the device to automatically connect to the wireless network without requiring to input any passphrase.

The *WiFi Direct* protocol [10] is built upon the IEEE 802.11 infrastructure and it enables the devices to form P2P groups by negotiating which device will be the Group Owner and which devices will be the clients. WiFi Direct is mainly used for data sharing, video streaming and gaming.

## 3    Association Attacks: A Taxonomy

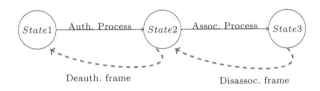

State1: Unauthenticated and Unassociated
State2: Authenticated and Unassociated
State3: Authenticated and Associated

**Fig. 2.** Dissassociation and deauthentication

As explained above, the goal of association attacks is to trick the target wireless stations into associating to an attacker controlled AP. Association attacks can be categorized based on the feature of the Network Manager that they exploit (Fig. 3). We divide them into two main categories: (a) the *automatic association attacks* where the only prerequisite is that the victim node is within the range of the attacker-controlled AP, which are analyzed in Sect. 3.1; and (b) the attacks that *require user interaction*, which are analyzed in Sect. 3.2. Finally, in Sect. 3.3 we calculate and discuss the exploitability scores of the attacks.

### 3.1    Automatic Association Attacks

In order to perform an automatic WiFi association attack, the victims stations need to run their Access Point Selection algorithm so that they can be later lured into the rogue network by abusing different features of their network manager.

This can be achieved by traversing the WiFi stations to a state where they are not authenticated nor associated with any AP. In this state, the victim stations will be enforced to run the Access Point Selection algorithm to connect with an

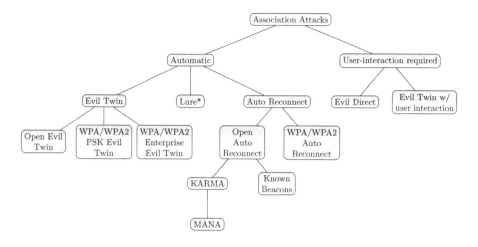

**Fig. 3.** Classification of WiFi association attacks

AP and maintain connectivity. The most common way to traverse authenticated and associated WiFi stations to an unauthenticated and unassociated state is by forging "Deauthenticate" and "Disassociate" packets as shown in Fig. 2. This can be easily achieved by an attacker, since a known issue with 802.11 is that the management packets are not cryptographically protected against eavesdropping, modification or replay attacks [19]. Alternatively, radio jamming is another common method to block or interfere with authorized wireless communications. An attacker can use an Software Defined Radio (SDR) or cheap off the-shelf WiFi dongles to transmit radio signals and make a wireless channel unusable for other devices [25].

Another way to enforce WiFi stations to run their Access Point Selection algorithm is by enforcing them to restart the WiFi feature itself. This can be done either programmatically (e.g. malware applications within the device may be able to restart the WiFi service) or by abusing the Enable WiFi automatically feature. By broadcasting a WPA/WPA2 network that exists in the PNL of the victim device, it is possible to enforce the device that has this feature enabled, to turn its WiFi feature on and run the Access Point Selection algorithm.

**Evil Twin.** During an Evil Twin attack [21,29], the adversary copies the ESSID and the encryption type of the wireless network that the victim device is connected to and sets up an AP that broadcasts the same attributes. If the malicious AP offers a stronger signal, and due to the operation of WiFi roaming, the victim device will automatically connect to the rogue network.

The Evil Twin attack is common against public hotspots that are usually employed along with a captive portal mechanism and are commonly deployed in airports, hotels and coffee shops. The adversary can easily replicate both the ESSID and the encryption type (Open) of these networks and assuming that the rogue AP offers a stronger signal, the victim stations will automatically connect to the malicious network.

The Evil Twin attack is also possible in WPA/WPA2 WiFi networks with known or disclosed Pre-Shared Keys (PSK) or in infrastructures whose members are dynamically joining and leaving the network (e.g. a conference WiFi). In such cases, the secret is either published or known by many parties, thus it can be easily known by a malicious party. Knowing the PSK, the adversary can replicate the ESSID and the encryption of the legitimate Access Point and as in open setups, the clients of these networks will automatically connect to the rogue Access Point. Finally, the Evil Twin attack is also popular against Enterprise networks [6,20] that are widely used in large corporations. If the victim stations are not validating the server certificate presented by the AP, the corporate setups are vulnerable to Evil Twin.

**Attack Requirements:**

- Victim device is connected to a wireless network
- Physical position within the Wi-Fi range of the victim device
- Knowledge of the wireless network's SSID that the victim device is connected
- In case the victim is connected to WPA/WPA2 network, knowledge of it secret (e.g. PSK)

**Attack Steps:**

1. Obtain position within the Wi-Fi range of the network that the victim device is connected
2. Spawn a network with the same SSID and encryption type as the network that the victim device is connected. Rogue network's signal strength needs to be stronger than the legitimate.

**Lure\*.** The Lure\*-type attacks are abusing the "automatically connect to high-quality open networks" that is found in some Operating Systems. The first attack of this type was Lure10 [13] that used to exploit the WiFi Sense feature found on Windows 10 and Widows Phone 8.1. This attack relied on the victim's device being fooled into believing it is within the geographical area of a WiFi Sense-tagged open wireless network. This could be achieved by broadcasting beacon frames of that area and eventually tricking the Windows Location Service [23]. Finally the attacker would successfully mimic the WiFi Sense network in that area (broadcasting the same SSID was found to be enough) and the victim users would connect to the rogue AP.

While the Lure10 attack is no longer applicable since the removal of the WiFi Sense feature by Microsoft, a similar attack vector recently appeared on certain Android devices with the introduction of the Google Assistant, which also enables the automatic connection to open networks.

**Attack Requirements:**

- Physical position within the Wi-Fi range of the victim device
- A feature that allows automatic connection to vendor-suggested hotspots is enabled on the victim's device
- Knowledge of a vendor-suggested hotspot's SSID
- Requirements for Location Service or GPS spoofing should also be satisfied

**Attack Steps:**

1. Obtain position within the Wi-Fi range of the victim device
2. If needed, traverse the WiFi station to a state where it is not authenticated nor associated with any AP
3. Spoof GPS or Location Service in order to "transfer" the victim in the vendor-suggested hotspot's location
4. Spawn a rogue network with the same SSID as the vendor-suggested network

**Auto Reconnect Exploitation.** In order to exploit the auto-reconnect feature, the adversary will spawn a network that is stored in the PNL of the target device. In contrast to the Evil Twin where the rogue network is copied based on the network that the target device is currently connected to, in this attack the rogue network is *not* required to exist in the wireless range of the victim device. If the victim's device is not authenticated to any network, it will automatically join the rogue network that was spawned by the attacker, regardless the fact that the attributes of this network may have been added to the PNL a long time ago in a complete different environment.

In the Open Auto Reconnect scenario, the attacker only needs to replicate the SSID of the network that exists in the PNL, while in the case of WPA/WPA2 encryption, the Pre-Shared Key (PSK) is also required. If the PSK of a WPA/WPA2 network is not known, an attacker may leverage public crowd-sourced databases to retrieve the secret and successfully mimic the network that exists in the victim's PNL. This attack typically requires some familiarity with the victim user and his whereabouts in order for the adversary to guess the attributes of a network in the target device's PNL. If the "available to all system users" flag is enabled, the attack surface is increased; networks that were stored as part of the association process of other users in the target system can be leveraged to carry out the attack.

Even if the whereabouts of the victim user are not known, an attacker that has achieved local access to the remote station (e.g. by infecting the victim device with a malware) will be able to add a network to the PNL of that host that can be leveraged later to carry out the attack. These kind of "backdoor" networks may also be added to the victim stations by physical means. Notably, in a host running Windows 10, even if the workstation is locked, an adversary with physical access may still connect to a wireless network that will be eventually added to the PNL of this device [24].

**Attack Requirements:**

- Physical position within the Wi-Fi range of the victim device
- Auto-Reconnect flag is enabled on victim's device
- Knowledge of an unencrypted wireless network's SSID that exists in the victim's PNL
- In case of WPA/WPA2 network, knowledge of the secret (e.g. PSK)

**Attack Steps:**

1. Obtain position within the Wi-Fi range of the victim device
2. If needed, traverse the WiFi station to a state where it is not authenticated nor associated with any AP
3. Spawn a wireless network with the same SSID as the unencrypted wireless network that exists in the victim's PNL

**KARMA and MANA.** While Open Auto Reconnect attacks exploits the "auto-reconnect" feature, the KARMA attack [15] also exploits the active scanning for networks that stations have associated with in the past. In this attack, a rogue AP is introduced that masquerades as a public network that nearby WiFi clients are actively searching for. Victim stations that are actively looking for open networks stored in their PNL will automatically join the rogue AP.

MANA [22] is an attack that took KARMA a step further by configuring a rogue AP that not only replies to directed probes, but additionally it responds to the victim device's broadcast probe requests (e.g. using the same response). Furthermore, a "loud" mode was introduced where the rogue AP is responding to each device's probe request frames with a list of networks that have been searched for by other devices within the range of the rogue AP.

**Attack Requirements:**

- Physical position within the Wi-Fi range of the victim device
- Auto-Reconnect flag is enabled on victim's device
- The victim device performs active scanning for networks stored in its PNL
- At least one unencrypted wireless network exists in victim's PNL

**Attack Steps:**

1. Obtain position within the Wi-Fi range of the victim device
2. If needed, traverse the WiFi station to a state where it is not authenticated nor associated with any AP
3. Respond positively to directed probe requests that are intended for unencrypted networks
4. Additionally, respond to broadcast probe requests using the same response

**Known Beacons.** The Known Beacons attack [8,14] is also a special instance of an Open Auto Reconnect attack, which is usually applied when the attacker has no prior knowledge of the victims' PNL and is applicable against all modern operating systems. In an attempt to guess the SSID of an open network that exists in the victim device's Preferred Network List, the attacker will broadcast dozens of beacon frames from a "dictionary" of common SSIDs. The dictionary includes entries with popular SSIDs that are commonly used by network administrators (e.g. 'wireless', 'guest', 'cafe', 'public'), SSIDs of global WiFi networks (e.g. 'xfinitywifi', 'attwifi', 'eduroam', 'BTFON'), SSIDs of hotspots that exist in hotels, airports and other places of public interest (e.g. 'hhonors_public', 'walmartwifi'). Finally, location-specific SSIDs based on the victim users whereabouts can be collected with wardriving [17] or by looking at public databases of 802.11 wireless networks.

**Attack Requirements:**

- Physical position within the Wi-Fi range of the victim device
- Auto-Reconnect flag is enabled on victim's device
- There is at least one wireless network from the victim's PNL in the dictionary of popular SSIDs

**Attack steps:**

1. Obtain position within the Wi-Fi range of the victim device
2. If needed, traverse the WiFi station to a state where it is not authenticated nor associated with any AP
3. Broadcast dozens of beacon frames from a dictionary of common SSIDs

### 3.2 Association Attacks Requiring Interaction

In contrast to the previous category where the attacks can be launched solely at the will of the attacker, in this case the attacks require some user interaction by the victim user (or a victim user initiated process). For this reason, their estimated risk is usually lower. However, these attacks are applicable in cases where the requirements for automatic association attacks are not satisfied.

**EvilDirect Attack.** The WiFi Direct protocol defines a Group Owner (GO) to allow other clients to connect with. EviDirect attacks [7] the WiFi Direct protocol by spawning a rogue GO that operates on the same channel as the original and has the same MAC address and SSID. If the rogue GO accepts any invitation requests faster than the legitimate one, the adversary will be able to hijack the wireless communications.

The fundamental problem with EvilDirect lies in the underlying WiFi Protected Setup Push Button Configuration (WPS-PBC) protocol which is susceptible to an active attack where the attacker offers an AP in the PBC state on another channel to induce an Enrollee to connect to the rogue network. These techniques require the victim users to actively use the WPS-PBC and WiFi Direct functionalities. Notably, we discovered that this attack is more viable on Windows10 where the WPS-PBC virtual button is automatically pushed just by selecting a network with WPS capabilities on the networks manager's list and without the end-user's explicit consent.

**Attack Requirements:**

- Physical position within the Wi-Fi range of the victim device
- Victim user initiates a WPS-PBC request

**Attack Steps:**

1. Obtain position within the Wi-Fi range of the victim device
2. Wait until the victim user activates WiFi Direct on the device
3. Accept the invitation request faster than the legitimate GO

**Evil Twin (Requiring User Interaction).** As in the case of the automatic Evil Twin, this attack is also based on the replication of a legitimate AP, however it requires some user interaction. The replicated rogue Access Points have at least one of their attributes (i.e. SSID and encryption type) different from the legitimate AP. In our experience, this may happen for two reasons: In the first case, the adversary cannot replicate the encryption type of the legitimate AP (e.g. because the PSK is unknown). In this scenario, the adversary will commonly perform a downgrade attack by spawning an Open-type network. Interestingly, from our research, it appears that only macOS systems will issue a warning for downgrade attacks.

In the second case, the adversary targets an Open-type network in an infrastructure where new members are dynamically joining the network (e.g. in public areas). In this scenario, it is reasonable for the attacker to spawn a rogue network with an SSID that precedes alphabetically from the target's AP SSID. Since network managers order the networks of the same signal power in an alphabetic order, the adversary raises the chances of having the rogue AP shown first in the network manager's list, hence victim users are more likely to select it. The attacker can take this a step further by spawning intermediate networks (i.e. by mounting an SSID flooding attack) in an attempt to push the legitimate SSID further down the Network Manager's list.

**Attack Requirements:**

- Physical position within the Wi-Fi range of the victim device
- Victim user is fooled into choosing to connect to the rogue Access Point

**Attack Steps:**

1. Obtain position within the Wi-Fi range of the victim device
2. Spawn a rogue Access Point that has at least one of its attributes different from the legitimate AP
3. Fool victim user into selecting the rogue Access Point

### 3.3 Association Attacks Exploitability

We used the exploitability sub-score equation that exists in CVSS 3.1 [4] to calculate the exploitability scores that reflect the ease and technical means by which each association attack can be carried out. We assumed an attacker that is positioned within the Wi-Fi range of an area with a moderate number of users

**Table 1.** Exploitability matrix of association attacks

| Association attack | Exploitability metrics | | | | Exploitability score (0–3.9) |
|---|---|---|---|---|---|
| | Attack vector | Attack complexity | Privileges required | User interaction | |
| Open Evil Twin | Network | High | None | None | 2.2 |
| WPA/WPA2 PSK Evil Twin | Network | High | None | None | 2.2 |
| WPA/WPA2 Enterprise Evil Twin | Network | High | None | None | 2.2 |
| Lure* | Network | High | None | None | 2.2 |
| Auto-Reconnect Open | Network | High | None | None | 2.2 |
| Auto-Reconnect WPA/WPA2 | Network | High | None | None | 2.2 |
| Known Beacons | Network | Low | None | None | 3.9 |
| KARMA | Network | Low | None | None | 3.9 |
| MANA | Network | Low | None | None | 3.9 |
| EvilDirect | Network | Low | None | Required | 2.8 |
| Evil Twin w/ user interaction | Network | High | None | Required | 1.6 |

(e.g. 50–100 devices). Finally, we considered that an attack is successful if at least one device is associated with the attacker-controlled AP.

In Table 1 we outline all association attacks with their exploitability metrics and the calculated scores. It is notable that KARMA, MANA and Known Beacons attacks have the higher exploitability score due to their automatic nature and their low complexity. The attack with the lowest exploitability score is "Evil Twin w/ user interaction" because of the required user interaction and the difficulty of the conditions that need to be satisfied to mount the attack.

# 4 Analysis of Network Managers' Behavior

## 4.1 Attack Implementation

We implemented Evil Twin and Auto-Reconnect attacks against 802.11 clients using Python standard library modules. We included them in the first release of Wifiphisher that was published under GPLv3 [2]. The rest of the association attacks and de-authentication techniques, were implemented as "ifiphisher extensions" which are scripts in Python that are executed in parallel and expand the functionality of the main Wifiphisher engine. For time-critical operations we developed "roguehostapd" [1], a fork of hostapd, that communicates with the main Wifiphisher engine by providing Python bindings with ctypes.

Running Wifiphisher requires at least one wireless network adapter that supports AP and Monitor mode in order to sniff and inject wireless frames. Wi-Fi drivers should also support the Netlink socket family.

**Table 2.** Usability features on modern Operating Systems

| Operating System | Auto-reconnect | | Avail. to all system users | Probes for prev. conn. networks | Auto-enable WiFi | Auto-connect to high-quality WiFi networks | Connect to network with locked screen |
|---|---|---|---|---|---|---|---|
| | Open | WPA/WPA2 | | | | | |
| Windows10 | ✓¹ | ✓ | ✓ | | | | ✓ |
| macOS | ✓ | ✓ | ✓ | | | | |
| Android | ✓ | ✓ | | | ✓ | ✓¹ | |
| iOS | ✓ | ✓ | | | | | |

| Comments | (1) The feature is available but is disabled by default |
|---|---|

## 4.2 Result Analysis

We examined the behavior of modern Operating Systems against known association attacks that were described in the previous sections of this paper. Specifically, in desktop systems, we analyzed the behavior of Windows10 and macOS 10.15, while in mobile devices, we examined Android 9 and iOS 12.4.

In Table 2 we summarize all existing usability features that are supported by the examined Operating Systems, and we also identify which features are enabled by default. The dissimilarities are notable. It can be concluded that each OS was designed with a different threat model in mind given that the risk involved with these usability features is known for some time now. For example, Windows10 will not allow automatic connection to previously connected open networks by default. However, the vendor seems to accept the risk of a physical attacker adding a network to the PNL (i.e. adding a network with locked screen is enabled) while the rest of the OS show the exact opposite behavior.

Mobile devices appear to have more usability features enabled by default than desktop operating systems. We find this reasonable since mobile devices rely on both user-owned and externally-managed WiFi connectivity.

It also seems that most of the vendors have stopped the probes to previously connected networks in order to hamper the effectiveness of KARMA and MANA attacks. However, they do accept the risk involved with leaving the Auto-reconnect feature enabled that makes them susceptible to Known Beacons.

In Table 3 we outline all association attacks and we show the Operating Systems that are vulnerable to each one of them. We can conclude that even though network managers have removed some of the risky features (for example those related with the KARMA attack), other association attacks are still active. Known Beacons appears to be the most effective WiFi association attack against modern Operating Systems. It is also worth mentioning that in a real scenario and depending on the identified vulnerabilities/effective usability features, an attacker will use a combination of the above attacks, for example KARMA and Known Beacons at the same time.

**Table 3.** Current landscape of association attacks

| Association Attack | Exploitability Score | Exploited Usability Features | | | | | Vulnerable Operating Systems | | | |
|---|---|---|---|---|---|---|---|---|---|---|
| | | Auto Reconnect | | Avail. to all system users | Probes for prev. conn. networks | Other | Windows10 | macOS | Android | iOS |
| | | Open | WPA/WPA2 | | | | | | | |
| Open Evil Twin | 2.2 | | | | | | ✓ | ✓ | ✓ | ✓ |
| WPA/WPA2 PSK Evil Twin | 2.2 | | | | | | ✓ | ✓ | ✓ | ✓ |
| WPA/WPA2 Enterprise Evil Twin | 2.2 | | | | | | ✓ | ✓ | ✓ | ✓ |
| Lure* | 2.2 | | | | | ✓[2] | | | ✓[5] | |
| Auto-reconnect Open | 2.2 | ✓ | | ✓[1] | | | ✓[4] | ✓ | ✓ | ✓ |
| Auto-reconnect WPA/WPA2 | 2.2 | | ✓ | ✓[1] | | | ✓ | ✓ | ✓ | ✓ |
| Known Beacons | 3.9 | ✓ | | ✓[1] | | | ✓[4] | ✓ | ✓ | ✓ |
| KARMA | 3.9 | ✓ | | ✓[1] | ✓ | | | | | |
| MANA | 3.9 | ✓ | | | ✓ | | | | | |
| EvilDirect | 2.8 | | | | | ✓[3] | ✓ | ✓ | ✓ | ✓ |
| Evil Twin /w user interaction | 1.6 | | | | | | ✓ | ✓ | ✓ | ✓ |

| Comments | (1) The feature increases the success rates but is not required for the attack to be successful <br> (2) Automatically connect to high-quality open networks <br> (3) WiFi Direct    (4) Not vulnerable by default    (5) Specific versions only |
|---|---|

# 5 Conclusions

Since 802.11 leaves room for custom implementations regarding the WiFi association phase, Operating System vendors tend to prioritize usability features instead of security. In this paper we have analyzed how these usability features can be exploited by various WiFi association attacks and we have validated the behavior of modern OS network managers, by implementing these attacks using Wifiphisher. Users that want to protect themselves from automatic association attacks need to disable the relevant features and revoke the Wi-Fi permission for all installed applications. Using a VPN solution right after associating with an access point is also an effective countermeasure assuming that the VPN client properly authenticates the other endpoint. As a future work, we plan to extend our analysis in other WiFi protocol features and to propose protocol extensions that will provide adequate security against WiFi association attacks.

**Acknowledgement.** This research has been co-financed by the European Union and Greek national funds through the Operational Program Competitiveness, Entrepreneurship and Innovation, under the call RESEARCH-CREATE-INNOVATE (project code: T1EDK-01958).

This work has been partly supported by the University of Piraeus Research Center.

# References

1. Roguehostapd github page. https://github.com/wifiphisher/roguehostapd
2. Wifiphisher github page. https://github.com/wifiphisher/wifiphisher
3. Wi-fi protected setup specification version 1.0h. 2006 (2015)
4. Common vulnerability scoring system version 3.1: Specification document (2019). https://www.first.org/cvss/specification-document
5. Pwning WiFi networks with bettercap and the PMKID client less attack, February 2019. https://www.evilsocket.net/2019/02/13/Pwning-WiFi-networks-with-bettercap-and-the-PMKID-client-less-attack/
6. Cassola, A., Robertson, W., Kirda, E., Noubir, G.: A practical, targeted, and stealthy attack against WPA enterprise authentication. In: NDSS Symposium 2013, June 2013. https://doi.org/10.1109/IAW.2005.1495975
7. Altaweel, A., Stoleru, R., Gu, G.: EvilDirect: A new Wi-Fi direct hijacking attack and countermeasures. In: 2017 26th International Conference on Computer Communication and Networks (ICCCN), pp. 1–11, July 2017. https://doi.org/10.1109/ICCCN.2017.8038416
8. Dagelić, A., Perković, T., Vujatović, B., Čagalj, M.: SSID oracle attack on undisclosed Wi-Fi preferred network lists. Wirel. Commun. Mob. Comput. **2018**, 15 p. (2018). https://doi.org/10.1155/2018/5153265. Article ID 5153265
9. Barbera, M.V., Epasto, A., Mei, A., Perta, V.C., Stefa, J.: Signals from the crowd: uncovering social relationships through smartphone probes. In: Proceedings of the 2013 Conference on Internet Measurement Conference, pp. 265–276. ACM (2013)
10. Camps-Mur, D., Garcia-Saavedra, A., Serrano, P.: Device-to-device communications with Wi-Fi direct: overview and experimentation. IEEE Wirel. Commun. **20**(3), 96–104 (2013). https://doi.org/10.1109/MWC.2013.6549288
11. Chatzisofroniou, G.: Efficient Wi-Fi phishing attacks. Tripwire blog (2017)
12. Chatzisofroniou, G.: Introducing wifiphisher. In: BSidesLondon 2015 (2017)
13. Chatzisofroniou, G.: Lure10: Exploiting windows automatic wireless association algorithm. In: HITBSecConf 2017 (2017)
14. Chatzisofroniou, G.: Known beacons attack. CENSUS S.A. blog (2018)
15. Dai Zovi, D.A., Macaulay, S.A.: Attacking automatic wireless network selection. In: Proceedings from the Sixth Annual IEEE SMC Information Assurance Workshop, pp. 365–372, June 2005. https://doi.org/10.1109/IAW.2005.1495975
16. Group, I.W.: Part 11: Wireless LAN medium access control (MAC) and physical layer (PHY) specifications: higher-speed physical layer in the 5 GHZ band. In: IEEE Std 802.11 (1999). https://ci.nii.ac.jp/naid/10011815988/en/
17. Hurley, C.: WarDriving: Drive, Detect, Defend: A Guide to Wireless Security (2004)
18. Jana, S., Kasera, S.K.: On fast and accurate detection of unauthorized wireless access points using clock skews. IEEE Trans. Mob. Comput. **9**(3), 449–462 (2010). https://doi.org/10.1109/TMC.2009.145
19. Nobles, P.: Vulnerability of IEEE802.11 WLANs to MAC layer dos attacks. In: IET Conference Proceedings, pp. 14–14(1), January 2004. https://digital-library.theiet.org/content/conferences/10.1049/ic.2004.0670
20. Nussel, L.: The evil twin problem with WPA2-enterprise. SUSE Linux Products GmbH (2010)
21. Roth, V., Polak, W., Rieffel, E., Turner, T.: Simple and effective defense against evil twin access points. In: Proceedings of the First ACM Conference on Wireless Network Security, pp. 220–235. ACM (2008)
22. SensePost: Manna from heaven. DEF CON 22 (2015)

23. Tippenhauer, N.O., Rasmussen, K.B., Pöpper, C., Capkun, S.: iPhone and iPod location spoofing: Attacks on public WLAN-based positioning systems. Technical report/ETH Zürich, Department of Computer Science 599 (2012)
24. Vanhoef, M.: Windows 10 lock screen: abusing the network UI for backdoors (and how to disable it). Mathy Vanhoef blog (2017)
25. Vanhoef, M., Piessens, F.: Advanced Wi-Fi attacks using commodity hardware. In: Proceedings of the 30th Annual Computer Security Applications Conference, ACSAC 2014, pp. 256–265. ACM, New York (2014). https://doi.org/10.1145/2664243.2664260
26. Vanhoef, M., Piessens, F.: Key reinstallation attacks: forcing nonce reuse in WPA2. In: Proceedings of the 2017 ACM SIGSAC Conference on Computer and Communications Security, CCS 2017, pp. 1313–1328. ACM, New York (2017). https://doi.org/10.1145/3133956.3134027
27. Venkataraman, A., Beyah, R.: Rogue access point detection using innate characteristics of the 802.11 MAC. In: Chen, Y., Dimitriou, T.D., Zhou, J. (eds.) SecureComm 2009. LNICST, vol. 19, pp. 394–416. Springer, Heidelberg (2009). https://doi.org/10.1007/978-3-642-05284-2_23
28. Viehbck, S.: Wi-Fi protected setup online pin brute force vulnerability (2011)
29. Yang, C., Song, Y., Gu, G.: Active user-side evil twin access point detection using statistical techniques. IEEE Trans. Inf. Forensics Secur. 7(5), 1638–1651 (2012)

# A Security Analysis of the Danish Deposit Return System

Ivan Garbacz, Rosario Giustolisi[(⊠)], Kasper Møller Nielsen, and Carsten Schuermann

IT University of Copenhagen, Copenhagen, Denmark
{ivga,rosg,kmni,carsten}@itu.dk

**Abstract.** The process that allows one to get rewarded for returning a container through reverse vending machines (RVM) involves people and technology. In fact, it typically sees a set of human parties (e.g. customers, cashiers) and technical parties (e.g., RVMs, databases, scanners) to collaborate in order to enable effective recycling. In this paper, we advance a formal treatment of the Danish Deposit Return System (DRS). We investigate the security of the ceremony that people are expected to perform in the context of DRS using field observation and automated reasoning tools. We give a particular focus to the security threats due to people interacting with the technology behind DRS. The findings of our investigation enable novel considerations of the ceremony weaknesses and make it possible to delineate potential mitigations.

## 1 Introduction

The introduction of technology into everyday life is normally considered secure, as are the companies providing such technology. Examples include automatic bike rental systems, online food ordering services, or, as we discuss in this paper, automatic deposit-return systems for cans and bottles, as they are commonly used all over Denmark. However, it is difficult to state precisely what security of such systems means and what it would imply. The reason is that socio-technical systems have a completely different attack surface than purely social systems, where interactions are human to human, or purely technical systems, where the operational context is deemed irrelevant. This attack surface can be, if not properly considered, a threat to confidentiality of private information, or in our case, the financial soundness of transactions, and therefore to the reputation of the company deploying the technology or its suppliers.

In this paper, we consider a *ceremony* as a technical system extended with its human users [3] and demonstrate that an analysis of the processes defining the ceremony can yield insights that protect the company's assets, its brand and its reputation. We study the different Danish bottle and can deposit return system (DRS) deployed in Danish supermarket chains Kvickly, Coop, and Netto, and analyse formally the security ceremonies that they require using automated reasoning tools. All DRS under consideration use a paper-based voucher system,

T. Groß and T. Tryfonas (Eds.): STAST 2019, LNCS 11739, pp. 124–139, 2021.
https://doi.org/10.1007/978-3-030-55958-8_7

generated by a reverse vending machine (RVM) and refunded by the cashier. In our study, we focus on three simple security requirements (1) if a voucher was cashed, then bottles of corresponding deposit value were indeed returned, (2) if a voucher is redeemed for a value, then the voucher was printed on an eligible RVM machine, and (3) a voucher cannot be used more than once.

The main contribution of this paper is that it is possible to reason about security ceremonies of this kind, with field observation and formal tools, and that interesting observations can be made about the security of Danish DRS.

The mechanised argument is carried out in Tamarin [10]. In order to define an appropriate model, we reverse engineer the DRS technologies in use and the accompanying processes, as we had no access to design documents, implementation or process definition details. From the knowledge gathered this way, we devise different socio-technical security contexts, which we model through different behavioural actions of inattentive customers or neglectful employees. In summary, the formal analysis approach makes the notion of DRS security more precise: some DRS are reasonable secure with respect to our model, while others are completely insecure. Some DRS could even be tricked into accepting counterfeit vouchers of arbitrary value that could easily be generated on a thermal printer at home.

**Outline.** This paper is organised as follows. In Sect. 2 we describe our reverse engineering activities resulting in a model of the security ceremony for different Danish DRS. In Sect. 3 we detail the formal analysis including the different behavioural actions. Our model includes some technical but mostly rules modelling humans. In Sect. 4, we assess results and describe our findings. In Sect. 5, we discuss related work before we conclude in Sect. 6.

## 2   Modelling the Ceremony

In Denmark, the deposit return scheme is typically implemented by supermarket chains through reverse vending machines (RVM). The customer experience is similar, independent of the store. However, different supermarket chains use different technology, and hence the technical protocol may vary although this is transparent to the customer. For example, RVMs deployed in Kvickly and Coop supermarkets are similar, but they produce different vouchers compared to the RVMs deployed in Netto supermarkets.

Since there is hardly any information about the technology behind deposit return systems available, besides a few patents, this work follows a reverse engineering approach and reconstructs the technical aspects and the ceremony of DRS. In particular, this work adopts the road map for reverse engineering proposed by Müller et al. [11] and focuses on field observation as a primarily investigative technique to gather information regarding the ceremony.

## 2.1    The Reverse Vending Machines

Reverse vending machines (RVM) are the main technological element in the DRS, hence it is essential to gather as much information as possible regarding the functioning of RVMs to build a correct ceremony. Most of the RVMs in Denmark are built by Tomra, and their specifications available to the public in the form of patents. This work considers three Tomra machine models: T-710, T-820, and T9. Every machine is built into a wall, which has a room on the other side which can be accessed through a locked door. An RVM can either accept a single empty container at a time or a beverage crate. Each container is validated on the basis of its weight, barcode, and size. In general, an RVM accepts only glass containers that have a barcode. The sole exemption is the traditional shape of the Danish beer bottle, which does not need to be equipped with a barcode for being accepted. Cans, instead, are accepted with or without barcode. However, the latter case entails no reward for the customer.

From a security perspective, Tomra has filed several patents for detecting fraud attempts in reverse vending machines [7,12,17]. However, the effort is almost exclusively concentrated on making sure that the machine does not accept invalid containers. Thus, we can assume that no RVM would accept an invalid container. Such an assumption can be confirmed by our observations of the machines. In particular, we had access to look through one of the Tomra RVMs while being emptied from its containers.

**Fig. 1.** An example of a voucher printed by a Tomra T-710 machine

In Denmark, RVMs are equipped with thermal printers that print paper vouchers. A voucher attests the number of containers filled by the customer and entails a reward to them. An example of a voucher is in Fig. 1. A voucher includes the following information

- The redemption value in Danish kroner
- A machine-readable serial number (SN1)
- The number of containers
- The model of the RVM
- A non-machine-readable serial number (SN2)
- Time and date of the printing of the voucher

## 2.2   The Machine-Readable Serial Number (SN1)

To the best of our knowledge, there is no document covering how the RVM generates the information included in the voucher, especially how the serial numbers are generated. According to the patents filed by Tomra [6,16], the company has implemented some security measures against presentation of home-made vouchers. In particular, some RVMs implement voucher control by means of a communication from the RVM to a cloud-based service solution provided by Tomra [20]. Once the filling of the RVM is completed by the customer, the RVM generates the voucher and sends both redemption value and SN1 to the Tomra servers. When later the voucher is presented for rewarding, this is controlled against the Tomra server, which authorises the payment to the customer. According to the patents, other solutions that do not require constant communication with the Tomra server may be implemented. For instance, the RVM can be set to communicate locally with a computer hosted at store premises, which periodically updates the list of valid vouchers to the in point of sale stations.

Since no public specification of SN1 is available, we have derived it empirically by analysing the vouchers printed by the different Tomra machines this work has taken in consideration (i.e. T-710, T-820, T9) hosted in three different stores (i.e. Kvickly, Coop, and Netto). Kvickly and Coop belong to the same supermarket chain. In our case, the Kvickly store hosts three T-710 machines, the Coop store hosts two T-820 machines, and the Netto store hosts one T9 machine.

**Kvickly and Coop Stores.** Several vouchers with different values were collected at different times and dates. A sample of the batch of vouchers collected at Kvickly from a T-710 is in Fig. 2a. It can be seen that, independently from date and time, SN1 is fixed when the RVM is filled with one container worth of 1.00 Kr. However, SN2 still slightly changes. This is because the three vouchers in Fig. 2a were printed by three different machines. This is confirmed by the second batch of vouchers (see Fig. 2b) obtained from the same store. The second batch also reveals that SN1 slightly changes accordingly the value of the containers filled in the RVM. The first nine digits are always fixed while the $10^{th}$ and the $13^{th}$ digits change. It can be seen that the $10^{th}$ digit represents the total value of the voucher. It is also confirmed that the same approach is used at the Coop supermarket as depicted in Fig. 2c. Here the $2^{nd}$ digit of the SN1 digits changes because the voucher is printed in a different store. However, the rest of the SN1 reflects the value of the containers.

**Fig. 2.** The four different batches of vouchers obtained from different Tomra machines at Kvickly, Coop, and Netto. (a) the SN1 digits are fixed in each voucher; (b) some of the SN1 digits reflect the value of the voucher; (c) only the 2$^{nd}$ digit differs among Kvickly and Coop stores; (d) the SN1 digits increment by one unit at Netto

Finally, in order to fully predict all the digits of the SN1, it is necessary to understand how the last digit is generated. We found that the last digit $SN1_{13}$ is the check digit from the EAN-13 standard, which can be computed as

$SN1_{13} = x - y$ where

$\quad y = SN1_{[1...12]} \cdot [1\ 3\ 1\ 3\ 1\ 3\ 1\ 3\ 1\ 3\ 1\ 3] \ \wedge \ x = \lceil y \rceil$ s.t. $x \bmod 10 = 0$

For example, the SN1 in Fig. 1 can be computed as

$$y = [2\ 3\ 3\ 9\ 9\ 0\ 0\ 0\ 0\ 4\ 0\ 0] \cdot [1\ 3\ 1\ 3\ 1\ 3\ 1\ 3\ 1\ 3\ 1\ 3]$$
$$= 2 + 9 + 3 + 27 + 9 + 0 + 0 + 0 + 0 + 12 + 0 + 0 = 62.$$
$$x = \lceil 62 \rceil = 70$$
$$SN1_{13} = x - y = 70 - 62 = 8.$$

**Netto Stores.** The T9 machine at Netto generates the SN1 in a different way. It can be seen that the value of the voucher is not anymore reflected on any of the SN1 digits. Instead, by analysing three vouchers printed in sequence by the machine, we found that the SN1 is implemented as a counter that increments by one unit every time a voucher is printed. Notably, the SN1 digits can be also fully predicted at Netto stores since the last digit of the SN1 is still a check digit from the EAN-13 standard.

**Discussion.** The analysis of the vouchers printed at Coop confirms that the SN1 and all the other information printed in the vouchers can be fully predicted. Since a voucher can be redeemed at any of the stores of the same supermarket chain, we can rule out that barcodes are sent to the store's local computer. Also, since any two vouchers with the same value turn out to contain the same SN1, it is unclear how the Tomra servers can prevent a fake voucher to be redeemed provided that other vouchers with the same value where printed. We believe that in this case there is no communication from the RVM and that the scanner reads the value of the voucher from the SN1 only. However, as we shall see later, we assume that such communication exists in the formal analysis of the Kvickly and Coop DRS ceremony.

Netto stores have a different way to generate the SN1, and the value is not stored in the SN1. Thus, we believe that the RVM should communicate to either Tomra servers or a store's local computer the details of the voucher. However, as for Kvickly and Coop stores, the SN1 is still fully predictable, but in this case one needs to know the value of the counter of the RVM.

## 2.3   Ceremony Description

Having seen the modelling of RVM and SN1, we can present a full description of the ceremony, as depicted in Fig. 3. It begins with the customer approaching

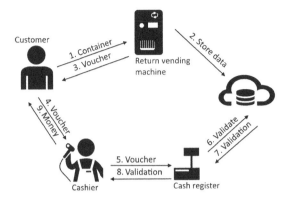

**Fig. 3.** The Danish deposit return system ceremony

the RVM and inserting a number of containers (step 1). The RVM may either accept or reject each of the containers. It will stop accepting new containers when either the customer pushes the button to complete the filling phase or the RVM is full and cannot accept further items. Then, the RVM generates the data to be printed in the voucher, and, optionally sends them to the Tomra servers (step 2). The RVM prints the voucher (step 3) that can be redeemed at the cash register at *any* of the stores belonging to the supermarket chain (step 4). There, the cashier scans the barcode encoding the SN1 (step 5). As seen above, the cash register may check the validity of the voucher against the Tomra server or a local computer (step 6 and 7). Then, the cashier may either stamp the voucher with the supermarket mark or rip it and put it in the cash register (step 7). Finally, the cashier reads the import redeemable from the cash register (step 8) and hands to the customer the money matching the value read from the cash register (step 9).

## 3  Formal Analysis

We analyse the ceremony of the Danish DRS using an automated tool for the formal verification of security protocols. Besides the modelling of the technological part of the DRS ceremony, it is required to model behaviours of the people interacting with the DRS. Thus, we model *behavioural actions* that people may perform as an extension of the canonical description of the ceremony. A behavioural action may or may not be prescribed by the ceremony. In the latter case, they may produce a deviation from the canonical description of the ceremony. For example, the action in which a cashier throws away a voucher is a consistent action with respect to the DRS ceremony and represents a possible deviation from its canonical description. The goal of the analysis is to check whether such deviations affect the security of the ceremony. Thus, three behavioural actions are derived as follows

- *the aware humans*, in which no one deviates from the canonical description of the ceremony;
- *the inattentive customer*, in which customers may share their vouchers with other parties (possibly the attacker);
- *the unaware cashier*, in which the cashier may throw a voucher somewhere else than the cash register.

The three behavioural actions outlined above are not meant to be comprehensive but includes what we think are the most basic ones for the DRS case. They mainly serve to demonstrate the viability of analysis security ceremony using a formal approach. Also, they enable one to assess whether the ceremony is secure despite the deviations that originate from the actions.

**The Tamarin Prover.** Tamarin [10] is an interactive protocol verifier that can prove reachability and equivalence-based properties in the symbolic model. It has an expressive language based on multiset rewriting rules and comes with a built-in attacker model (i.e. the Dolev-Yao attacker). However, it allows one to specify any threat model. Each rule operates on a multiset of facts and has a premise and a conclusion. Facts are predicates that store state information and may be linear (i.e. can be consumed only once) or persistent (i.e. can be consumed arbitrarily often by rules). The execution of the rules creates a labelled transition system of the protocol in which all facts in the premise of a rule are consumed by the facts in the conclusion.

## 3.1  Modelling Choices

Modelling a security ceremony into a symbolic model requires one to make some abstraction choices. The first choice is to develop the equational theory needed to model the ceremony. The equational theory allows one to model arbitrary cryptographic and non-cryptographic functions. In the case of the DRS ceremony, we model the following non-trivial functions (Table 1).

**Table 1.** Part of the equational theory to model the DRS ceremony in Tamarin

| | |
|---|---|
| (*Voucher scanning*) | $getVoucherLeft(voucher(SN1, value)) = SN1$ |
| (*Voucher scanning*) | $getVoucherRight(voucher(SN1, value)) = value$ |
| (*Cash out*) | $getMoney(money(value) = value$ |

The function *voucher* captures the printing of a voucher by the RVM. The function *getVoucherLeft* captures the scanning of the voucher and returns the SN1. Similarly, the function *getVoucherRight* gets in the voucher and returns the value of the voucher. Finally, the function *getMoney* models the cashier handing to the customer the amount of money matching the value read from the cash register.

Another modelling choice regards the modelling of physical objects such as vouchers or money. The presence and the handing over of physical objects are typical of ceremonies since they involve people. However, physical objects are normally not modelled in security protocols as these involve only the exchange of pieces of information. The main difference between objects and pieces of information is that the former cannot be reproduced and once they are handed over, they are not anymore available to the sender. Conversely, a piece of information can be replicated, stored, and made available to the sender. In Tamarin, handing and getting an object can be elegantly modelled using linear facts, in which resources are expandable. The sending and the receiving of pieces of information are modelled using persistent facts.

Another important choice regards the modelling of SN1 barcodes. We have seen that in Kvickly and Coop stores the SN1 is a function of the number of containers filled into the RVM. Hence, we model the SN1 barcode accordingly. For simplicity, we assume the number of containers to be constant. This is not the case for Netto stores, in which the SN1 barcode is a function of the previous barcode. Here, we model the SN1 as a random value, otherwise the verification in Tamarin may incur into non-termination. Note that this is a securely sound over-approximation of the model since, as we have seen before, the SN1 is predictable provided one knows the previous barcode printed by the RVM. However, we assume that the attacker has no access to such barcode (but he may have access to other barcodes). This assumption is sound since any attack found in such a scenario would be valid also in the scenario where the barcode can be predicted.

### 3.2   Human Rules

Behavioural actions can be easily modelled in Tamarin as rules. For reason of space, we comment only on the main rules of the ceremony that model behavioural actions[1]. The rule that expresses a customer receiving a voucher from the RVM (i.e. step 3 of the ceremony) and handing it to the cashier (i.e. step 4 of the ceremony) can be modelled as

```
rule H1SendToH2:
    [AgSt($H1,'H1_1',conts_I),In_O($V,$H1,'voucher_VToH1',voucher_O)]
    --[H1SendToH2($H1,voucher_O,conts_I)]->
    [AgSt($H1,'H1_2',conts_I),Out_O($H1,$H2,'voucher_H1ToH2',voucher_O)]
```

This rule is part of the canonical description of the ceremony, hence it contributes to the modelling of the aware humans. In the premise, the fact AgSt expresses a customer H1 who knows how many containers have been filled conts_I and receives the voucher_O. In the conclusion, the customer hands the voucher to the cashier H2 but memorises how many containers have been filled out. The suffixes _I and _O stand for information and object respectively.

---

[1] The full Tamarin code is available at the link https://www.dropbox.com/s/qrinq3yc9kkrq4e/DRS_Tamarin.zip?dl=0.

Information facts are kept on conclusions while object facts are not. Handing is captured by channels In_O and Out_O, which are modelled as linear facts.

The rules concerning the inattentive customer can be summarised as

```
rule H1SendToBadH:
    [AgSt($H1, 'H1_1', conts_I), In_O($V, $H1, 'voucher_H1ToH2',voucher_O)]
    --[H1SendToBadH($H1, voucher_O, conts_I)]->
    [AgSt($Badh, 'H1_2', conts_I),
     Out(<getVoucherLeft(voucher_O),getVoucherRight(voucher_O),$H1>)]

rule H2GetFromBadH:
    [AgSt($H2,'H2_0', validation_I), In(<voucher_O, $Badh>)]
    --[H2GetFromH1($H2, voucher_O, validation_I)]->
    [AgSt($H2, 'H2_1', <voucher_O, validation_I>),
     Out_O($H2, $Re, 'voucher_H2ToRe',voucher_O)]
```

The rule H1SentToBadH is similar to the canonical rule seen above for the aware humans, but with a different conclusion, in which the customer hands the voucher to the attacker. In this case, only H1 appears in the fact Out since the recipient is the attacker. Similarly, the rule H2GetFromBadH enables the cashier to get a voucher from any one, including the attacker. These rules deviate thus extend the canonical description of the DRS ceremony.

The unaware cashier can be captured with a rule that specifies another deviation from the canonical description of the ceremony. In Tamarin, this is modelled as

```
rule H2SendToH1andThrowsIt:
    [AgSt($H2,'H2_1', <voucher_O, validation_I>)
    ,In_I($Re,$H2,<'value','verification'>,<value_I, verification_I>)
    ,In_O($Re, $H2, 'money_ReToH2', money_O)]
    --[H2SendToH1($H2, voucher_O, validation_I, verification_I,
        money_O, value_I),
      Eq(validation_I, verification_I)]->
    [Out_O($H2, $H1, 'money_H2ToH1', money_O),
     Out(<voucher_O, verification_I>)]
```

In the premise of the rule, the cashier H2 receives a signal from the cash register Re about the validity verification_I of the voucher (step 6). In the conclusion, the cashier hands the money to the customer (step 9) and throws away the voucher, which becomes available to the attacker.

## 4   Findings

We analyse the DRS ceremony against three security requirements

- *Cash for container*, which says that if a voucher is redeemed for a value, then some containers of equal value should have been returned earlier.
- *Cash for voucher*, which says that if a voucher is redeemed for a value, then a voucher was actually printed by an RVM.

– *Unique voucher*, which says that a voucher can be used only once to get money.

The three requirements above capture what we believe are the basic security properties for a DRS. They can be modelled in Tamarin using first-order logic. The requirement of cash for container can be modelled as

```
lemma CashForContainer:
"( All H1 value_I conts_I #k. H1GetFromH2(H1, value_I, conts_I)@k ==>
  (Ex conts_O conts_I #j. H1SendToV(H1, conts_O, conts_I)@j & j<k))
"
```

where `H1GetFromH2` and `H1SendToV` are labels for the rules that capture respectively step 9 and step 1 of the ceremony.

Similarly, the requirement of cash for voucher is captured by the following lemma

```
lemma CashForVoucher:
"( All H1 value_I conts_I #i. H1GetFromH2(H1, value_I, conts_I) @i ==>
  (Ex H2 SN1_I voucher_O #j.
  VSendToH1(H2, SN1_I, value_I,conts(conts_I), voucher_O) @ j & j<i))
"
```

The label `VSendToH1` corresponds to the rule in which the RVM prints the voucher (step 3).

Finally, the requirement of unique voucher can be modelled as

```
lemma UniqueVoucher:
"( All H2 voucher valid1 valid2 money value H2_2
    valid1_2 valid2_2 money_2 value_2 #i #j.
    H2SendToH1(H2, voucher, valid1, valid2, money, value)@i &
    H2SendToH1(H2_2, voucher, valid1_2, valid2_2, money_2, value_2)@j ==>
    #i=#j)
"
```

The label `H2SendToH1` captures the step in which the cashier hands the money to the customer (step 9). The terms `valid1` and `valid2` refer respectively to the successful validation signal that the cashier receives from the register and to the verification message that the server sends to the register. There is also a difference between `money` intended as coins and banknotes, and the piece of information regarding their `value`. Note that all the parameters of the two labels but `voucher` are different. The temporal marks `i` and `j` are crucial: if step 9 is executed twice with the same voucher, it should be referring to the same action, that is, all the parameters have indeed the same values.

In Table 2 are the results obtained by checking the ceremonies in Tamarin. Concerning the ceremonies at Kvickly and Coop stores, the tool proves that the ceremony with aware humans meets cash for container and cash for voucher. The requirement of unique voucher is not met because two different RVMs print the same SN1 barcode as this depends on the number of containers filled by the customer. Tamarin finds attacks for all three properties when inattentive

**Table 2.** The result of the ceremony analysis of the Danish DRS

|  | Kvickly & Coop | | | Netto | | |
|---|---|---|---|---|---|---|
|  | Aware | Inattentive | Unaware | Aware | Inattentive | Unaware |
| Cash for container | ✓ | ✗ | ✓ | ✓ | ✗ | ✓ |
| Cash for voucher | ✓ | ✗ | ✗ | ✓ | ✗ | ✓ |
| Unique voucher | ✗ | ✗ | ✗ | ✓ | ✓ | ✓ |

customer actions are considered as part of the ceremony. We found that the common issue that leads to falsify the properties is that the attacker may create fake vouchers based on what he has seen earlier. Namely, the attacker can create vouchers that were never printed by any RVM. This is also possible because the attacker knows that the SN1 only depends on the number of containers. For the same reason, the ceremonies at Kvickly and Coop stores fail at ensuring cash for voucher when actions from unaware cashier are considered: the Tamarin trace shows that the attacker can just hand the voucher to the cashier a second time if the latter does not destroy it properly. Notably, the attack is possible even if the vouchers are synced and controlled through the Tomra servers, as the voucher is based solely on the number of containers filled in by customers. It is enough that a number of customers have filled in the same number of container, for the Tomra servers have multiple vouchers with the same SN1.

The DRS ceremony for the Netto stores meets all the requirements when aware humans are considered. However, if one considers an inattentive customer, cash for container and cash for voucher cannot be ensured. This is because the attacker, once he knows the SN1, can print the voucher on its own and be refunded in place of the legitimate customer. However, both cash for container and cash for voucher are met for unaware cashier since the SN1 are uniquely generated and, once they are redeemed, the Tomra servers remove the SN1 from the list of valid barcodes, making it impossible for an attacker to redeem the corresponding vouchers again. The requirement of unique voucher is met in all scenarios. However, Tamarin cannot prove unique voucher for unaware cashier if the Tomra server sends only an acknowledgement about the validity of a specific voucher. We found that it is required that the server explicitly sends back the valid SN1 to the cash register, and the latter checks the correctness of this against the scanned voucher.

## 4.1   Discussion

Having analysed formally the ceremonies for the Danish DRS, we can conclude that, according to our model, the Kvickly and Coop ceremony is less secure than the one in Netto stores. The main problem with that ceremony is that one can generate a voucher by guessing the number of containers that other customers may have previously filled into any of the RVMs that belong to the supermarket chain. This is worsened by the fact that vouchers have the same SN1 independently from which RVM they have been generated, hence an attacker can likely be successful on redeeming a fake voucher holding the same SN1.

The Netto ceremony sees the RVMs generating the SN1 based on an internal counter. Thus, each voucher is unique and is validated against a check with the Tomra servers. The Netto ceremony is secure in all scenarios but inattentive customers. However, we analysed the ceremony assuming that the attacker has no access to the internal counter of an RVM. Hence, the Netto ceremony is potentially vulnerable if one knows the current counter of an RVM. We believe that such potential vulnerability can be easily removed by using digital signatures, which would make the vouchers not predictable any more. The presence of digital signatures in paper ticketing has been already developed in public transportation. The signatures are generated by the public transportation server, encoded as QR codes, and then scanned by the ticket inspectors who hold portable scanners that store the verification key [4]. The Danish deposit return system can be modelled in a similar way. The voucher can be signed by the RVM, while the cash register can store the verification key. Since the digital signature of an SN1 cannot be forged, vouchers cannot be fully predicted by the attacker unless he knows the signing key. We modelled the Netto ceremony with digital signatures in Tamarin and the outcome of our analysis confirms that the ceremony would meet at least the same level of security of the original Netto ceremony. However, in the case of inattentive customers, an attacker can still make a copy of a voucher and redeem them in place of the customer. We believe that this attack cannot be avoided unless the customer is actively involved in the generation and validation of the voucher, for example using a PIN.

## 5    Related Work

Formal approaches for the analysis of socio-technical systems have been recently proposed in a few works. Basin et al. [1] formalised models of humans in security protocols and analysed two-factor authentication protocols in Tamarin as case studies. They considered three main human models. The first is the *infallible human* model, in which the human actions follow the prescribed steps of the protocol. In this paper, it corresponds to the aware humans. The second model is the *untrained human*, in which the human actions are completely controlled by the Dolev-Yao attacker. The last model is the *rule-based human*, which is defined as the untrained human with specific restricting rules that limit the arbitrary behaviour of the Dolev-Yao attacker. Conversely, this paper models the inattentive customer and unaware cashier actions as rules that extend the canonical description of the ceremony.

Johansen and Jösang [5] discussed probabilistic models of humans, while Probst et al. [14] proposed novel formal approaches to analysing socio-technical systems. Bella and Coles-Kemp [2] provided a model for the analysis of security ceremonies termed *the ceremony concertina* and demonstrated it by formally analysing the Amazon user registration ceremony using the Inductive Approach [13]. Giustolisi et al. [15] analysed the TLS certificate validation in different browsers in front of socio-technical properties using UML and model checking tools. Stojkovski et al. [18] recently proposed a model to define socio-technical misalignments between a technical system and its users, and formally verified an end-to-end email encryption system against a set of misalignment properties. Differently from the works outlined above, which consider a single human role, this paper provides a formal account on human-to-human interactions as it considers a ceremony with customers and cashiers.

Martina et al. [9] and more recently Martimiano and Martina [8] proposed a shift from the classical Dolev-Yao attacker model to a more dynamic and human-centred threat model. In this paper, we still rely on the Tamarin built-in Dolev-Yao attacker, although we believe that the analysis of our case study into a different threat model may be beneficial to gain even more accurate and deep understanding of the security of the ceremony.

# 6  Conclusion

This paper has shown that the socio-technical analysis of a security ceremony can be pivoted on field observation and formal verification tools. Field observation enables the reverse engineering of ceremonies, as they usually lack proper documentation. Thus, field observation produces a specification that can be fed into a formal verification tool. The latter provides a precise way to dissect the security implications of the ceremony and allows one to formulate and verify potential mitigations.

To the best of our knowledge, this paper has provided the first security analysis of a DRS considering its human players. Although DRS is a well-established technology in Denmark and other countries in the world, it has been found that RVM manufactures devote most of their efforts to the detection of fake containers rather than detecting the refunding of fake vouchers. This work has also found that minor changes in the technology behind DRS may lead to severe security implications, although the technology comes from the same manufacturer and human interactions are identical. Fixing the technology to cope with the behavioural actions that people may perform outside the box is yet an open problem. Other countries adopt a voucher-less scheme in which customers are provided with personal cards. Customers use their cards to collect points that can be redeemed for rewards. While personal cards may mitigate threats due to inattentive customers, they pose novel privacy threats by exposing customers' habits in purchasing cans and bottles. We are not aware whether the findings of this work are applicable to other manufacturers and countries. We have contacted both Dansk Retursystem and Tomra on the issue and, at the time of writing this paper, we are waiting for a reply.

This work aims at contributing to the establishment of holistic approaches to security. Future work should focus on how systematically model out-of-the-box human interactions into behavioural actions that can be fed into a formal verification tool. A desirable feature of such a model is to make it independent from the specific ceremony so that it would be possible to build a formal framework for the analysis of less restricted security ceremony. As regards the analysis of DRS, we believe that it would be interesting to investigate other scenarios such as the one with additional behavioural actions as well as analysing the implications of scenarios with multiple behavioural actions from different people at the same time. However, the Dolev-Yao attacker may be too powerful to appreciate the subtleties entailed by such scenarios, hence we think that a different threat model than the Dolev-Yao attacker should be considered. Finally, it would be interesting to analyse recent voucher-less and fully digital DRS proposals in which customers receive their refunds using an app [19]. The more pervasive the technology becomes, the more socio-technical analysis is required.

## References

1. Basin, D., Radomirovic, S., Schmid, L.: Modeling human errors in security protocols. In: 2016 IEEE 29th Computer Security Foundations Symposium (CSF), pp. 325–340, June 2016
2. Bella, G., Coles-Kemp, L.: Layered analysis of security ceremonies. In: Gritzalis, D., Furnell, S., Theoharidou, M. (eds.) SEC 2012. IAICT, vol. 376, pp. 273–286. Springer, Heidelberg (2012). https://doi.org/10.1007/978-3-642-30436-1_23
3. Ellison, C.: Ceremony design and analysis. IACR eprint (2007)
4. Giustolisi, R.: Free rides in Denmark: lessons from improperly generated mobile transport tickets. In: Lipmaa, H., Mitrokotsa, A., Matulevičius, R. (eds.) NordSec 2017. LNCS, vol. 10674, pp. 159–174. Springer, Cham (2017). https://doi.org/10.1007/978-3-319-70290-2_10
5. Johansen, C., Jøsang, A.: Probabilistic modelling of humans in security ceremonies. In: Garcia-Alfaro, J., et al. (eds.) DPM/QASA/SETOP-2014. LNCS, vol. 8872, pp. 277–292. Springer, Cham (2015). https://doi.org/10.1007/978-3-319-17016-9_18
6. Jorgensen, A.: Method, system, reverse vending machine and use thereof for handling empty packaging, November 2005. https://patents.google.com/patent/US20050246225A1/en. US20050246225A1
7. Kavli, T.O., Njastad, J., Saether, G.: Method and apparatus for detecting fraud attempts in reverse vending machines, November 2012. https://patents.google.com/patent/US9189911. US9189911B2
8. Martimiano, T., Martina, J.E.: Daemones Non Operantur Nisi Per Artem. In: Matyáš, V., Švenda, P., Stajano, F., Christianson, B., Anderson, J. (eds.) Security Protocols 2018. LNCS, vol. 11286, pp. 96–105. Springer, Cham (2018). https://doi.org/10.1007/978-3-030-03251-7_11
9. Martina, J.E., dos Santos, E., Carlos, M.C., Price, G., Custódio, R.F.: An adaptive threat model for security ceremonies. Int. J. Inf. Secur. 14(2), 103–121 (2014). https://doi.org/10.1007/s10207-014-0253-x
10. Meier, S., Schmidt, B., Cremers, C., Basin, D.: The TAMARIN prover for the symbolic analysis of security protocols. In: Sharygina, N., Veith, H. (eds.) CAV 2013. LNCS, vol. 8044, pp. 696–701. Springer, Heidelberg (2013). https://doi.org/10.1007/978-3-642-39799-8_48
11. Müller, H.A., Jahnke, J.H., Smith, D.B., Storey, M.A., Tilley, S.R., Wong, K.: Reverse engineering: a roadmap. In: Proceedings of the Conference on The Future of Software Engineering, ICSE 2000, pp. 47–60. ACM, New York (2000)
12. Nordbryhn, A., Hansen, A.H.H.: Fraud detection, February 2019. https://patents.google.com/patent/EP3440641A1/en. EP3440641A1

13. Paulson, L.C.: The inductive approach to verifying cryptographic protocols. J. Comput. Secur. **6**(1–2), 85–128 (1998)
14. Probst, C.W., Kammüller, F., Hansen, R.R.: Formal modelling and analysis of socio-technical systems. In: Probst, C.W., Hankin, C., Hansen, R.R. (eds.) Semantics, Logics, and Calculi. LNCS, vol. 9560, pp. 54–73. Springer, Cham (2016). https://doi.org/10.1007/978-3-319-27810-0_3
15. Giustolisi, R., Bella, G., Lenzini, G.: Invalid certificates in modern browsers: a socio-technical analysis. IOS J. Comput. Secur. **26**(4), 509–541 (2018)
16. Saether, G.: Means in a reverse vending machine (RVM) for receiving, handling, sorting and storing returnable items or objects, July 2010. https://patents.google.com/patent/US7754990B2/en. US7754990B2
17. Saether, G., Sivertsen, R., Lunde, T., Njastad, J.: Fraud detection system and method, August 2018. https://patents.google.com/patent/US20180232745A1/en. US20180232745A1
18. Stojkovski, B., Vazquez Sandoval, I., Lenzini, G.: Detecting misalignments between system security and user perceptions: a preliminary socio-technical analysis of an E2E email encryption system. In: 4th European Workshop on Usable Security (2019)
19. Tomra Systems ASA: myTOMRA app. https://www.mytomra.com.au/home/the-mytomra-app/. Accessed 05 July 2019
20. Tomra Systems ASA: Voucher control. https://www.tomra.com/en/collection/reverse-vending/tcs-digital/voucher-control. Accessed 05 July 2019

# Moving to Client-Side Hashing for Online Authentication

Enka Blanchard[1(✉)], Xavier Coquand[2], and Ted Selker[3]

[1] Digitrust, Loria, Université de Lorraine, Nancy, France
[2] Bsecure, Paris, France
[3] University of Maryland, Baltimore County, USA
https://www.koliaza.com

**Abstract.** Credential leaks still happen with regular frequency, and show evidence that, despite decades of warnings, password hashing is still not correctly implemented in practice. The common practice today, inherited from previous but obsolete constraints, is to transmit the password in cleartext to the server, where it is hashed and stored. We investigate the advantages and drawbacks of the alternative of hashing client-side, and show that it is present today exclusively on Chinese websites. We also look at ways to implement it on a large scale in the near future.

**Keywords:** Hashing · Web standards · Authentication

## 1 Introduction

Despite multiple decades of insistence from the cybersecurity and cryptography communities, password hashing is still far from a solved problem in practice. Two issues are even more critical today than they were more than 25 years ago, when vulnerabilities were first found in MD5. The first is that, although it was first mentioned as important to security in the 1960s, long before the existence of the Internet, password hashing is still not as commonplace as it should. Many recent database leaks with passwords in clear reveal that even some of the largest service providers still do not follow what was already best practices when they were created. The most recent example is Facebook's revelation in March 2019 that they kept a log file with more than 200 million cleartext passwords that was accessible by more than 2000 developers. The second issue is that hashing techniques have changed, and distributed computation on specialised hardware has made many hashing algorithms obsolete for password purposes. Well applied modern hashing techniques are still exceedingly rare, with the only major leaks that showed this level of security coming from online password managers such as LastPass [22,42].

There are many explanations for such problems, most of them with a social component. First, developers who implement the security procedures do not always have the relevant training [2,14]. This is linked to a culture of going faster, at the expense of good security practices [1]. This, in turn, comes from the fact

© Springer Nature Switzerland AG 2021
T. Groß and T. Tryfonas (Eds.): STAST 2019, LNCS 11739, pp. 140–156, 2021.
https://doi.org/10.1007/978-3-030-55958-8_8

that service providers generally suffer from negative outcomes only when security breaches become public. Even in such cases, the incentives are not always strong enough to effect real change—Yahoo! suffered from three leaks of increasing magnitude between October 2016 and October 2017, which could have been prevented had security been reinforced after the first [41].

There are many ways to address this issue, but blaming the developers has not worked so far [14]. As such, we investigate the possibility of client-side password hashing to be an alternative to the standard practice of server-side hashing. Its main advantage is that client-side hashing, as opposed to server-side, is easily detectable and analysable. This creates accountability, means that it becomes possible to impose a direct cost on companies with poor security practices. Thus, we can give a strong incentive to companies to reform their practices before they suffer from major public security breaches.

This paper is organised as follows. We start by looking at the current state of the art, both on how to hash securely and how current service providers fail to do so. We then turn to client-side hashing, by looking at how prevalent it is before listing its advantages and drawbacks. We finish by looking at how large scale changes could be made in the near future, and discussing potential improvements and complications.

## 2    Password Hashing Today

Problems were first found with the practice of storing all the passwords unencrypted in a single text file in the 1970s [37]. The general password architecture that was developed at the time has not evolved much in the decades since. The best practice still consists in hashing the password with a salt, storing this hash on the server, and comparing the hashes to make a decision when the user tries to login again. Client-based hashing was not always a possibility, due to compatibility issues with legacy protocols [35]. This is not true anymore—although there is still a generally unspoken assumption that all hashing should be done server-side. The server hashing cost was even a major point of contention in a recent password hashing algorithm competition [20], without the authors mentioning the possibility and impact of client-side hashing.

### 2.1    Best Practices

As the general architecture has not changed much in the past decades, the main questions are still the same: Which hashing function to use? How to salt the password? How to prevent side-channel attacks?

*Hashing Algorithm.* After problems were found in the first two common hashing algorithms—MD5 and SHA-1—the two principal general-purpose hashing algorithms currently considered to be secure are SHA-2 and SHA-3—or rather, algorithms from these families. However, this has a caveat. They are secure insofar as the string to hash has high entropy, in which case finding a preimage for the function becomes a hard problem. Hashing a complete message with these algorithms is then secure. However, if the number of possibilities for the original message is limited, one can use brute-force and hash all the potential messages. Unlike online attacks where $10^{10}$ bogus login attempts are easily noticeable, it is easy to compute that many hashes offline, on special-made machines. This is one of the main risks with database leaks, as even consumer machines can nowadays brute-force more than 1 billion such hashes per second [11, 15, 43].

With that kind of capability, dictionary-augmented brute-forcing becomes a strong option, as most passwords deviate only poorly from real words. This is true no matter the kind of hashing algorithm used: if the space of all possible inputs remain small and the search can be parallelised efficiently, it is enough to hash all probable inputs to get the inverse of most hashes. To address this, two main algorithms were initially used, PBKDF2 and bcrypt, which can run recursively $n$ times on their own output to artificially increase the computing time [49]. This slows down the algorithm in an unavoidable way, negating the gains due to more powerful machines but is still vulnerable to parallel brute-forcing. Argon2 is a more recent solution, specifically made to be hard to parallelise by requiring an arbitrarily large amount of memory [8], and is now one of a set of good alternatives [20]. All the alternatives provide an adjustable parameter to increase the time and space complexity of hashing.

*Salt.* The second common component in the hashing process is the *salt*—a pseudorandom string that is concatenated with the password before hashing. This is done to prevent attacks that make use of a large table of precomputed hashes, also known as a rain bow table [33]. The salts should be different from user to user—which is not always understood by service providers. If a single salt is used for a whole database, it prevents attacks using generic rainbow tables, but allows the computation of a website-specific rainbow table, only marginally improving security. Salts are often used as an example of data stored only on the server's side. However, in this context of password hashing, the only goal of the salt is to prevent precomputed tables. As such, the salt can just be the login and website name, which is unique and always available client-side. When using one service to login into another, one must however be careful and make sure that the right website name is used.

*Side-Channels.* Even using secure hashing with unique salts is not enough if adversaries have opportunities to obtain the passwords through other means. There is a large variety of side-channel attacks that are relevant, but two are particularly important. The first lies in stealing the password itself when it is transmitted in cleartext, but that has been thankfully made mostly obsolete by the switch from HTTP to HTTPS [47]. The second comes from unsecure password management on the server side, for example the storage of log files with incoming requests (including cleartext passwords), as was done until recently by Facebook [32]. Never storing sensitive data is a first step towards security, with the advantage of being easier than never receiving it in the first place.

*PAKE.* There already exists an alternative protocol that addresses the issues of server-side hashing: Password Authenticated Key Exchange (PAKE) [7], and its derivatives, among which the Secure Remote Password protocol (SRP) [50] is the best known. This protocol integrates asymmetric cryptography and ideas from zero knowledge protocols to prevent the server from having enough information to independently recomputing the password without mounting costly brute-force attacks.

Various problems have plagued different PAKE implementations and prevented widespread use, among which we can mostly cite patent problems, as well as security issues in earlier versions of SRP [17], as it is already two decades old. The main issue, however, is that it is quite a complex protocol, and cannot be implemented as easily as a simple hashing function. Some more modern alternatives exist, such as OPAQUE [25], but they are still far from being commonly used.

## 2.2   Recent Database Leaks

Credential leaks are becoming increasingly commonplace, with weekly reports of stolen credentials [41], not only from start-ups and smaller corporations but also from the biggest companies. As vulnerabilities in both MD5 and SHA-1 have been public for more than a dozen years, one could expect that most service providers would update their policies (even if hashing server-side), but this is sadly not the case. Because of this, some leaks reach catastrophic proportions, as can attest the discovery in mid-March 2019 that Facebook had stored between 200 and 600 million passwords in cleartext instead of hashing, going as far back as 2012 [32]. Facebook revealed that the stored passwords were only accessible to employees—and were accessed by about 2000 of them—leaving open the question of why they had stored them in the first place. Less than a month later, it was revealed that the social network had also asked some of its users to provide their login details for their main email addresses, breaching all forms of privacy concerns [27]. This is not a freak occurrence, as Twitter and GitHub both revealed similar failures to encrypt their confidential information in the previous ten months [31,48].

In an extensive analysis [24], Jaeger et al. looked at 31 credential leaks going from 2008 to 2016, totalling close to 1 billion email/password pairs worldwide. Of the leaks considered, more than half consisted of entirely unencrypted stored credential pairs (including gmail.com in 2014 and twitter.com in 2016, although they could not make sure the data was authentic), and only one, ashleymadison.com, used a strong level of encryption—bcrypt—while still making some mistakes. The main mistake made was storing MD5 hashes of case-insensitive versions of the passwords, from which it was possible to compute a preimage, leaving the option of computing the full password by hashing the 1000 or so remaining possibilities through bcrypt [16]. Table 1, partially extracted from [24], shows the main authenticated leaks they analysed.

**Table 1.** Partial list of leaks analysed by Jaeger et al. with number of credentials leaked, date and encryption method used in each case, extracted from [24].

| Website | Encryption | # accounts leaked | Leak date |
|---|---|---|---|
| myspace.com | SHA-1 | 358986419 | 2008 |
| gawker.com | DES | 487292 | Dec. 2010 |
| aipai.com | MD5 | 4529928 | Apr. 2011 |
| csdn.net | clear | 6425905 | Oct. 2011 |
| tianya.cn | clear | 29642564 | Nov. 2011 |
| vk.com | clear | 92144526 | 2012 |
| linkedin.com | SHA-1 | 112275414 | Feb. 2012 |
| imesh.com | MD5+salt | 51308651 | Sep. 2013 |
| xsplit.com | SHA-1 | 2990112 | Nov. 2013 |
| 51cto.com | MD5+salt | 3923449 | Dec. 2013 |
| xiaomi.com | MD5+salt | 8281358 | May 2014 |
| 000webhost.com | clear | 15035687 | Mar. 2015 |
| sprashivai.ru | clear | 3472645 | May 2015 |
| ashleymadison.com | bcrypt | 36140796 | July 2015 |
| 17.media | MD5 | 3824575 | Sep. 2015 |
| mpgh.net | MD5+salt | 3119180 | Oct. 2015 |
| r2games.com | MD5+salt | 11758232 | Oct. 2015 |
| nexusmods.com | MD5+salt | 5918540 | Dec. 2015 |
| mate1.com | clear | 27402581 | Feb. 2016 |
| naughtyamerica.com | MD5 | 989401 | Apr. 2016 |
| badoo.com | MD5 | 122730419 | June 2016 |

One common problem with this list is that we can only discover that service providers were using obsolete security techniques after the damage is done, or even much later if they do not immediately disclose observed breaches [26]. This is where client-side hashing comes into play, as it is much easier to detect.

## 3    Detecting Client-Side Hashing

One of the main interests of client-side hashing is that it is observable by the user. Detecting it, however, often requires work. Some service providers still rely on security through obscurity, and make their scripts obfuscated to make attacks harder. Except in rare cases, passwords are by now generally encrypted (with a symmetric encryption algorithm) before leaving the client's machine. As such, checking whether the password is still visible in outgoing packets would only catch the very worst cases, where the password is neither hashed nor encrypted. Thankfully, there are at least two different methods to check whether *sufficiently secure* hashing is being performed.

## 3.1   Syntactic and Semantic Analyses

The first method is the most precise of the two, and relies on—potentially automated—code analysis. One of the simplest way is to check the libraries called by the current webpage and infer from them (for example, the presence of no hashing library besides the inclusion of an MD5 function would be a red flag). An improvement would be to automatically detect the password field and follow the path of the relevant memory object (or to check whether any object sent in an outgoing packet is identical to the password). As it depends on the skill of the person analysing the code, this is the most versatile method and can even work with custom-made hashing methods, but cannot be entirely automated. It also struggles against hashing that relies on compiled code.

## 3.2   Computing Load Analysis

An alternative and more efficient method could be used in the near future to detect whether the website implements client-side hashing, and whether it is secure enough. One issue is that it is not immediately relevant, as the proportion of websites that would currently be considered secure would be infinitesimal. The idea is quite simple: any correct implementation of a secure password hashing algorithm requires a surge in memory and processor usage. Detecting it would be doable, although a surge could be linked to a different process. As such, it can mostly be used to quickly detect websites where the hashing is visibly insufficient. Both methods could also be combined to indicate a failure to correctly hash in most dangerous cases—while proving that it is correctly hashed would still be harder.

## 3.3   Manually Checking the Alexa Top 50

We decided to use manual semantic analysis to check which of the top 50 global websites—according to Amazon Alexa [4]—implemented client-side hashing. Table 2 shows the results of this small experiment. Figure 1 shows an example of cleartext password sent to the server (using TLS, but no hashing) on facebook.com and the equivalent on baidu.com.

*Analysis of the Websites with Client-Side Hashing.* Out of the top 50 websites, we only found 8 with client-side hashing. This is slightly misleading, however, as some of the concerned websites, including 360.cn and qq.com, use the same authentication system, made by baidu.com. Other websites—like csdn.net and taobao.com—do not redirect to baidu.com but reuse very similar authentication templates. Moreover, the 8 websites with client-side hashing correspond exactly to the 8 websites from the top 50 that are based in the People's Republic of China. There are different potential explanations, which we will now investigate.

## 3.4   Why Is Client-Side Hashing Rare?

This question we ask is twofold. First, why does every Chinese website implement client-side hashing, and second, why are they the only ones to do so? Alas, we do

**Fig. 1.** Request sent to facebook.com (top) and baidu.com (bottom) by TLS after clicking on the login button. For facebook.com, the cleartext password is shown on the bottom line, bordered in red. For baidu.com, the encrypted password is shown on the third line from the bottom, right after the username. (Color figure online)

**Table 2.** Result of a manual analysis on which websites implement client-side hashing. A YES was given to each website where the password was not simply symmetrically encrypted using TLS. All websites come from the Alexa Top 50 global websites on 07-07-2019, with the left column corresponding to ranks 1–25, and the right one to ranks 26–50.

| Website | Client-side | Website | Client-side |
|---|---|---|---|
| google.com | NO | youtube.com | NO |
| facebook.com | NO | baidu.com | **YES** |
| wikipedia.org | NO | qq.com | **YES** |
| yahoo.com | NO | amazon.com | NO |
| taobao.com | **YES** | twitter.com | NO |
| tmall.com | NO | reddit.com | NO |
| instagram.com | NO | live.com | NO |
| vk.com | NO | sohu.com | NO |
| jd.com | NO | yandex.ru | NO |
| sina.com.cn | **YES** | weibo.com | **YES** |
| blogspot.com | NO | netflix.com | NO |
| linkedin.com | NO | bilibili.com | NO |
| twitch.tv | NO | pornhub.com | NO |
| login.tmall.com | NO | 360.cn | **YES** |
| csdn.net | **YES** | yahoo.co.jp | NO |
| mail.ru | NO | bing.com | NO |
| microsoft.com | NO | whatsapp.com | NO |
| naver.com | NO | aliexpress.com | NO |
| livejasmin.com | NO | microsoftonline.com | NO |
| alipay.com | **YES** | ebay.com | NO |
| xvideos.com | NO | tribunnews.com | NO |
| amazon.co.jp | NO | google.co.in | NO |
| github.com | NO | okezone.com | NO |
| imdb.com | NO | google.com.hk | NO |
| pages.tmall.com | NO | stackoverflow.com | NO |

not have access to the decision-making process that led to this state of affairs. However, we can make informed guesses by looking at regulations and incentive structures.

*Chinese Client-Side Hashing.* The PRC imposes strong constraints on the type of cryptography that can be used on its territory and by its companies [34], so it is normal to see a difference in the frameworks used. One trivial consequence is that the hashes on the relevant websites do not correspond to MD5 or SHA hashes, and their output cannot be easily identifiable as the output of a common hashing algorithm due to the character set and length parameters. A second visible difference is that websites generally discourage users from using passwords, privileging alternative methods such as unlocking through one's phone, as Google recently deployed on its own service. This means that they also generally implement some forms of 2-factor authentication based on cellphone usage. There are two advantages to this design, in a context where some ISO protocols could potentially be compromised [18,46]. The first is that it makes it easier to prevent foreign actors from being able to decrypt password data exchanged with—potentially compromised—ISO protocols while it is in transit. The second is that, as 2-factor authentication is used, tracking users—through triangulation, among other methods—becomes possible with the cooperation of telephone companies[1]. Strong state security incentives and a tighter cooperation—than in the western world—between the state and large technology companies [45] combined made it feasible to implement on a large (national) scale this kind of technological decision.

The improved security linked to client-based hashing could then be a side-effect of state-wide protection mechanisms against foreign actors. However, the real question is not why those 8 websites implement client-side hashing, but rather, why the others do not implement it.

*Server-Side Hashing in Other Countries.* There are many potential arguments as to why server-side hashing is so frequent, but the main explanation is probably the simplest: inertia and simplicity. In a world where large companies with hundreds of millions of users (such as Mate1) still store their passwords in cleartext, the question is not so much "why is the hashing not done on the client?" but rather "why is the hashing not done at all, or with obsolete tools?", as shown in Table 1. This is compounded by the fact that, unlike the general issue of hashing on which there was a quasi-unanimity and a common push from the security community for more than two decades, the issue of server-side versus client-side hashing is less known, and even academic endeavours didn't question some of the common assumptions until recently [20,35]. Two other issues amplify this inertia and are worth looking into.

The first is that there has been a long tradition of pitting security and functionality against each other. Until recently, common practice said that any improvement on the first came at the expense of the other. This view has recently been challenged, thankfully, as certain designs can in practice improve both [5]—similarly to how the increased complexity of password constraints in the 2000s actually worsened both security and functionality [29].

The second issue, related to the first, is the incentive structure that surrounds password security. Most online companies operate in an ecosystem where security is not a cost that is paid continuously but instead where they pay nothing

---

[1] This would be a natural extension of the 2002 law that forced cybercafe owners to keep a list linking login information and state ID for all their clients [44]—in a country where cybercafe was the main internet access point for more than a quarter of users in 2006 [9].

until a major leak is made public. As such, there is little in the way of incentives to push those companies to keep up to date against threats they are misinformed about. This translates to developer culture, where security can become an afterthought when the goal is to implement the different functionalities as fast as possible. Even developers aware of the security risks might end up with managerial directives that go against their warnings, as the potential damage can be underestimated until the damage is done [6]. This *reactive* way of handling security is alas poorly adapted to passwords as they have a domino effect on other services [23]. Solving this bad incentive structure—at least on this front— is one of the main advantages of making client-side hashing the norm, as shown in the next section.

## 4   Cost Analysis of Client-Side Hashing

Before we discuss how to implement client-side hashing on a large scale, it's time to summarise its advantages and drawbacks.

### 4.1   Advantages

*No Credential Reuse Attack.* The main advantage with client-side hashing is that, as the password never leaves the client machine, database leaks are much less serious. In any case, if an appropriate hashing algorithm and salt are used, an adversary with access to the database cannot reuse the credentials to mount an attack on a different service provider.

*Lower Server Costs.* The second advantage is that, as the hashing happens client-side, some server resources are freed, unlike when they have to compute expensive key derivation functions.

*Stronger Hashing.* The previous advantage means that there is no need to compromise between server utilisation and security, as determined by the slowdown factor of the hashing function. A lot of computing power can then be dedicated to hashing, at the client's expense (as they have a low probability of noticing).

*Makes Phishing More Difficult.* If the method becomes standardised, the use of the website address as salt can be detected (or corrupt password hashes generated instead). This can help against homograph attacks—where a unicode character that is visually similar is used to get realistic-looking impostor domain names [21]—as one among a set of other mitigation methods [19,36].

*Simplicity.* As the method can become standardised, and visible in its standardisation, it puts the onus on what happens on the client's side, instead of the server. This leaves more opportunities to improve the database design and the server optimisation, without jeopardising security.

*Accountability.* The final advantage is that, if implemented at scale, this method can create a social cost for companies that do not implement client-side hashing, as they become known for having lax security practices. In consequence, the cost is transferred to the developers, who have a direct interest in improving the security. This is opposed to what happens currently, as explained earlier, as most developers spend time on security issues only in a reactive manner, after the leak has already happened. This allows the system to have detectable issues that are not only observable through catastrophic failures.

## 4.2   Drawbacks

There are four central drawbacks to client-side hashing, depending on how it is implemented.

*Authentication Attacks After Leaks.* The first issue happens if an attacker manages to obtain a copy of the database. They could then copy the hash and send a valid authentication message to the website. Two factors mitigate this. The first is that it is quite trivial to prevent it by having double hashing, whereby the service provider also runs a minimal amount of hashing server-side, thus preventing this attack. In such a case, the server-side hashing does not require strong security parameters, and a simple SHA-256 is enough[2], as it is not the security bottleneck—as long as the client-side hashing is solid enough to prevent brute-force. The second factor is simply that an adversary able to steal the password database is also most probably able to steal and affect most other systems. As such, the impact would mostly concern buyers of said database rather than the original attacker.

*Computing Power Limits.* The second issue is that servers generally have more computing power than at least some of the client devices. As long as most clients authenticate through computers or modern mobile devices, this should not be problematic, as the computing power and, even more importantly, the memory available tend to be more than what many servers could generally afford for a single user, even in an unoptimised Javascript implementation. That said, with the advent of the Internet of Things, some devices with very low power could be involved and require password authentication, which could complicate the matter.

*Script Blocking.* A third potential issue—although it is quite minor—is that client-side hashing can be blocked by the client. This is especially true among users who are sensitive to security issues and block all scripts by default. The jump in memory and CPU use could also trigger warnings as they would occur in a way similar to cryptojacking[3] [12].

---

[2] MD5 would not work as it would be easy for an adversary with the leaked database to create an attack: instead of finding the original password, they would only need to find an MD5 collision for it.

[3] Cryptojacking corresponds to the hidden execution of code inside a browser to mine cryptocurrencies while the user is visiting a website.

*Incompatibility with Legacy Protocols.* The last issue is quickly disappearing, but is one reason why client-side hashing is still quite rare, through inertia. Some older protocols, especially homebrews, required a cleartext password to function [35].

## 5  Making Changes to the Hashing Process

As the overwhelming majority of hashing is done server-side today, changing this requires a relatively large amount of labour. We see three main avenues to make the relevant changes, that could all be attempted in parallel.

### 5.1  A Service-Centric View

From a service provider point of view, the interest in switching to client-side hashing are akin to those of switching to hashing from initially having stored passwords in cleartext, with a few key differences. The first is that the relative security gains are weaker, whether in terms of real security or in terms of public blame if the security is broken. There is little difference between "adequate" and "strong" security procedures when compared to having "inadequate" security. On the other hand, switching to client-side hashing saves on server costs and code complexity, unlike switching from cleartext to hashed passwords. Hence, although the costs of switching are smaller, the benefits are correspondingly weaker. Moreover, all these are moot points if the incentive structure stays the same, as even the first switch to hashed passwords isn't universal yet.

There is one way to change this incentive structure, by involving major browser developers. A client-side hashing detection system could be integrated into a browser, and give a warning to users when passwords are not handled correctly. This detection system would of course be imperfect and let some websites badly handle passwords while not showing warnings. That said, it could be enough to create a real cost on the service providers, who might lose users to security concerns. Ideally, this could happen in a way similar to what was seen during the switch from HTTP to HTTPS, by first adding warnings and then blocking service providers with unsecure practices (unless the user confirms that they are aware of the risks). Despite the complexity of the architectural changes required [30], browser warnings changed the incentives and had a fast and large-scale impact [13,40]. Finally, convincing one such actor might also probably be enough for the others to follow suit, as other browsers would have some pressure to be perceived as secure to the users as the one displaying the warnings. Adopting some standard header could also help differentiate between websites with probably obsolete security practices and the rest, which would be composed of websites with good security practices and high quality phishing websites [28].

### 5.2  A User-Centric View

From the end user's perspective, the issue is different, as there is a wide variability of possibilities when it comes to users' goals, constraints, and expertise.

As long as independent service providers switch to client-side hashing, the process is mostly invisible to users[4], and should have no negative effects. User costs would only appear in one of two cases: if a browser starts implementing warning systems, interrupting users' actions, or if a user decides to take matters in their own hands by using an extension that implements a warning system. We'll start by looking at how the second could happen.

*An Extension to Warn Users.* The first and easiest short term solution is to create a short script—a priori in the form of a browser extension—to detect whether the password is sent in cleartext to the service provider. This script could be based on some of the methods mentioned earlier, such as detection of the password string in the outgoing packets, or use of computing resources. It could be displayed next to the padlock corresponding to HTTPS connections, in the form of a warning in the address bar—or potentially even more aggressively as a pop-up. The effects on the user would be partially detrimental as it would distract from their current task, although it could help some users avoid using passwords on unsecure websites. The main advantage of this would however be the incentive structure it would create to switch systems if widely deployed.

There is one potential drawback of this method in the form of a privacy risk similar to the one we just started observing on HTTPS padlocks [10,39]. If the warning system shows not only indications of risky websites but also of safe ones, corrupting the warning system itself becomes a worthy goal. As such, users could be more easily fooled by phishing attempts that manage to show good password security than they would with neither positive nor negative warnings. That might be less of an issue because, unlike HTTPS, warning systems for client-side hashing would easily detect bad practice but struggle to detect truly good practice[5], but still bears keeping in mind.

*Detecting and Hashing Passwords on the Client.* A more extreme case for more technically inclined—and concerned—users would be to use a different kind of extension, as a stopgap measure. Instead of checking whether the password is sent in cleartext, it would be possible to automatically detect password fields— as Google Chrome does—and offer a second field through the extension. After the user types their password in that second field, the hashed result could be directly input into the original field. This bypasses a few issues and adds some level of security, but would also be harder to optimise than if done natively by the service provider. One concern then would be that the user's password could not be directly used on a different device without the extension. The website

---

[4] The only way for it to be visible is if it unduly increases delays by asking too many rounds of hashing on a low-powered device, but this is a matter of parameter optimisation where wide margins could be taken by default to avoid this issue.

[5] For example, to be sure the password is not sent in cleartext, one would need to make sure that the password field is accessed exactly once as input to the hash function, otherwise any reversible function could be used before transmitting, dodging accusations of cleartext sending. Similarly, the website could trigger some expensive computation without using it to fool resource monitors.

changing its domain name would also create problems that are harder to address from this client-centric view.

## 6    Discussion

We have shown that client-side hashing benefits from multiple advantages, and that its drawbacks often come from older constraints and are quickly becoming less relevant. Despite this, among the most used websites, it is only used today by Chinese service providers, as part of a larger security suite common to many of them. After observing the issues caused by server-side hashing, we provide some ideas to detect such hashing techniques at a larger scale than what we manually did. We also propose integrating them into common browsers to change the incentive structure for developers and companies involved in the security ecosystem. We finish by offering some alternatives for end users, such that all solutions mentioned could be used in parallel.

The changes we propose are minimal and have some self-perpetuating mechanisms, exactly because expecting a sudden and non-trivial change from a large security ecosystem would be idealistic. There are of course alternatives to the solutions proposed, such as Time-based One-time Password algorithms [38], which solve many issues mentioned. The problem, as with all other security improvements, is getting large actors to make the requisite changes. A different alternative is to use password managers—which the hashing extension we mention imitates in some ways—but this brings us back to older security models by shifting all costs to the user. Moreover, password managers still have low penetration on mobile devices and are not always compatible with all users' constraints [3].

We see two ways to go further in the direction we explored. First, it seems wise to investigate whether the increasing role played by low-power devices in the Internet of Things could create bottlenecks security-wise. Second, to increase the amount of hashing time available, one could hash the password letter by letter, using the lapse between keystrokes to hash what is available for a set duration and using this as a salt for the next hash. This is not currently done, and could potentially create security vulnerabilities, so a thorough cryptanalysis of this method should be done with the currently used password hashing functions. On the usability side, there is also the question of finding an ideal delay to resist parallelised attacks without creating a time cost for users on lower-end devices.

**Acknowledgements.** We're grateful to participants of the Privacy and Security Workshop, IU Gateway Berlin, for their comments. This work was supported partly by the french PIA project "Lorraine Université d'Excellence", reference ANR-15-IDEX-04-LUE.

## References

1. Acar, Y., Backes, M., Fahl, S., Kim, D., Mazurek, M.L., Stransky, C.: How internet resources might be helping you develop faster but less securely. IEEE Secur. Priv. **15**(2), 50–60 (2017). https://doi.org/10.1109/MSP.2017.24

2. Acar, Y., Fahl, S., Mazurek, M.L.: You are not your developer, either: a research agenda for usable security and privacy research beyond end users. In: IEEE Cybersecurity Development – SecDev, pp. 38, November 2016. https://doi.org/10.1109/SecDev.2016.013

3. Alkaldi, N., Renaud, K.: Why do people adopt, or reject, smartphone password managers? In: Proceedings of EuroUSEC. eprint on Enlighten: Publications (2016)

4. Amazon Alexa: 500 global sites (2019). http://alexa.com/topsites/

5. Baskerville, R., Rowe, F., Wolff, F.C.: Functionality vs. security in is: tradeoff or equilibrium. In: International Conference on Information Systems, pp. 1210–1229 (2012)

6. Baskerville, R., Spagnoletti, P., Kim, J.: Incident-centered information security: managing a strategic balance between prevention and response. Inf. Manage. **51**(1), 138–151 (2014)

7. Bellovin, S.M., Merritt, M.: Encrypted key exchange: password-based protocols secure against dictionary attacks. In: Proceedings 1992 IEEE Computer Society Symposium on Research in Security and Privacy, pp. 72–84. IEEE (1992)

8. Biryukov, A., Dinu, D., Khovratovich, D.: Argon2: new generation of memory-hard functions for password hashing and other applications. In: IEEE European Symposium on Security and Privacy - EuroS&P, pp. 292–302. IEEE (2016)

9. Center, C.I.N.I.: 18th statistical survey report on the internet development in China. Technical report CINIC (2006)

10. Cimpanu, C.: Extended validation (EV) certificates abused to create insanely believable phishing sites (2017). https://web.archive.org/web/20181012025730/www.bleepingcomputer.com/news/security/extended-validation-ev-certificates-abused-to-create-insanely-believable-phishing-sites/

11. Dürmuth, M., Kranz, T.: On password guessing with GPUs and FPGAs. In: Mjølsnes, S.F. (ed.) PASSWORDS 2014. LNCS, vol. 9393, pp. 19–38. Springer, Cham (2015). https://doi.org/10.1007/978-3-319-24192-0_2

12. Eskandari, S., Leoutsarakos, A., Mursch, T., Clark, J.: A first look at browser-based cryptojacking. In: 2018 IEEE European Symposium on Security and Privacy Workshops (EuroS&PW), pp. 58–66. IEEE (2018)

13. Felt, A.P., Barnes, R., King, A., Palmer, C., Bentzel, C., Tabriz, P.: Measuring HTTPS adoption on the web. In: 26th USENIX Security Symposium (USENIX Security 17), pp. 1323–1338 (2017)

14. Florêncio, D., Herley, C., van Oorschot, P.C.: An administrator's guide to internet password research. In: LISA, vol. 14, pp. 35–52 (2014)

15. Ge, C., Xu, L., Qiu, W., Huang, Z., Guo, J., Liu, G., Gong, Z.: Optimized password recovery for SHA-512 on GPUs. In: IEEE International Conference on Computational Science and Engineering - CSE - and Embedded and Ubiquitous Computing - EUC, vol. 2, pp. 226–229. IEEE (2017)

16. Goodin, D.: Once seen as bulletproof, 11 million+ ashley madison passwords already cracked (2015). https://web.archive.org/web/20180803014106/arstechnica.com/information-technology/2015/09/once-seen-as-bulletproof-11-million-ashley-madison-passwords-already-cracked/

17. Green, M.: Let's talk about pake (2018). https://web.archive.org/web/20190426024348/blog.cryptographyengineering.com/2018/10/19/lets-talk-about-pake/

18. Hales, T.C.: The NSA back door to NIST. Not. AMS **61**(2), 190–192 (2013)

19. Hannay, P., Baatard, G.: The 2011 IDN homograph attack mitigation survey. In: Proceedings of the International Conference on Security and Management (SAM 2012) (2012)

20. Hatzivasilis, G., Papaefstathiou, I., Manifavas, C.: Password hashing competition-survey and benchmark. IACR Cryptol. ePrint Arch. **2015**, 265 (2015)
21. Holgers, T., Watson, D.E., Gribble, S.D.: Cutting through the confusion: a measurement study of homograph attacks. In: USENIX Annual Technical Conference, General Track, pp. 261–266 (2006)
22. Independent Security Evaluators: Password managers: Under the hood of secrets management. Technical report, ISE (2019). https://web.archive.org/web/20190301171335/www.securityevaluators.com/casestudies/password-manager-hacking/
23. Ives, B., Walsh, K.R., Schneider, H.: The domino effect of password reuse. Commun. ACM **47**(4), 75–78 (2004). https://doi.org/10.1145/975817.975820
24. Jaeger, D., Pelchen, C., Graupner, H., Cheng, F., Meinel, C.: Analysis of publicly leaked credentials and the long story of password (re-)use. In: Proceedings of the International Conference on Passwords (2016)
25. Jarecki, S., Krawczyk, H., Xu, J.: OPAQUE: an asymmetric PAKE protocol secure against pre-computation attacks. In: Nielsen, J.B., Rijmen, V. (eds.) EUROCRYPT 2018, Part III. LNCS, vol. 10822, pp. 456–486. Springer, Cham (2018). https://doi.org/10.1007/978-3-319-78372-7_15
26. Karyda, M., Mitrou, L.: Data breach notification: issues and challenges for security management. In: Mediterranean Conference on Information Systems (2016)
27. Khandelwal, S.: Facebook caught asking some users passwords for their email accounts (2019). https://web.archive.org/web/20190404071339/amp.thehackernews.com/thn/2019/04/facebook-email-password.html
28. Kisa, K., Tatli, E.: Analysis of http security headers in turkey. Int. J. Inf. Secur. Sci. **5**(4), 96–105 (2016)
29. Komanduri, S., et al.: Of passwords and people: Measuring the effect of password-composition policies. In: Proceedings of the SIGCHI Conference on Human Factors in Computing Systems, CHI 2011, pp. 2595–2604. ACM, New York (2011). https://doi.org/10.1145/1978942.1979321
30. Kranch, M., Bonneau, J.: Upgrading https in mid-air. In: Proceedings of the 2015 Network and Distributed System Security Symposium, NDSS (2015)
31. Krebs, B.: Twitter to all users: Change your password now! (2018). https://web.archive.org/web/20190402093127/krebsonsecurity.com/2018/05/twitter-to-all-users-change-your-password-now/
32. Krebs, B.: Facebook stored hundreds of millions of user passwords in plain text for years (2019). https://web.archive.org/web/20190322091235/krebsonsecurity.com/2019/03/facebook-stored-hundreds-of-millions-of-user-passwords-in-plain-text-for-years/
33. Kumar, H., Kumar, S., Joseph, R., Kumar, D., Singh, S.K.S., Kumar, P.: Rainbow table to crack password using md5 hashing algorithm. In: IEEE Conference on Information and Communication Technologies - ICT, pp. 433–439. IEEE (2013)
34. MartinKauppi, L.B., He, Q.: Performance Evaluation and Comparison of Standard Cryptographic Algorithms and Chinese Cryptographic Algorithms. Master's thesis (2019)
35. Mazurek, M.L., et al.: Measuring password guessability for an entire university. In: Proceedings of the 2013 ACM SIGSAC Conference on Computer Communications Security, CCS 2013, pp. 173–186. ACM, New York (2013). https://doi.org/10.1145/2508859.2516726
36. McElroy, T., Hannay, P., Baatard, G.: The 2017 IDN homograph attack mitigation survey. In: Proceedings of the 15th Australian Information Security Management Conference (2017)

37. Morris, R., Thompson, K.: Password security: a case history. Commun. ACM **22**(11), 594–597 (1979). https://doi.org/10.1145/359168.359172
38. M'Raihi, D., Machani, S., Pei, M., Rydell, J.: RFC6238: TOTP: Time-based one-time password algorithm (2011). https://tools.ietf.org/html/rfc6238
39. Peng, P., Xu, C., Quinn, L., Hu, H., Viswanath, B., Wang, G.: What happens after you leak your password: Understanding credential sharing on phishing sites. In: AsiaCCS 2019, pp. 181–192, July 2019. https://doi.org/10.1145/3321705.3329818
40. Schechter, E.: Moving towards a more secure web (2016). https://web.archive.org/web/20190405120627/security.googleblog.com/2016/09/moving-towards-more-secure-web.html
41. Shape: 2018 credential spill report. Technical report, Shape Security (2018)
42. Siegrist, J.: Lastpass hacked - identified early and resolved (2015). https://web.archive.org/web/20190412054716/blog.lastpass.com/2015/06/lastpass-security-notice.html/
43. Sprengers, M.: GPU-based password cracking. Master's thesis, Radboud University Nijmegen (2011)
44. State Council of the People's Republic of China: Regulations on administration of business premises for internet access services, article 23 (2002)
45. Swaine, M.D.: Chinese views on cybersecurity in foreign relations. China Leadersh. Monit. **42**, 1–27 (2013)
46. Tryfonas, T., Carter, M., Crick, T., Andriotis, P.: Mass surveillance in cyberspace and the lost art of keeping a secret. In: Tryfonas, T. (ed.) HAS 2016. LNCS, vol. 9750, pp. 174–185. Springer, Cham (2016). https://doi.org/10.1007/978-3-319-39381-0_16
47. Vyas, T., Dolanjski, P.: Communicating the dangers of non-secure http (2017). https://web.archive.org/web/20190524003142/, https://blog.mozilla.org/security/2017/01/20/communicating-the-dangers-of-non-secure-http/
48. Whittaker, Z.: Github says bug exposed some plaintext passwords (2018). https://web.archive.org/web/20190331110732/www.zdnet.com/article/github-says-bug-exposed-account-passwords/
49. Wiemer, F., Zimmermann, R.: High-speed implementation of bcrypt password search using special-purpose hardware. In: International Conference on ReConFigurable Computing and FPGAs - ReConFig, pp. 1–6. IEEE (2014)
50. Wu, T.: The SRP authentication and key exchange system. Technical report, RFC Editor (2000)

# Privacy Control

# A Privacy-Preserving Infrastructure for Driver's Reputation Aware Automotive Services

Gianpiero Costantino[1], Fabio Martinelli[1], Ilaria Matteucci[1(✉)],
and Paolo Santi[1,2]

[1] Istituto di Informatica e Telematica, Consiglio Nazionale delle Ricerche, Pisa, Italy
{gianpiero.costantino,fabio.martinelli,ilaria.matteucci}@iit.cnr.it
[2] MIT Senseable City Laboratory, Cambridge, MA, USA

**Abstract.** Even though the introduction of ICT in transportation systems leads to several advantages in terms of efficiency of transport, mobility, traffic management, and in improved interfaces between different transport modes, it also brings some drawbacks in terms of increasing security challenges, also related to human behavior. For this reason, in the last decades, attempts to characterize drivers' behavior have been mostly targeted towards risk assessment and, more recently, to the training of machine learning software for autonomous driving. In this paper, we propose, for the first time, to use driver behavioral characterization to build a general *reputation profile*, that can be used to create innovative, reputation-aware automotive services. As a first step towards realizing this vision, we present guidelines for the design of a privacy preserving vehicular infrastructure that is capable of collecting information generated from vehicles sensors and the environment, and to compose the collected information into driver reputation profiles. In turn, these profiles are exchanged in a privacy preserving way within the infrastructure to realize reputation-aware automotive services, a sample of which are described in the paper. As a fundamental component of the infrastructure, we show that: *i*) multi-dimensional reputation profiles can be formed building upon the recently introduced notion of driver DNA; *ii*) multi-dimensional comparison of profiles can be achieved by means of a reputation lattice rooted in the notion of algebraic c-semiring; and *iii*) a secure two-party mechanism can used to provide services to drivers on the basis of their reputation and/or DNA's parameters.

**Keywords:** Drivers' reputation profile · Privacy preserving infrastructure · Vehicular network · Reputation-aware services

## 1 Introduction

Recalling the directive of the European Union 2010/40/EU, made on the 7th of July 2010 [20], Intelligent Transportation Systems (ITS) are "*advanced applications, which [. . . ] aim to provide innovative services relating to different modes of*

© Springer Nature Switzerland AG 2021
T. Groß and T. Tryfonas (Eds.): STAST 2019, LNCS 11739, pp. 159–174, 2021.
https://doi.org/10.1007/978-3-030-55958-8_9

*transport and traffic management and enable various users to be better informed and make safer, more coordinated and 'smarter' use of transport networks"*. In particular, the directive defines an ITS as a system in which Information and Communications Technology (ICT) is applied in the field of road transport, including infrastructures, like tunnels and vehicles. In fact, advances in both vehicle and personal communication technologies are creating increasing opportunities for collecting data within and around the car. With thousands of signals customarily generated by today's vehicles, a car can be considered a veritable mobile sensing platform that produces a few Gigabytes of data per hour [19].

Besides creating potential privacy and security issues when this immense amount of data is connected to the Internet, as implied by the transition to connected and autonomous vehicles, opportunities for unprecedented understanding and optimization of what happens in vehicular infrastructure arise. Within this context, a problem of particular interest is how to leverage vehicular and/or smartphone data to characterize driver behavior. Its characterization is especially interesting for the auto insurance industry, since it can be used to produce accurate risk profiles and personalized policy rates [22]. Characterizing driver behavior finds application also in the development of autonomous driving technologies, where "good" driving styles can be used to train the car control software and give a human feeling to autonomous driving.

This paper suggests a possible use of driver behavior characterization that substantially evolves its role beyond what currently considered in the insurance and autonomous vehicle industry. Building upon the recently proposed notion of Driver DNA [12], we herein propose that vehicle-collected data can be used to compute a "driver reputation" profile that synthetically summarizes a driver's reputation within the vehicular ecosystem. Reputation profiles of circulating drivers can, then, be exchanged in a privacy preserving way with surrounding vehicles or infrastructure to enable innovative management of road infrastructure and driver-aware ITS services, as described in Sect. 5. A key component of the envisioned notion of driver reputation is a framework that enables secure and private exchange of driver reputation profiles between vehicles and between a vehicle and the road infrastructure. The initial design of such a framework is the focus of the present paper, in which we introduce a privacy-preserving infrastructure able to evaluate the reputation of drivers and to provide them with customized services based on their reputation evaluation.

*The paper is organized as following:* Section 2 reports some literature about driver behavior characterization through vehicles parameters and possible applications and services designed accordingly. Section 3 presents a possible approach to profile a driver, estimate her reputation, and eventually compare different drivers' profile. Section 4 describes our proposed infrastructure able to collect information and to exchange reputation profiles in a privacy-preserving way. Section 5 proposes some ideas of possible services that the infrastructure can provide to "good " drivers, i.e., drivers with a high reputation while Sect. 6 describes our prototype of privacy preserving comparison functions with experimental results. Finally, Sect. 7 analyse the presented work and discuss some points regarding it while Sect. 8 draws the conclusion of the paper and outlines future research directions.

## 2   Related Work

In the last few years, interest about the characterization of driver behavior according to information collected from the vehicle has consistently increased. However, to the best of our knowledge, none of the existing work attempts to link driver behavior to the notion of reputation and trust as proposed herein.

One of the early works in this field is presented in [4], where the authors proposed a traffic simulation model incorporating assumptions about what a safe drivers' behavior should be. The main outcome of the paper is the comparison between results obtained in the simulation and the real world.

Other recent works [9,26] present approaches to identify reckless drivers based on a combination of speed and acceleration. Both measures are retrieved from different ICT systems present in the vehicle itself. Indeed, in [9], the authors used GPS-enabled mobile phones as a low-cost opportunity for collecting instantaneous vehicle speed and other information. In [26], the information was retrieved from SD Card and GPS on vehicle.

In [10], the driver is considered as part of the vehicle system (driver-in-the-loop), more specifically as the control unit of the entire system. In this way, the authors described three methods to identify driver behavior as a comparison with the actual and the expected behavior of the system by considering different aspects of the drive-in-the-loop vehicle system.

Works about how to link the driver behavior with traffic accidents, safety on roadside network, and possible rewarding are mostly related to the insurance world. For instance, reference [22] is about the risk of reckless drivers and how insurance reward can depend on the driver behavior. Adapting insurance fee to driver behavior is promoted as a method to incentivize drivers to drive more carefully and reduce accidents.

To our best knowledge, the idea of characterizing driver's behavior with the final aim of computing a comprehensive driver's reputation profile and to realize reputation-aware vehicular services is novel to this paper.

About reputation-aware vehicle service, several services for ITS have been introduced in the literature. Following the standardization work of European Telecommunications Standards Institute (ETSI), ITS applications (or service) have been categorized in a number of classes. While their requirements and operational constraints have been defined in ETSI, security specifications are not fully defined and mostly left to the single developers. For instance, secure and privacy aware versions of two representative classes of ITS applications are Driver Assistance – Road Hazard Warning, and Community Services. In case of road hazard warning, there is ample literature that studies under what conditions the communication network (V2V and V2I communication) is able to provide the adequate level of responsiveness necessary to enable early hazard detection [11]. Since security and privacy requirements as mandated by the proposed architecture will introduce significant communication/computational overhead, there is a need of carefully analyzing and testing the interplay between security level, communication performance, and achieved effectiveness in providing secure and early warning to the drivers.

## 3    Defining Driver Reputation

This section describes a possible way of defining the notion of driver reputation. We start by observing how to objectively quantify driver reputation starting from vehicle collected data is a very challenging problem by itself. While intuitively understandable by the human mind – it is relatively easy, when you sit beside a driver, to judge if she is "good" or "bad" at driving –, the notion of "good" driving style, which should be the basis for establishing a driver's reputation, is evasive from a quantitative viewpoint.

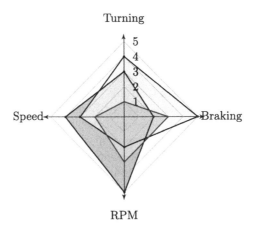

**Fig. 1.** Radar graph representation of a Driver's DNA.

Recently, the notion of Driver DNA [12] has been proposed to concisely represent a driver's driving style starting from car-collected data analysis, integration with road and weather information, and comparison with peer drivers. The Driver DNA, as defined in [12], is composed of four parameters which cannot be directly compared with each other. Individually, each parameter is measured with a rank ranging between 0 (lowest score) and 5 (highest score). The four parameters are: braking ($b$), turning ($t$), speeding ($s$), and RPM ($rpm$) (revolutions per minute). The first parameter (braking intensity) is used to quantify a driver's aggressiveness, the second (steering wheel angle) is used to quantify comfort in driving, the third parameter (driving above speed limit), which is also combined with weather information, is directly related to accident risk, while the fourth parameter (engine RPM) is used, when compared with values obtained by peer drivers, as a proxy of a driver's fuel efficiency.

Following [12], we represent the profile of each driver as a tuple of four elements $(b_i, t_i, s_i, rpm_i)$, with $b_i, t_i, s_i, rpm_i \in [0, 5]$, one for each parameter we are going to consider to identify the driver's DNA. Using the profile, we associate to each driver a reputation value.

As the four parameters composing driver DNA cannot be directly compared – i.e., a score of 4 in braking cannot be compared to a score of 4 in speeding – the authors of [12] suggests graphically representing a driver's driving style as a radar graph of the four dimensions, where a relatively larger area of the radar graph indicates a relatively better driver.

Starting from this idea, we enhance the driver's characterization by adding the notion of *driver's reputation* as a unique value that identifies the goodness or recklessness of the driver. In fact, we consider as driver *reputation score* $R_{D_i}$ the internal area identified by the radar graph derived by the four parameters of the driver's DNA. As seen from Fig. 1, the area of a radar graph can be calculated as the sum of the areas of the four triangles composing the graph, each having two of the parameters composing the profile as perpendicular sides. Hence, given the 4-tuple $P_{D_i} = (b_i, t_i, s_i, rpm_i)$ associated with driver $D_i$, her reputation $R_{D_i}$ can be computed as follows:

$$R_{D_i} = \frac{(b_i \times t_i) + (t_i \times s_i) + (s_i \times rpm_i) + (rpm_i \times b_i)}{2}$$

Note that the order of parameters in the graph influenced the result of the area. Thus, considering the 4-tuple $(b, t, s, rpm)$, we label the graph starting from the right-hand side with the first element of the tuple, i.e., $b$, and then we proceed counterclockwise to label the other directions with the remaining parameters, as in Fig. 1. To ensure consistency, the same order of parameters is used to compare different driver's profile.

As it will become clear later on, a single reputation score associated to a driver might not be sufficient to enable reputation-aware automotive services as described in the following. For this reason, we set forth the notion of *reputation profile* for a driver, which we define as:

$$RP_{D_i} = ((b_i, t_i, s_i, rpm_i), R_{D_i})$$

i.e., the profile and the synthetic reputation score.

According to this definition of reputation, we have to characterize "good" and "bad" driver behavior. Different strategies may be followed, e.g., the median value of each measure, i.e., 2.5, as threshold value to distinguish between good and bad. Hence, a driver has a *good* behavior when her reputation score is higher than 12.5, and a *bad* behavior, otherwise.

Once it has been calculated, the reputation score becomes part of the driver profile in addition to the other information in the profile. Hence, keeping also the information in the profile, that is richer than the single score $R_{D_i}$ it is possible to allow services responsive to specific aspects of driving, such as, fuel-efficiency, accident-risk, etc.

Moreover, two drivers could be directly compared through their reputation score. However, it is possible that two drivers have the same reputation scores but for very different reasons. Indeed, being the parameters values independent and not comparable to one another, the results of the ordering of driver's profiles is a *lattice* as the one in Fig. 2. We refer to it as *reputational lattice* in which all the driver with the same reputation score are at the same level of the lattice. Having the same reputation score, are classified in the same way with respect to the ITS. In this case, we use the driver's information to distinguish among drivers. In fact, a better assessment of driver reputation can be achieved by accounting for the individual parameters that compose a driver's DNA.

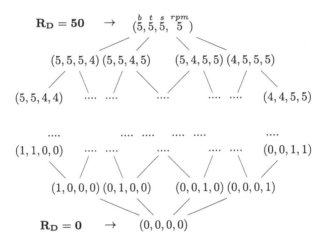

**Fig. 2.** Reputational lattice.

Using the lexicographic order on tuples of values, it is possible to prioritize one parameter over another (depending on the order of the components in the lexicographic order itself), and to compare different driver profiles to customize transportation services according to their reputation.

*Example 1.* Let us consider three drivers profiles:

$$P_{D_A} = (\overset{b}{2}, \overset{t}{3}, \overset{s}{4}, \overset{rpm}{5})$$

$$P_{D_B} = (\overset{b}{5}, \overset{t}{4}, \overset{s}{3}, \overset{rpm}{2})$$

$$P_{D_C} = (\overset{b}{3}, \overset{t}{1}, \overset{s}{2}, \overset{rpm}{3})$$

represented in Fig. 1. The reputation score of the three drivers is calculated as follows:

$$R_{D_A} = \frac{(2 \times 3 + 3 \times 4 + 4 \times 5 + 5 \times 2)}{2} = 24$$

$$R_{D_B} = \frac{(5 \times 4 + 4 \times 3 + 3 \times 2 + 2 \times 5)}{2} = 24$$

$$R_{D_C} = \frac{(3 \times 1 + 1 \times 2 + 2 \times 3 + 3 \times 3)}{2} = 10$$

Hence, driver $D_A$ and driver $D_B$ have the same reputation higher than 12,5, so they are considered as good drivers. Driver $D_C$ is a reckless driver, since her reputation is less than 12,5, and consequently, less than the reputation of the other two drivers. However, if we want to compare the three drivers with respect to the *braking parameter*, we note that, the worst driver is $D_A$. Moreover, $D_A$ is a good driver but the value of the braking parameter is less than 2.5 (it is 2), hence with respect to this parameter, it is considered an "aggressive" driver.

# 4  Our Privacy Preserving Infrastructure

We assume to work in an Intelligent Transportation Systems as the one depicted in Fig. 3. It is composed of three layers *Ground, Fog,* and *Cloud.* The infrastructure we have in mind is based on Fog [23–25] and Cloud computing. The *Ground layer* involves all vehicles that interact with the fog layer to manage and share in-vehicle information. Vehicles contain a large number of internal sensors, e.g., photonic sensors, LiDARs, and communication systems, that can be used, among other things, to sense the quality of the road, traffic, vehicle trajectories, weather conditions, and so on. The *Fog layer* is composed by fog nodes, that are smart components of the road infrastructure, and can be located, for instance, at a gas station, a smart traffic light, a pay toll station, and so on. The fog node is able to collect and exchange data with vehicles and other components of the infrastructure in a safe and secure way. In the same way, fog nodes communicate with the cloud to perform more complex calculation, in case there are required to provide a better service to the drivers. Once smart devices at the fog layer collect information from vehicles, the data can be forwarded to the *Cloud layer.* In this layer, all data coming from the different devices at the fog layer are collected, where upon some analytic operations are executed to obtain both new derived information able to improve the safety of the stakeholders, or to provide customized applications to the infrastructure nodes. The Cloud layer will also contribute to implement the security and privacy aspects [15].

We also assume that each driver in the ITS reported in Fig. 3 is characterized by a multi-dimensional reputation profile, which should be considered as a valuable and private information to the driver. Reputation profiles of drivers become a sort of passport in the infrastructure. Thus, they can be exchanged in a secure and private way with surrounding vehicles and roadside infrastructure to realize innovative reputation-aware vehicular services, a sample of which are described in Sect. 5.

## 4.1  Secure Two Party Computation

Given the importance of a driver's reputation profile in the envisioned scenario, the proposed infrastructure shall guarantee that such profiles are exchanged in a

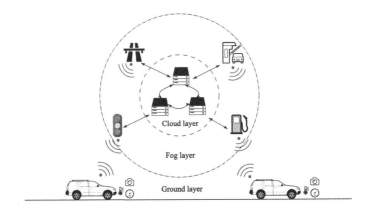

**Fig. 3.** The proposed three-layers infrastructure.

privacy preserving way. To this aim, we enhance each fog node with the ability of performing a simple algorithm for *secure two party computation* (2PC). The algorithm allows drivers to discover whether they fulfill the conditions to obtain a certain service provided by the fog layer of the infrastructure, without disclosing their profiles. The 2PC technique was first presented in [1] with the goal of solving the Millionaires' problem: two parties, Alice and Bob, each holding some private data $x$ and $y$, want to discover whom of them is richer, i.e., whether $x > y$ or $x < y$, without disclosing out to the other party the amount of money and without using a Trusted Third Tarty (TTP).

In literature, there are several 2PC frameworks. Some examples are listed below:

– FairPlay [18] can be considered the first influential 2PC framework. It allows users to write functions using a high level language, called SFDL, and to compile SFDL functions into garbled boolean circuit. A limit of Fairplay is given by the limited number of commands and operations that is possible to express through SFDL. FairPlay has strong security properties in the context of two-party computation. The framework is shown to be secure against a malicious party; in particular *i*) a malicious party cannot learn more information about the other party's input than it can learn from a TTP that computes the function; and *ii*) a malicious party cannot change the output of the computed function.
– A few years later, the same researchers have released FairplayMP [3], which is the extension of Fairplay that works with more than two parties.
– MobileFairplay [8] ports Fairplay to Android Smart-phones. In particular, MobileFairplay takes as input functions written and complied using the SFDL language and extends the application domains also to Android devices.
– MightBeEvil [14] and CBMC-GC [13], similarly to Fairplay, take as input functions written in high-level language, that can be run in a private way. In case of CBMC-GC, functions are written using the $C$ language, then transformed into boolean circuits by the CBMC-GC compiler, and executed as

illustrated in [16]. A version for Android Smart-phones of CMCG-GC was presented in [7], showing much better performances compared with Fairplay for Android Smart-phones.

– *CBMC-GC* v2.0 [5,6] is a new optimized compiler to generate circuits for 2PC and Multi-Party Computation MPC) starting from ANSI-C source code.

## 5   Privacy-Preserving Reputation-Aware Vehicular Services

Vehicles in the considered infrastructure can ask for services, getting different quality and or prices depending on their driver's reputation profile. Typically, we can assume that to obtain, say, a special discount on a service, a driver must provide her profile to be compared with an access threshold used by the service provider. This comparison function hits the driver's privacy since the service provider will be able to know the entire profile in case of full profile disclosure, or at least a single parameter in the reputation profile. To protect the privacy of the drivers, we implemented the comparison function in a privacy-preserving manner that make use of the 2PC technique CBMC-GC v1.0. The presented method allows drivers to discover whether they meet the conditions for obtaining a certain service level without disclosing their profile (Fig. 4).

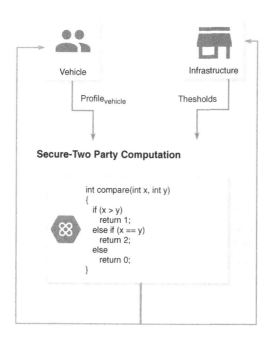

**Fig. 4.** 2PC flow for profile comparison

Examples of innovative "reputation-aware" services enabled by the proposed infrastructure are described below:

**Reputation-Aware Fuel Cost.** Currently, fuel cost is decided at the level of the single gas station, and it is applied independently of the driver's attitude to save or waste fuel while driving. In an effort to incentivize fuel-efficient driving style, one might think of a scenario where fuel cost is personalized to reflect a driver's fuel efficiency. When entering a gas station, the vehicle onboard software sends driver's reputation information – in this specific case, both her reputation score and her fuel efficiency score – to the fog node installed at the gas station. After proper authentication, the driver will be offered a personalized fuel price: a relatively lower price for drivers with relatively higher reputation, and vice versa.

**Reputation-Aware Tolling.** Similarly to the case of fuel price, also access to road infrastructure is currently oblivious to driving style, and is typically done based on the type of vehicle. However, a driver with a relatively higher risk profile (e.g., more aggressive, or speeding more frequently) might pose a relatively higher prospect cost to the infrastructure manager than a relatively more cautious driver, due to the higher risk of incurring accidents, damage road components, etc. One can then envision a scenario in which the price to access road infrastructure (highways, bridges, etc.) is personalized based on a driver's reputation profile. Similarly to the gas station scenario, the vehicle onboard software shares driver's reputation information with the fog node interfacing with the tolling system, and a driver is charged a variable amount that reflects her accident and damage risk profile.

# 6   Prototype of Privacy-Preserving Functions

To evaluate the feasibility of privacy-preserving, reputation-aware services as described in Sect. 5, we built a test-bed with a client-server paradigm where an Android Radio unit (Fig. 5) acts as client and represents the onboard computational unit of a vehicle, and a server that mimics as node of the infrastructure, i.e., a fog node. To achieve privacy-preserving comparison, we leveraged CBMC-GC on the fog node, while for the vehicles we use the Android porting of CBMC-GC. In our test-bed, the fog node runs on a Ubuntu 16.04.5 virtual machine with a dual core and 2 Gbyte of RAM, and the client on a Radio with Android 6.0, Quad-core at 1.2 GHZ and 1 Gbyte of RAM.

**Security Consideration of CBMC-GC.** The authors claim that their framework provides security in the *honest-but-curious* attacker model in which an attacker follows all the steps of the protocol as per specifications. However, attacker's goal is to get information on the other party during the message exchanging phase, with the purpose of acquiring at least part of the private profile.

Another situation to point out is that there is an asymmetry on the provided security guarantees as customary in 2PC. This makes very difficult to prevent one

**Fig. 5.** Our android radio used in the test-bed.

party from terminating the protocol prematurely, and not sending the outcome of the computation to the other party. This situation can be discovered by the weak party, but cannot be recovered from.

## 6.1  Evaluation

As first step, we compare the driver reputation with the reputation threshold fixed on the fog node to discriminate between "good" and "bad" drivers. If the value of the vehicle reputation is larger than the threshold, the vehicle gets 1, otherwise 0. In case of equal values, the output is 2. The source code for this function is reported in Listing 1.1.

**Listing 1.1.** C function to compare driver's reputation

```
int compare(int x, int y) {
  if (x > y)
    return 0;
  else if (x == y)
    return 2;
  else
    return 1;
}

void comparerep(int INPUT_A_thr, int INPUT_B_rep) {
  int OUTPUT_rep = compare(INPUT_A_thr, INPUT_B_rep);
}
```

Figure 6a shows the time needed to execute the function listed in the code 1.1 using CBMC-GC and grouped in the table represented in Fig. 6b. In particular, we compare the running time when executing the vehicle part on the Android Radio, and when executing it on the same place of the fog node. This comparison is labelled as *Radio* and *Localhost* on the figure and table. The reported times are obtained by running the code in Listing 1.1 ten times. The two lines in the figure represent the average calculated for each of the ten executions. So, the

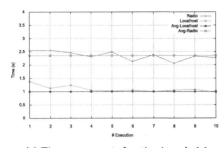

(a) Times to compute function in code 1.1

| Localhost (sec) | Radio (sec) |
|---|---|
| 1,381 | 2,553 |
| 1,127 | 2,558 |
| 1,246 | 2,456 |
| 1,049 | 2,311 |
| 1,026 | 2,486 |
| 1,052 | 2,134 |
| 0,999 | 2,377 |
| 1,049 | 2,063 |
| 1,074 | 2,330 |
| 0,971 | 2,270 |

(b) Performances of execution of code 1.1

**Fig. 6.** Global reputation comparison function

average time to execute the function in the privacy-preserving manner using the radio is of 2, 354 s. Instead, when the STC protocol is run in localhost the average time is of ∼1s.

If the driver is considered "good", then, a finer comparison on parameter is made. In fact, the code in Listing 1.2 illustrates the $C$ function written to make the comparison for each of the considered parameters:

**Listing 1.2.** C function to compare driver's parameters

```
int compare(int x, int y) {
   if (x > y)
      return 1;
   else if (x == y)
      return 2;
   else
      return 0;
}

void profile(int INPUT_A_brake, int INPUT_B_brake, int INPUT_A_turn, int
    INPUT_B_turn, int INPUT_A_speed, int INPUT_B_speed, int INPUT_A_rpm,
    int INPUT_B_rpm) {
   int OUTPUT_brake = compare(INPUT_A_brake, INPUT_B_brake);
   int OUTPUT_turn = compare(INPUT_A_turn, INPUT_B_turn);
   int OUTPUT_speed = compare(INPUT_A_speed, INPUT_B_speed);
   int OUTPUT_rpm = compare(INPUT_A_rpm, INPUT_B_rpm);
}
```

The main function *profile* takes as input the driver's profile and four different thresholds of each service provided by the infrastructure. The driver's input has as prefix *INPUT_A_*, instead the thresholds have as prefix *INPUT_B_*. These numbers are simple integer and in the profile are numbers that range from 0 to 5. Same interval is given to the threshold number.

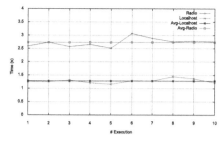

(a) Times to compute function in code 1.2

| Server (sec) | Radio (sec) |
|---|---|
| 1.254 | 2.593 |
| 1,253 | 2,737 |
| 1,313 | 2,575 |
| 1,211 | 2,658 |
| 1,158 | 2,518 |
| 1,285 | 3,068 |
| 1,281 | 2,891 |
| 1,442 | 2,762 |
| 1,366 | 2,789 |
| 1,213 | 2,766 |

(b) Performances of execution of code 1.2

**Fig. 7.** Paramater comparison function

Then, the code contains a single function that simply compares each reputation parameter with the corresponding threshold. In particular, the *compare* function provides as output three different states, which are:

- *1*: if the value of the driver is higher than the threshold;
- *0*: if the value of the driver is lower than the threshold;
- *2*: if the values are the same.

Hence, each reputation-based service will apply the discount on the basis of the comparison results. For instance, the **Reputation-aware fuel cost** service will apply the discount when the result of the comparison function is 1 for the RPM parameter, while the service **Reputation-aware tolling** will apply the discount when the comparison function output is 1 for the speed parameter.

So, each time that the *compare* function is called, the output of the comparison is given to the $OUTPUT\_*$ variable that can be read at the end of the STC execution.

Figure 7a shows the time needed to execute the function listed in the code 1.2 using the CBMC-GC framework. Times are reported in the table in Fig. 7b. Also in this case, we compare the running time when executing the vehicle part on the Android Radio, and when executing it on the same place of the server. The average time to execute the function in the privacy-preserving manner using the radio is of $2,736$ s. Instead, when the STC protocol is run in localhost the average time is of $1,278$ s.

Summarizing, the results of our prototype evaluation clearly shows the feasibility of the proposed privacy-preserving framework, as the running times of the related secure functions are below 3 s in all the considered scenarios and hardware configurations.

# 7   Discussion

In the current paper, we based on the driver DNA on the radar graph introduced in [12] and we considered it as initial starting and studying step for our reputation calculations. However, the type of parameters as well as the number of those considered in the reputation formula may be extended or replaced with others. In addition, parameters selection depends on the support of the vehicles architecture. In fact, values are gathered from the internal network of a vehicle, for instance the CAN bus, and, to properly read this information, a hardware support may be needed to get accurate values for each parameter involved in the reputation formula. In our experiments, the adoption of our Android Infotainment system allowed us to get the needed parameters that were directly decoded from the information derived from the CAN bus of the vehicle.

Another aspect that can be considered but it is not part of the present work, is the manipulation of the information coming from the vehicle internal network to calculate the reputation formula. The presence of a physical attacker on the vehicle is not taken under consideration and this will not alter the calculus of the driver's reputation. To prevent this issue, different actions should be taken under consideration. However, it is not in the scope of this paper. For instance, the adoption of a secure internal vehicular protocol may reduce or avoid the presence of attacks on the physical bus to alter the transmitted content. Works on this topic are [2,17,21].

# 8    Conclusion and Future Work

In this paper, the notion of driver's reputation profile is introduced as a unique, multi-dimensional information associated to a driver's behavior. As an example, we have described how reputation profiles can be built starting from the *driver DNA* and a synthetic *reputation score*, respectively. Moreover, we propose a private vehicular infrastructure based on both fog and cloud networks, which is able to both collect the information needed to compute driver reputation profiles, and to provide reputation-aware services to the driver themselves. The proposed infrastructure and related reputation-aware automotive services have the potential to stimulate drivers to behave correctly to a much larger extent than what achieved by current practice based on risk profiling and personalized insurance rates. Through prototype implementation, we have tested and positively assessed the feasibility of a privacy-preserving implementation of the framework.

This work is intended to open more avenues for future research, rather than to present a fully developed system. In particular, we plan to assess the proposed framework on real test cases considering design and development of vehicles' evolution. This may require a more complex calculation of the reputation formulas that, for instance, consider benefits from the adoption of an hybrid engine that gets the support of the electric power. It could also require to move form a secure two party computation approach to a multi-party one in which reputation values are exchanged among more than two entities.

Another interesting points that we will investigate as future work is the multi-user driving scenario. Nowadays, modern vehicles support different driving styles that come out from different drivers. So, based on the current management of multiple-users, like traditional computers that supports different logins, the reputation of a user may be more accurate considering this additional feature.

**Acknowledgement.** This work has been partially supported by the GAUSS national research project (MIUR, PRIN 2015, n 2015KWREMX) and by H2020 EU-funded projects C3ISP (GA n700294).

# References

1. Andrew, C., Yao, C.: Protocols for secure computations. In 23rd IEEE Symposium on FOCS, pp. 160–164 (1982)
2. Bella, G., Biondi, P., Costantino, G., Matteucci, I.: TOUCAN: a protocol to secure controller area network. In: Proceedings of the ACM Workshop on Automotive Cybersecurity, AutoSec@CODASPY 2019, Richardson, TX, USA, 27 March 2019, pp. 3–8 (2019)
3. Ben-David, A., Nisan, N., Pinkas, B.: FairplayMP: a system for secure multi-party computation. In Proceedings of the CCS Conference, pp. 257–266. ACM, New York (2008)
4. Bonsall, P., Liu, R., Young, W.: Modelling safety-related driving behaviour-impact of parameter values. Transp. Res. Part A Policy Pract. **39**(5), 425–444 (2005)
5. Buescher, N.: CBMC-GC-2 (2018). https://gitlab.com/securityengineering/CBMC-GC-2
6. Buescher, N., Holzer, A., Weber, A., Katzenbeisser, S.: Compiling low depth circuits for practical secure computation. In: Askoxylakis, I., Ioannidis, S., Katsikas, S., Meadows, C. (eds.) ESORICS 2016. LNCS, vol. 9879, pp. 80–98. Springer, Cham (2016). https://doi.org/10.1007/978-3-319-45741-3_5
7. Costantino, G., Maiti, R.R., Martinelli, F., Santi, P.: Private mobility-cast for opportunistic networks. Comput. Netw. **120**, 28–42 (2017)
8. Costantino, G., Martinelli, F., Santi, P., Amoruso, D.: An implementation of secure two-party computation for smartphones with application to privacy-preserving interest-cast. In: Proceedings of the 18th International Conference Mobicom, pp. 447–450. ACM (2012)
9. Eboli, L., Mazzulla, G., Pungillo, G.: Combining speed and acceleration to define car users' safe or unsafe driving behaviour. Transp. Res. Part C Emerg. Technol. **68**, 113–125 (2016)
10. Filev, D., Lu, J., Tseng, F., Prakah-Asante, K.: Real-time driver characterization during car following using stochastic evolving models. In: 2011 IEEE International Conference on Systems Man and Cybernetics (SMC), pp. 1031–103 (2011)
11. Fracchia, R., Meo, M.: Analysis and design of warning delivery service in intervehicular networks. IEEE Trans. Mobile Comput. **7**(7), 832–845 (2008)
12. Fugiglando, U., Santi, P., Milardo, S., Abida, K., Ratti, C.: Characterizing the "driver DNA" through can bus data analysis. In: Proceedings of the 2nd ACM International Workshop on Smart, Autonomous, and Connected Vehicular Systems and Services, CarSys 2017, pp. 37–41. ACM, New York (2017)
13. Holzer, A., Franz, M., Katzenbeisser, S., Veith, H.: Secure two-party computations in ANSI C. In: Proceedings of the CCS Conference, CCS 2012, NY, USA, pp. 772–783 (2012)
14. Huang, Y., Chapman, P., Evans, D.: Privacy-preserving applications on smartphones. In: Proceedings of the 6th USENIX conference on Hot topics in security, HotSec 2011, Berkeley, CA, USA, p. 4 (2011). USENIX Association

15. European Telecommunications Standards Institute: ETSI TS 102 940: Intelligent Transport Systems (ITS); Security; ITS communications security architecture and security management, September 2010. https://www.etsi.org/deliver/etsi_ts/102900_102999/102940/01.01.01_60/ts_102940v010101p.pdf
16. Kolesnikov, V., Schneider, T.: Improved garbled circuit: free XOR gates and applications. In: Aceto, L., Damgård, I., Goldberg, L.A., Halldórsson, M.M., Ingólfsdóttir, A., Walukiewicz, I. (eds.) ICALP 2008. LNCS, vol. 5126, pp. 486–498. Springer, Heidelberg (2008). https://doi.org/10.1007/978-3-540-70583-3_40
17. Kurachi, R., Matsubara, Y., Takada, H., Adachi, N., Miyashita, Y., Horihata, S.: CaCAN-centralized authentication system in CAN (controller area network). In: 14th International Conference on Embedded Security in Cars, ESCAR 2014 (2014)
18. Malkhi, D., Nisan, N., Pinkas, B., Sella, Y.: Fairplay—a secure two-party computation system. In: Proceedings of the 13th conference on USENIX Security Symposium, SSYM 2004, Berkeley, CA, USA, vol. 13, p. 20 (2004). USENIX Association
19. Massaro, E., et al.: The car as an ambient sensing platform. Proc. IEEE **105**(1), 1–5 (2017)
20. The European Parliament and of the Council. Directive 2010/40/eu. eur-lex.europa.eu. 7 July 2010
21. You, I., Jung, E.-S.: A light weight authentication protocol for digital home networks. In: Gavrilova, M.L., et al. (eds.) ICCSA 2006. LNCS, vol. 3983, pp. 416–423. Springer, Heidelberg (2006). https://doi.org/10.1007/11751632_45
22. Rønning, A.: Rewarding safe drivers could make roads safer. ScienceNordic. 12 September 2013. http://sciencenordic.com/rewarding-safe-drivers-could-make-roads-safer. Accessed 22 March 2021
23. Satyanarayanan, M., Bahl, P., Caceres, R., Davies, N.: The case for VM-based cloudlets in mobile computing. IEEE Pervasive Comput. **8**(4), 14–23 (2009)
24. Stojmenovic, I., Wen, S.: The fog computing paradigm: scenarios and security issues. In: Federated Conference on Computer Science and Information Systems, 7–10 September 2014, pp. 1–8 (2014)
25. Vaquero, L.M., Rodero-Merino, L.: Finding your way in the fog: towards a comprehensive definition of fog computing. SIGCOMM Comput. Commun. Rev. **44**(5), 27–32 (2014)
26. Zeeman, A.S., Booysen, M.J.: Combining speed and acceleration to detect reckless driving in the informal public transport industry. In 16th International IEEE Conference on Intelligent Transportation Systems, ITSC 2013, The Hague, The Netherlands, 6–9 October 2013, pp. 756–761 (2013)

# Case Study: Disclosure of Indirect Device Fingerprinting in Privacy Policies

Julissa Milligan, Sarah Scheffler[✉], Andrew Sellars, Trishita Tiwari,
Ari Trachtenberg, and Mayank Varia

Boston University, Boston, USA
sscheff@bu.edu

**Abstract.** Recent developments in online tracking make it harder for individuals to detect and block trackers. This is especially true for device fingerprinting techniques that websites use to identify and track individual devices. Direct trackers – those that directly ask the device for identifying information – can often be blocked with browser configurations or other simple techniques. However, some sites have shifted to indirect tracking methods, which attempt to uniquely identify a device by asking the browser to perform a seemingly-unrelated task. One type of indirect tracking known as *Canvas fingerprinting* causes the browser to render a graphic recording rendering statistics as a unique identifier. Even experts find it challenging to discern some indirect fingerprinting methods. In this work, we aim to observe how indirect device fingerprinting methods are disclosed in privacy policies, and consider whether the disclosures are sufficient to enable website visitors to block the tracking methods. We compare these disclosures to the disclosure of direct fingerprinting methods on the same websites.

Our case study analyzes one indirect fingerprinting technique, *Canvas fingerprinting*. We use an existing automated detector of this fingerprinting technique to conservatively detect its use on Alexa Top 500 websites that cater to United States consumers, and we examine the privacy policies of the resulting 28 websites. Disclosures of indirect fingerprinting vary in specificity. None described the specific methods with enough granularity to know the website used Canvas fingerprinting. Conversely, many sites did provide enough detail about usage of direct fingerprinting methods to allow a website visitor to reliably detect and block those techniques.

We conclude that indirect fingerprinting methods are often technically difficult to detect, and are not identified with specificity in legal privacy notices. This makes indirect fingerprinting more difficult to block, and therefore risks disturbing the tentative armistice between individuals and websites currently in place for direct fingerprinting. This paper illustrates

S. Scheffler—Supported by a Clare Boothe Luce Graduate Research Fellowship and a Google Ph.D. Fellowship.
This material is based on work supported by the National Science Foundation under Grants CNS-1414119, CCF-1563753, and CNS-1915763.

T. Groß and T. Tryfonas (Eds.): STAST 2019, LNCS 11739, pp. 175–186, 2021.
https://doi.org/10.1007/978-3-030-55958-8_10

differences in fingerprinting approaches, and explains why technologists, technology lawyers, and policymakers need to appreciate the challenges of indirect fingerprinting.

# 1 Introduction

Companies employ a variety of "fingerprinting" techniques to track consumers' identities online. These fingerprints are used to identify – or at least significantly narrow the range of possibilities for – repeated visits to a site by the same device or individual, or within the same location or web browsing session. In this work, we focus on device fingerprinting over the web: code on the server of a website (rather than in email or dedicated applications) that seeks to uniquely identify each consumer device that visits the site. Device fingerprinting can often identify a single device in a manner that persists across browsing sessions, that is throughout usage at different physical and virtual locations and among different people. We provide a brief summary of direct and indirect methods for device fingerprinting in the next section, and we refer interested readers to the following surveys for more detail [1,2,7,19].

From a purely technological viewpoint, the current evolution of device fingerprinting is akin to a cat-and-mouse game. Companies seek increasingly detailed data and collection techniques to increase their confidence that they have identified a similar device across different visits. Individuals can respond by declining to visit certain sites or using blocking software that seeks to prevent those companies from obtaining information that could be used to identify the visitors. Companies can then refuse to serve their site to individuals using blockers, and so on. This cat-and-mouse game plays out across many websites.

Anecdotally, much of the web seems to have settled upon a kind of détente at the intersection of technology and policy: companies disclose that they track devices and use reasonably transparent (or at least detectable) "direct" tracking technologies, and the small percentage of consumers who do object to such tracking use technological tools such as ad blockers to inhibit tracking. Many companies nevertheless welcome these tracking-inhibiting visitors on their sites.

"Indirect" or "inference-based" fingerprinting works differently, using methods that serve a purpose unrelated to tracking, like the HTML5 Canvas API, to develop a unique device identifier. Because these techniques are typically dual-use – that is, they can fingerprint a user or alternatively perform different user-friendly function on the website – it is more challenging to detect whether they are used as trackers. Indeed, there are few public tools that can detect or block indirect fingerprinting, and these tools might themselves be detected by websites and used to fingerprint [17].

A privacy-aware user might therefore turn to a company's privacy policy to determine whether a site uses indirect fingerprinting techniques. One purpose of such privacy policies is to tell consumers what type of data the site collects. A technologically savvy individual could, in theory, review the disclosed fingerprinting methods and design a technical response that meets her comfort level, which the website could accept or reject. In practice, many sites strike a balance between disclosure and readability, and thus they purposely avoid some technical details about how data is collected. But if a privacy policy does not contain technical details about which indirect tracking methods it uses, creating a technical block against indirect fingerprinting becomes much more difficult.

In this paper, we examine changes in tracking technology over the past half-decade, and study how websites explain Canvas fingerprinting in their privacy policies. We illustrate the differences between direct and indirect fingerprinting. We analyze the disclosure of indirect fingerprinting in privacy policies to consider how these techniques may destabilize the delicate direct-fingerprinting truce between websites and visitors. Finally, we consider whether these differences are important to potential technical and legal responses.

## 2  Device Fingerprinting

### 2.1  Direct Fingerprinting

One common way to identify a device is to directly ask the device for identifying information. For example, websites can use one of several Application Programming Interface (API) calls to elicit a client browser to send device information, such as its operating system or Internet Protocol (IP) address, or to store identifying information locally for future use (e.g., cookies). Widely-deployed techniques that websites use in this manner include:

- Collecting header information transmitted through the standard HTTP exchange, and using the uniqueness of that data to develop a distinguishable profile;
- Embedding discreet objects (web beacons, tracking pixels, or clear GIFs) within a common third-party website, which can be used to track access patterns; or
- Placing a cookie on the site, either directly or through a third-party tracker.

These techniques enable web servers both to personalize web services (e.g., for language or region) and to fingerprint the device, often simultaneously or in an intertwined manner.

Direct fingerprinting methods are easy to detect, understand, and reset. When used, direct fingerprinting techniques are typically simple to detect because they operate similarly on all websites and rarely obfuscate their true intention. Novice users can use a web browser's built-in features or download a plugin to identify their use. Additionally, expert consumers can examine a log of all interactions between the web server and the client browser to understand precisely the type of information obtained by the server and (unless it is encrypted at rest or in transit by the server) read its contents. Once detected, many direct fingerprinting methods have "reset" mechanisms that decouple future visits to a website from previous ones; for instance, deleting a cookie with a unique identifier can have this effect.

Individuals can also proactively block unwanted direct tracking by appropriately configuring their client. For example, if a visitor does not want a web server to learn her device's operating system, she can configure her browser to block or falsify the responses to common requests that reveal her operating system, including the User-Agent field of the HTTP header, and the navigator.userAgent and navigator.platform properties of the navigator object within JavaScript. Indeed, modern web browsers give users the ability to block or control cookie storage, and third-party tools like Adblock Plus and Privacy Badger allow users to selectively block connections and cookies from websites that are known to serve ads, web beacons, and other direct trackers. These blocks can be persistent, in that blocking one direct request for specific information will block all future requests for the same information. In this way, a user is empowered to transform the binary choice presented by accessing a website – use the website with these tracking features, or do not use the website at all – into a negotiated environment. She can use the website and control some of the information that the website obtains about her.

## 2.2    Inference-Based, or Indirect, Fingerprinting

In contrast, *inference-based device fingerprinting* is a newer set of tracking techniques that use different tools to achieve the same goal. Rather than directly querying the browser about its localizing features, the server will instead instruct the browser to perform a seemingly-unrelated computing task such as rendering text, audio, a picture, or an animation. Different devices with different configurations, installed libraries, and hardware will perform the task in slightly different ways, and these subtle differences can be measured and summarized by the server, creating a fingerprint for the device. Many techniques for web servers to conduct indirect device fingerprinting have arisen over the last decade, including:

- Measurements of JavaScript performance [13] and conformance [16],
- Font enumeration [10],
- Graphics Processing Unit (GPU) behavior measurement [3],
- VRAM detection [2, p. 5],
- Sensor data access [6], and
- Techniques that use HTML5 APIs [18].

One of these HTML5 APIs is known as the Canvas API. Normally used for rendering graphics or video on a screen [15], the Canvas can also be used to fingerprint devices [14] by instructing the client device to render some text or gradients in the client browser, and then reading back the exact pixel data of the image rendered by the browser. The image used in a popular open-source fingerprinting script fingerprintjs2 is shown in Fig. 1. The resulting fingerprints are highly effective because they are both highly distinguishing (a large number of machines yield different renderings) and highly stable (the same machine repeatedly yields the same result). The team behind the anonymity-seeking Tor Browser has called Canvas fingerprinting "the single largest fingerprinting threat browsers face today" [20], aside from plugins such as Flash. Indeed, Englehardt and Narayanan [8] also performed an extensive study in 2016 on the top 1 million websites, and found that 14,371 of those websites employed Canvas fingerprinting. Of these, they found that 98.2% of the Canvas fingerprinting scripts came from third party websites from around 400 domains.

In this study, we focus on Canvas fingerprinting because it is a reasonably detectable indirect fingerprinting method that has been well-studied over the last six years, and there are consequently well-justified heuristics provided by Acar et al. [1] and Englehardt and Narayanan [8] that distinguish fingerprinting uses of Canvas from non-fingerprinting uses.

**Fig. 1.** Graphic sent to clients to draw in Canvas fingerprinting script within open-source fingerprinting script https://github.com/Valve/fingerprintjs2, commit 563dbde. The way in which the graphic is drawn can be used to fingerprint the client's device.

Unlike direct tracking techniques, there are relatively few tools available to detect or understand Canvas fingerprinting. To analyze whether a Canvas query is being used at all requires a deeper inspection of the interchange between server and client than inspecting one's own HTTP header, identifying a cookie request, or observing third-party websites calls in the chain of HTTP requests made when loading a website. Even if an individual does observe the use of a Canvas query, it is hard to know whether it is used to fingerprint a device or for some other legitimate graphical purpose. A Canvas API call could use the information from the web client to create a unique fingerprint, to check whether the client rendered an image correctly, or to determine how to properly organize information on the client's screen. To distinguish between these options, the user would need to predict how the server is (or will be) processing the resulting data.

Furthermore, tools that allow consumers to automatically mask, reset, or block Canvas queries are not as well-known as their counterparts to block direct tracking. For example, Adblock Plus, a common ad-blocker, has 11 million average daily users on Firefox. In contrast, no public tools to effectively block the fingerprinting existed in 2014 [1], and only a few browser add-ons/extensions are available today. The most popular Firefox add-on for blocking Canvas fingerprinting has only about 46,000 average daily users as of August 2019.

These tools also may not persistently block the fingerprinting, because the precise way that a website configures a Canvas query to fingerprint a device may change over time. Common tools to block direct fingerprinting tend to target fixed web content and objects – most commonly HTTP header information, cookies, and connections to third-party websites. With Canvas queries, however, the fingerprinting scripts could easily be changed, obfuscated, or combined with commonly used scripts. This could make it more difficult to detect or block fingerprinting scripts without breaking the functionality of many websites. In our experiments, we were able to easily detect Canvas fingerprinting websites that use minor variations of five dedicated fingerprinting scripts. It is possible we did not detect existing obfuscated fingerprinting techniques.

# 3    What Do Privacy Policies Say About Fingerprinting?

We studied the ways tracking techniques are discussed in privacy disclosures to better understand how users might learn about direct versus indirect tracking. Specifically, we examined 28 privacy policies of websites that appear to use Canvas queries for fingerprinting purposes. In the United States, the collection of consumer browsing data on commercial websites is generally regulated by the Federal Trade Commission, which polices unfair and deceptive acts or practices in or affecting commerce.[1] When a company is not operating in a sector that is specifically regulated by another statute (e.g., healthcare or finance), the primary obligation on companies is to provide accurate information about how the site collects and discloses user data so that a reasonable consumer has meaningful choice about whether to submit to those practices.[2]

A privacy policy for a company could reveal information about fingerprinting by disclosing the specific information it gathers, or by discussing the techniques it uses to obtain information. Many policies use some combination of these disclosures. With respect to fingerprinting, a policy could specifically explain whether and/or how the company uses fingerprinting technology, or it could discuss what data it collects, leaving the inference about which fingerprinting technique it uses to the consumer. Of course, it could also disclose both technology and data. We examine the level of specificity of these privacy policy disclosures below. These disclosures provide a useful base from which to consider further whether indirect fingerprinting methods, such as Canvas, are well-known or widely-publicized techniques.

## 3.1    Methodology

To find instances of Canvas fingerprinting on popular websites, we conducted two web crawls of the Alexa top 500 websites using the code accompanying Acar et al.'s 2014 study [1]. Run 1 ran on January 15, 2019 from 2:19 am to 1:55 pm EST and found Canvas fingerprinting on 40 out of 470 successful connections. Run 2 ran from January 15 at 4:22 pm EST to January 16 at 3:48 pm EST and found Canvas fingerprinting on 42 out of 484 successful connections. In total, across both runs, we found 49 unique websites that had fingerprinting scripts.

---

[1] 15 U.S.C. §45(a)(1),(n).

[2] See, e.g., *In re Liberty Fin. Cos., FTC No. C-3891.*

Because our expertise is focused on privacy law within the United States, we manually inspected these 49 webpages and filtered them based on the following two criteria.

1. The website's main page is written in English (30 of 49 websites).
2. The website and its associated privacy policy are written for an audience of U.S. consumers. We discarded 1 site with the country-specific domain .co.uk and 1 site for an Indian bank lacking a physical presence in the U.S.

We manually reviewed the privacy policies of the remaining 28 websites[3] between January–July 2019 to determine which disclosures in their policies are intended to inform consumers about their use of Canvas fingerprinting. At least one legal scholar and one technologist on our team read each privacy policy and identified all statements that explicitly or implicitly refer to device fingerprinting.

## 3.2   Results

All 28 privacy policies share two features in common: they all indicate that the site uniquely identifies individual devices, and none of them state specifically that the site uses Canvas fingerprinting. Otherwise, the 28 privacy policies vary substantially in the specificity of disclosures regarding tracking techniques. We identified three categories of privacy policy disclosures of Canvas fingerprinting: (1) broad, technology-agnostic language, (2) disclosure of specific direct fingerprinting techniques but not indirect techniques, and (3) specific mention of collecting "device fingerprints" as distinct from other device-specific identifiers.

One set of privacy policies uses very broad and technology-agnostic language that covers the capture of granular, device fingerprinting data, but provides little guidance on specific techniques or types of information captured. For example, the privacy policy of the website CNET (which is part of CBS, and uses CBS' general Privacy Policy) states that it collects "[u]nique identifiers and connection information" of various sorts [4]. Other sites simply note that they collect "information about your use of the Website, and/or mobile application" [5].

A second group of policies provide more detailed information about how a site collects data using older tracking technologies, and less specific information about the types of data they collect through fingerprinting. The majority of privacy policies investigated fell into this category. Yelp, for example, states that it may store data "such as your browser type, type of computer or mobile device, browser language, IP address, WiFi information such as SSID, mobile carrier, phone number, unique device identifier, advertising identifier, location (including geolocation, beacon-based location, and GPS location), and requested and referring URLs" [22]. This list appears to specifically call out the data typically

---

[3] These sites are americanexpress.com, aol.com, asos.com, bestbuy.com, cambridge.org, capitalone.com, cnet.com, coinmarketcap.com, dell.com, drugs.com, fiverr.com, forbes.com, foxnews.com, homedepot.com, ikea.com, livescore.com, msn.com, nike.com, shutterstock.com, slickdeals.net, sonyliv.com, speedtest.net, thesaurus.com, udemy.com, upwork.com, weather.com, yelp.com, and zillow.com.

obtained from direct tracking techniques like cookies or HTTP header information. The list is non-exhaustive, and fingerprinting appears to be covered under the open-ended "unique device identifier." That said, the specific disclosures appear more tailored to older tracking techniques than to fingerprinting. The Fox News Privacy Policy states that "[i]f you access the Fox News Services from a mobile or other device, we may collect a unique device identifier assigned to that device, geolocation data (including your precise location), or other transactional information for that device," which reads broadly enough to embrace Canvas data [12]. Forbes lists its collection by identification technique, specifically stating that it collects data through "cookies," "web beacons," and "log files." It also acknowledges that Forbes may retain any "information automatically collected about your usage of the Site" [11]. That open-ended disclosure may well encompass fingerprinting techniques, but the policy does not expressly identify Canvas or other indirect fingerprinting technologies in the same way it identifies some direct tracking techniques.

We also identified one policy that specifically states the website uses device fingerprinting, but it does not call out the fingerprinting technique that it uses – Canvas fingerprinting – or explain what data it collects using Canvas fingerprinting. Udemy's privacy policy lists "device or browser fingerprints" along with other tracking methods it uses [21]. Describing device fingerprinting specifically *in addition* to all the other information collected suggests that the website is indirectly obtaining a fingerprint by measuring the device's responses (e.g. to Canvas queries), as opposed to simply using direct queries, even of device-specific IDs.

### 3.3   Observations

In short, most privacy policies generally describe *what* information is collected rather than providing details on the *method* of collection. Those that do list specific tracking technologies tend to omit fingerprinting. And the site that listed fingerprinting did not state which methods of fingerprinting it deployed. This may suggest that the public and perhaps the lawyers who draft privacy policies may not yet be aware of more recent indirect fingerprinting techniques.

Of note, some of the privacy policies may be written to comply with the European Union's General Data Protection Regulation (GDPR) [9]. If the GDPR requires attorneys to more deeply understand and explain the website's tracking practices at a technical level, we would expect to see greater clarity in the way in which fingerprinting, or the data collected thereby, is described in privacy policies. Companies may seek to harmonize policies across jurisdictions, and this increased understanding and explanation could benefit people from non-EU member nations (like the United States) as well. However, that shift did not jump out in the policies we reviewed at this point in time.

More to the point, even when a policy states that the website uses fingerprinting, it may be difficult to identify which indirect fingerprinting methods the website uses. All companies in our review indicated that they collect information that could be used to identify a device – putting consumers on notice that the site likely correlates user browsing behavior over time. However, the policies we reviewed did not provide enough information about how data is collected to allow even savvy individuals to access the website while proactively blocking such collection or retrospectively resetting an identifier held by the website.

### 3.4   Consumer Responses

For direct fingerprinting methods, this gap appears to be surmountable. A consumer wishing to hide his browser type may alter her `User-Agent` and the relevant fields of the JavaScript `navigator` object, since these are the relevant methods a website might use to directly query this information. She need not know the details of the server's code, since there are limited methods to query this information directly.

However, for indirect fingerprinting methods, even a consumer who is both legally and technologically savvy finds little recourse to tracking from either of her areas of expertise. The individual must first know that a functionality seemingly unrelated to fingerprinting (like Canvas) can be used to fingerprint. She must then inspect each use of the functionality and infer whether the purpose is related to fingerprinting or not. This process could involve an inspection of client-side code (e.g. the JavaScript code generating the image in Fig. 1), or heuristics that make an educated guess as to how the server-side code will process the information it receives. The website's privacy policy does not provide her with any guidance on how to perform any of the above steps. Ultimately, to use the website without being fingerprinted, she must choose between being cautious by overzealously blocking useful website components, or being overconfident that she has blocked all the tracking that is personally objectionable and missing an indirect fingerprinting method.

## 4   Indirect Fingerprinting Shifts the Balance Between Individuals and Websites

Indirect fingerprinting can be technologically difficult to identify, and may not be specifically identified in privacy policies. These properties make indirect fingerprinting different than direct methods, where a rough armistice has evolved between consumers and websites.

### 4.1   Disturbing a Delicate Armistice

Direct fingerprinting techniques are often identifiable technologically. They can also be inferred from the disclosures made in the privacy policy, either because they are explicitly mentioned or because the policy discloses that it collects data typically obtained using direct fingerprinting. Once detected, tools are available (although not universally adopted) to thwart such attempts at fingerprinting. Many of these tools have been adopted by enough consumers that many websites complain about the use of these techniques and their effect on advertising revenue. Websites have a technological countermeasure of their own: they can detect and deny access to consumers who deploy ad-blocking technologies. While some websites use these anti-blocking tools, most websites opt to accept privacy-aware consumers who block direct fingerprinting. Put simply: we think the ad blocking arms race has reached a de facto armistice in which privacy-aware consumers can choose whether to block direct fingerprinting, and websites can choose whether to accept consumers who opt to block.

However, indirect fingerprinting disrupts this armistice. Indirect fingerprinting techniques are harder to technically detect and block, and easier for the company to change and obfuscate. These techniques can serve a functional end beyond fingerprinting a device, so it is harder to predict whether the website is using the relevant technique to persistently identify the user or for some other purpose. Indirect fingerprinting methods are not yet well-known to the general public, and privacy policies do not specifically describe indirect device finger-printing methods – even policies that do describe direct methods. In short, consumers do not have an accessible way to learn a website's indirect fingerprinting practices.

In the short term, individuals who are unaware of indirect fingerprinting techniques may mistakenly believe that tools like Adblock Plus and Privacy Badger are sufficient to prevent tracking. In the longer run, individuals (or the developers of privacy tools they use) will need to be aware of evolving ways to fingerprint devices indirectly using an existing API call, and develop methods to detect and block each of these new methods as they are invented.

## 4.2   A Path Forward

The authors of this article have different views about the best path forward and whether any alternative is better than the current state of affairs. The spectrum of options ranges from maintaining the status quo while calling attention to these new techniques, to removing consumer choice entirely and imposing privacy defaults by law.

The area between these options illustrates multiple tradeoffs. For example, changing FTC guidance to instruct websites to list all tracking practices would increase public information about indirect tracking but would make privacy policies longer, more cumbersome, and less comprehensible to non-technical readers. Requiring companies by law to provide legal or technological means to block and/or reset individual identifiers would increase consumer choice but would put new burdens on companies and could adversely impact competition.

It may be possible to use a combination of tools to increase consumer choice while minimizing other costs. For instance, a social campaign to heighten public awareness about device fingerprinting might spur consumers to choose sites that avoid fingerprinting. Alternatively, larger liability for breaches of unique device identifiers might lead websites to reconsider the value of gathering them.

This work brought together authors with different fundamental perspectives about the appropriate role for law and regulation in the context of privacy and consumer protection. Despite our differences, we reached consensus on the technological and legal state of affairs and improved our understanding of the trade-offs. We hope this paper lays the foundation for additional conversations and improves the quality of the debate.

# References

1. Acar, G., Eubank, C., Englehardt, S., Juarez, M., Narayanan, A., Diaz, C.: The web never forgets: persistent tracking mechanisms in the wild. In: Proceedings of the 2014 ACM SIGSAC Conference on Computer and Communications Security, pp. 674–689. ACM (2014)
2. Alaca, F., van Oorschot, P.C.: Device fingerprinting for augmenting web authentication: classification and analysis of methods. In: Proceedings of the 32nd Annual Conference on Computer Security Applications, pp. 289–301. ACM (2016)
3. Cao, Y., Li, S., Wijmans, E.: (Cross-)browser fingerprinting via OS and hardware level features. In: Proceedings of Network & Distributed System Security Symposium. The Internet Society (2017)
4. CBS: CBS privacy policy highlights (2019). https://www.cbsinteractive.com/legal/cbsi/privacy-policy/highlights. Accessed 26 Jan 2019
5. CoinMarketCap: Privacy and cookie policy (2019). https://coinmarketcap.com/privacy/. Accessed 9 July 2019
6. Das, A., Acar, G., Borisov, N., Pradeep, A.: The web's sixth sense: a study of scripts accessing smartphone sensors. In: Proceedings of the 2018 ACM SIGSAC Conference on Computer and Communications Security, pp. 1515–1532. ACM (2018)
7. Eckersley, P.: How unique is your web browser? In: Atallah, M.J., Hopper, N.J. (eds.) PETS 2010. LNCS, vol. 6205, pp. 1–18. Springer, Heidelberg (2010). https://doi.org/10.1007/978-3-642-14527-8_1
8. Englehardt, S., Narayanan, A.: Online tracking: a 1-million-site measurement and analysis. In: Proceedings of the 2016 ACM SIGSAC Conference on Computer and Communications Security, pp. 1388–1401. ACM (2016)
9. European Parliament and Council of the European Union: General Data Protection Regulation (2016)
10. Fifield, D., Egelman, S.: Fingerprinting web users through font metrics. In: Böhme, R., Okamoto, T. (eds.) FC 2015. LNCS, vol. 8975, pp. 107–124. Springer, Heidelberg (2015). https://doi.org/10.1007/978-3-662-47854-7_7
11. Forbes: Forbes.com privacy statement (2018). https://www.forbes.com/privacy/english/#5825f0013061. Accessed 26 Jan 2019
12. Fox News: Privacy policy (2018). https://www.foxnews.com/privacy-policy. Accessed 26 Jan 2019
13. Mowery, K., Bogenreif, D., Yilek, S., Shacham, H.: Fingerprinting information in JavaScript implementations. In: Proceedings of W2SP, vol. 2, no. 11 (2011)
14. Mowery, K., Shacham, H.: Pixel perfect: fingerprinting canvas in HTML5. In: Proceedings of W2SP, pp. 1–12 (2012)
15. Mozilla Developer Network Web Docs: Canvas API. https://developer.mozilla.org/en-US/docs/Web/API/Canvas_API
16. Mulazzani, M., et al.: Fast and reliable browser identification with JavaScript engine fingerprinting. In: Web 2.0 Workshop on Security and Privacy (W2SP), vol. 5 (2013)

17. Multilogin: How canvas fingerprint blockers make you easily trackable (2016). https://multilogin.com/how-canvas-fingerprint-blockers-make-you-easily-trackable
18. Nakibly, G., Shelef, G., Yudilevich, S.: Hardware fingerprinting using HTML5. arXiv preprint arXiv:1503.01408 (2015)
19. Nikiforakis, N., Kapravelos, A., Joosen, W., Kruegel, C., Piessens, F., Vigna, G.: Cookieless monster: exploring the ecosystem of web-based device fingerprinting. In: IEEE Symposium on Security and Privacy, pp. 541–555. IEEE (2013)
20. Perry, M., Clark, E., Murdoch, S., Koppen, G.: The design and implementation of the Tor browser [DRAFT] (2018). https://www.torproject.org/projects/torbrowser/design/
21. Udemy: Privacy policy (2019). https://www.udemy.com/terms/privacy/. Accessed 9 July 2019
22. Yelp: Yelp privacy policy (2018). https://www.yelp.com/tos/privacy_en_us_20180525. Accessed 26 Jan 2019

# Investigating the Effect of Incidental Affect States on Privacy Behavioral Intention

Uchechi Phyllis Nwadike and Thomas Groß[(⊠)]

Newcastle University, Newcastle upon Tyne, UK
thomas.gross@newcastle.ac.uk

**Abstract.** Incidental affects users feel during their online activities may alter their privacy behavioral intentions. We investigate the effect of incidental affect (fear and happy) on privacy behavioral intention. We recruited 330 participants for a within-subjects experiment in three random-controlled user studies. The participants were exposed to three conditions neutral, fear, happy with standardised stimuli videos for incidental affect induction. Fear and happy stimuli films were assigned in random order. The participants' privacy behavioural intentions (PBI) were measured followed by a Positive and Negative Affect Schedule (PANAS-X) manipulation check on self-reported affect. The PBI and PANAS-X were compared across treatment conditions. We observed a statistically significant difference in PBI and Protection Intention in neutral-fear and neutral-happy comparisons. However across fear and happy conditions, we did not observe any statistically significant change in PBI scores. We offer the first systematic analysis of the impact of incidental affects on Privacy Behavioral Intention (PBI) and its sub-constructs. We are the first to offer a fine-grained analysis of neutral-affect comparisons and interactions offering insights in hitherto unexplained phenomena reported in the field.

**Keywords:** Privacy behavioral intentions · Incidental affect states · Affect induction

## 1 Introduction

Online privacy behaviors, though not limited to requesting for personal contact information to be removed from mailing lists, keeping passwords safe, use of strict privacy settings [20] such as can be observed as users take deliberate steps to protect their personal details while browsing on the Internet. Despite the best intentions to avoid sharing personal information, users still get influenced by different factors to disclose same. These factors include incentives, loyalty points, privacy concerns to mention a few. There is sparse information on the

Pre-Registration: https://osf.io/c3jy8/.

T. Groß and T. Tryfonas (Eds.): STAST 2019, LNCS 11739, pp. 187–210, 2021.
https://doi.org/10.1007/978-3-030-55958-8_11

effect of affect states on privacy behavior despite existing literature in psychology and economics highlighting the role of emotion in human behavior [17] and decision making [17]. Though preliminary studies [4,31] have been conducted on the effect of fear, happy, anger affect states on privacy behavioral intentions, however no comprehensive study has been conducted to investigate the effect of the relationship between neutral, fear and happy affect states on privacy behavioral intentions. Researchers such as Wakefield [31], Li [16] or Coopamootoo and Groß [3] have called for further investigation to extend the existing knowledge on the effect of fear and happy affect states on privacy behavioural intentions.

In this paper we contribute a comprehensive study which systematically compares PANAS-X and PBI scores across neutral, fear and happy conditions and explores the relationship between affect states and privacy behavioral intentions.

Given that measurement of actual privacy behavior is difficult to achieve within a laboratory setting, privacy behavioral intentions are frequently used as a proximal measure [9,15]. Hence in our user study we will measure privacy behavioral intentions instead of privacy behavior. The aim of the user studies discussed in this paper is to investigate the effect of incidental affect states of induced fear and happy affect states on privacy behavioral intention. This will contribute towards bridging the highlighted research gap, extend the existing research knowledge and provide empirical evidence that would be useful for further research.

## 2   Background        ·

### 2.1   Affect, Emotion, and Mood

The terms mood, emotion and affect have been used interchangeably in literature in the past, however referred to a range of emotional intensity and also reflect fundamental differences including duration, frequency, intensity and activation pattern. The terms *affect* or *affective states* are often used to describe the experience of emotion or feeling, in general, going back to an early definition attempt of Scherer [27]. The terms *core affect, emotion* and *mood* have been differentiated further in subsequent years. Ekkekakis [7] made one of the most recent attempts to summarize the emergent consensus of the field as well as the differences between these constructs (cf. [7, Ch. 7] for a detailed analysis).

We note that the impact of affect on another task led to a classification of *incidental affect*, that is, affect independent from the task at hand, and *integral affect*, that is, affect related to the task at hand. The differences between incidental and integral affect have received attention in psychology research [11,14,30]. Let us consider these terms and converge on a definition for this paper.

**Core Affect.** Following the discussion by Ekkekakis [7], we perceive core affect is a broader concept than mood or emotion. Russell [25] defined (core) affect as the specific quality of goodness or badness experienced as a feeling state (with or without consciousness). We include his circumplex model of affect in Fig. 1.

Affect states can be triggered spontaneously by memories, exposure to stimuli, perception of one's immediate environment [2,29,30]. Subsequently, Russel and Feldman Barrett [26] offered an updated definition "core affect is defined as a neuro-physiological state consciously accessible as a simple primitive non-reflective feeling most evident in mood and emotion but always available to consciousness" also consulted by Ekkekakis [7]. The feeling being non-reflective has been pointed out as a critical attribute.

**Fig. 1.** Circumplex model of affect, adapted from Russel [24]. Note that fear is classified as negative-valence/high-arousal (110°, labeled by Russel as "afraid") and happiness is classified as positive-valence/high-arousal (10°, labeled as "happy"). PANAS-X includes the high-arousal items delighted (30°) and excited (50°) in its joviality scale.

**Emotion.** Lazarus [13] defined *emotion* "as a complex reaction of a person arising from appraisals and outcomes of self-relevant interactions with the environment, which could result in states of excitement, direction of attention, facial expressions, action tendencies, and behavior." Ekkekakis [7, Ch. 7] points out elaborating on the discussion by Lazarus that: "Because emotions are elicited *by* something, are reactions *to* something, and are generally *about* something, the cognitive appraisal involved in the person-object transaction is considered a defining element." (emphasis by the Ekkekakis).

**Mood.** Mood is typically differentiated from emotion by intensity and duration. Lazarus [13] discussed *mood* as follows: "While moods are usually less anchored to specific stimulus conditions and perhaps of longer duration and lesser intensity than emotions, may also be distinguished in terms of specific content." Similarly, Ekkekakis [7, Ch. 7] discusses that moods are "diffuse and global."

## 2.2    Affect Elicitation

This refers to the process of engaging study participants in specific tasks with the sole purpose of drawing out the required affect state of interest from individuals. Given the brief span associated with affect states it is difficult to determine how long a treatment should be in order to obtain and ascertain the affect's intensity and sustained effect throughout the user study duration. Emotion researchers have recommended that the inducement process should not last longer than minutes [22].

The methods used to elicit or induce affect states include the use of standardized stimulus in form of audio, video, autobiography recall, vignettes and pictures [28]. These methods are not used in isolation rather the authors recommend to use a combination of techniques. They proposed that different affect inducing methods have different success rates with evoking different affect states within the laboratory's setting [28]. The methods are further discussed below.

**Visual Stimuli.** This refers to the use of visually stimulating images such as video clips as stimuli. These materials can contain either evocative or non evocative elements which can induce specific affect states. Types of visual stimuli include pictures (e.g., gruesome images, a sunset over a calm sea) or films (e.g., defined scenes from horror or comedy films).

To induce fear, psychologists [2] have established standardized scenes from *"The Shining"* or *"The Silence of the Lambs."* To induce happiness, similarly, the restaurant scene from *"When Harry meets Sally"* was used. As a standard procedure, these stimuli videos are precisely defined and systematically evaluated for their impact on the participants' affective state. In the studies discussed later in this chapter, we selected the use of standardized stimulus video films. This technique was considered the most effective in inducing affect states with large effect sizes.

**Autobiographical Recall.** When using this method, participants are requested to recollect (and at times write) about real life evoking events from their past when they experienced a particular affect state the researchers are interested in. The researchers expect participants to relive the affect state felt at the time of the event or incident. Researchers who have used this method in use of their studies, recorded noticeable change in emotional effect in their participants' self reported responses and increased physiological responses such as heart rate, skin conductance [19].

## 2.3    Affect Measurement

The methods and tools used in measuring affect states can be classified into two categories, namely psychometric self-report instruments and psycho-physiological measurements.

Self report tools involve the use of scales, such as PANAS-X, which require input from the subject, reporting how he or she feels with respect to a defined timeframe (e.g., in this moment). In this study, we have selected the Positive and Negative Affect Schedule (PANAS-X) [32] as manipulation check of choice. While largely considered an effective measurement instrument [5,33], Ekkekakis [7, Ch. 12] pointed out that the PANAS-X items include core affects, emotions, as well as moods in the terminology set out above. We also note that the sub-scales on *fear* and *joviality* we use in this study would be considered an emotion in this terminology, infused with high negative and positive core affect, respectively. We note that in recent years, there was further criticism of the factorial structure and theoretical underpinnings of PANAS-X, especially when it comes to measuring low-activation states (outside of the scope of this study).

Psycho-physiological measurement tools do not require any subjective input rather it involves the measurement of physiological responses after exposure to a given stimulus. These responses could be facial expressions, heart beat, skin conductance, pupil movement to mention a few. While there has been supportive evidence for those tools, there is also criticism in constructivist views on emotions that physiological states are not necessarily indicative of specific emotions.

# 3   Related Work

To the best of our knowledge, we were the first to present an affect induction experiment designed to explore the effect of affect states on privacy behavioral intention (PBI) [21]. Our paper reports pilot studies and describes a design template to investigate the impact of happy and fear affect states on PBI. Subsequently, Coopamootoo [4] and Fordyce et al. [8] adopted said template in their research. So do we. Fordyce et al. applied the method to password choice.

The closest work to this study is Coopamootoo's work-in-progress (WIP) paper [4]. Both experiments are measuring incidental affect as proposed by Nwadike et al. [21] initially. for which we notice a number of differences: (i) While this study is only concerned with the impact of affect on PBI, the study by Coopamootoo also considered general self-efficacy as a human trait. (ii) While we induced incidental affects with standardized stimuli films, Coopamootoo used autobiographical recall of emotive events. (iii) While Coopamootoo uses tone analysis of participant-written text as predictor, we use PANAS-X as psychometric instrument. Our impression is that the tone analysis only measures the tone of a text input, but does not constitute a psychometric measurement of the current affective state of a participant.

We noticed that the correlations reported in the WIP paper [4, §5.3.4] are trivial to small ($r \leq 0.3$), with Protection Intention (PI) having the greatest reported correlation with self-efficacy ($r = 0.3$).

Coopamootoo's causal hypothesis $H_{c,1}$ was declared as "emotion [fear/happiness] and self-efficacy impact privacy intentions." The relations reported are (i) emotions impact trait self-efficacy (negatively) and (ii) self-efficacy impacts PI (positively). Strikingly, for relation (i) the corresponding study [4, Study 2, §4.2] administered the trait self-efficacy questionnaire in Step (b) *before* the affect induction protocol (Step (c)). Hence, the induced emotion could *not* have *caused* self-efficacy changes, hence could also not have acted as independent variable on self-efficacy as mediator for PI. Thus, the mentioned logical inconsistencies along with the statements of having tried out of multiple (yet, unspecified) models, raise questions on the validity of reported causal relation.

# 4  Aims

*Impact of Affect.* The study seeks to make a comparison of the influence of incidental affect states on Privacy Behavioral Intention (PBI) [34].

**RQ 1 (Impact of affect on PBI).** *To what extent does Privacy Behavioral Intention (PBI) [34] in the form of Information Disclosure Intention (IDI), Transaction Intention (TI) and Protection Intention (PI) change depending on induced incidental happy and fear states?*

This research question decomposes into multiple statistical hypotheses iterated over dependent variables (idi, ti, pi) pair-wise compared across conditions (neutral, happy, fear). Hence, we obtain nine null and alternative hypotheses pairs for comparisons on: neutral–happy (nh), neutral–fear (nf), happy–fear (hf). In addition to that, we investigate the pair-wise comparison of the combined pbi scores across conditions.

As primary analysis, we are most interested in, we consider the combined Privacy Behavioral Intention (PBI) pbi in the comparison between the happy–fear conditions.

$H_{hf,pbi,0}$ There is no difference in privacy behavioral intention (pbi) between cases with induced happiness and induced fear. $H_{hf,pbi,1}$ Privacy behavioural intention pbi differs between the happy and fear (hf) conditions.

The hypotheses are obtained iterating over

1. Conditions Comparisons $CC :=$
   (a) neutral–happy (nh),
   (b) neutral–fear (nf),
   (c) happy–fear (hf)
2. Dependent Variables $DV :=$
   (a) pbi: Combined Privacy Behavioral Intention (PBI) score,
   (b) idi: PBI Information Disclosure Intention (IDI) sub-scale score,
   (c) ti: PBI Transaction Intention (TI) sub-scale score,
   (d) pi: PBI Protection Intention (PI) sub-scale score.

$H_{CC,DV,0}$. There is no difference in privacy behavioral intentions scores of scale $DV$ between conditions specified in comparison $CC$. $H_{CC,DV,1}$ Privacy behavioural intention scores of scale $DV$ differ between the conditions specified in comparison $CC$. Note that $CC$ and $DV$ are variables that take values (nh, nf, hf) and (pbi, idi, ti, pi) as specified above. They thereby define a test family of 12 alternative and null hypothesis pairs.

*Manipulation Check.* We use the Positive and Negative Affect Schedule (PANAS-X) [32] as joint manipulation check *MC* across the three studies. A manipulation is considered successful if the following null hypotheses can be rejected. $H_{MC,jov,0}$ There is no difference in *MC*-measured joviality between happy and fear conditions. $H_{MC,jov,1}$ The *MC*-measured joviality differs between happy and fear conditions. $H_{MC,fear,0}$ There is no difference in *MC*-measured fear between happy and fear conditions. $H_{MC,fear,1}$ The *MC*-measured fear differs between happy and fear conditions. The pre-registration defined the PANAS-X (px) measurement as authoritative (Table 1).

**Table 1.** Operationalization: effect of fear on privacy behavioral intention.

|  | Levels | Instrument | Intervention/Variable |
|---|---|---|---|
| IV: Affect | Fear | Stimulus Video [23] | *The Shining* |
|  | Happy |  | *When Harry Met Sally* |
| IV Check | Fear | PANAS-X [32] | fear |
|  | Happy |  | joviality |
| DV: Privacy Behavioral Intention | | PBI [34] | pbi |
| *Sub-Scales:* | | | |
| Information Disclodure Intention | | | idi |
| Transaction Intention | | | ti |
| Protection Intention | | | pi |

*Regression Model.* We are interested in the relation between Privacy Behavioral Intention (pbi, idi, ti, pi) and measured affect PANAS-X (pxjov and pxfear).

**RQ 2 (Relation of measured affect and PBI).** *To what extent is there a linear relationship between the reported affect state (PANAS-X) and the PBI scales.*

We consider the following hypotheses for an overall model, with canonical hypotheses for the respective predictors. $H_{px,pbi,0}$ There is no linear relationship between measured affect and PBI scores. $H_{px,pbi,1}$ There is a systematic linear relationship between measured affect and PBI scores. We note that the overall PBI score relation is designated as primary hypothesis and the PBI-sub-scale relations designated as secondary hypotheses.

# 5  Method

The studies had been pre-registered at Open Science Framework[1]. The tables and graphs were produced directly from the data with the R package KnitR.

---

[1] https://osf.io/c3jy8/?view_only=cc90a7db0fbd48ad87bfb44176c224c8.

The statistical inferences conducted are two-tailed and operate on a significance level of $\alpha = .05$. We consider the per-condition pair-wise Wilcoxon Signed-Rank tests for Privacy Behavior Intention (PBI) and its sub-scales IDI, PI, and TI as a test family with 12 elements. A Bonferroni-Holm multiple-comparison correction (MCC) is applied directly to the $p$-values reported, indicated as $p_{MC(12)}$.

Even though the differences between DVs are at times not normally distributed, we use Hedges $g_{av}$ as unbiased dependent-samples effect size and its corresponding confidence interval for estimation purposes.

The three studies were conducted within online and offline settings: one laboratory and two online studies. We chose to run these studies in a combination of offline and online settings for two main reasons: because we wanted to measure facial expressions, which at the time could be done only within a lab setting; and also have access to a larger sample size.

## 5.1 Experiment Design Evaluation

We developed the experiment design in a series of pretests, which established the validity and reliability of the overall design as well as the procedure and instruments used therein. Figure 2 contains a flowchart depicting the development process in its entirety.

## 5.2 Sampling

Using flyers, and adverts on the crowdsourcing platforms- the participants involved in the user studies were recruited from different locations and at different time frames. The participants consist of institution's staff, students, workers on crowdsourcing platforms - Amazon Mechanical Turk and Prolific Academic. We adopted a simple sampling method based on participants' availability. The sample size were determined in an *a priori* power analysis using G*Power.

## 5.3 Ethics

The studies reported here adhered to the institution's ethics guidelines and an ethics approval was obtained before the studies were conducted.

*Affect Elicitation.* The affect induction techniques used were not expected to adversely affect the participants' affect states. Stimulus video clips which have been tested in psychological studies and considered as standardized clips [2] were used. These clips were considered suitable for use in user studies which involve emotion [2]. The participants were not expected to experience any discomfort different from that encountered in daily life activities. At the end of the online user studies, the participants were provided with links to free online counseling services and advised to contact the researcher if they were agitated by contents of the user study.

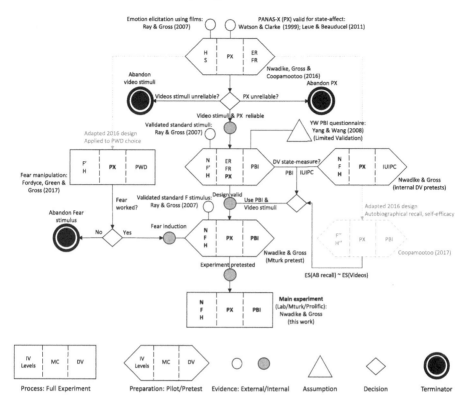

**Fig. 2.** Flowchart of the research process from 2016–2019, highlighting external evidence drawn upon, assumptions and design decisions made, as well as different pilots/pretests and external experiments informing this main study. We model Processes and Preparations as tripartite, consisting of 1. Independent Variable (IV) Levels, 2. Manipulation Check, and 3. Dependent Variable (DV). **IV Levels:** N = neutral (video *"Alaska's Wild Denali"*) [23]; H = happiness (video *"When Harry met Sally"*) [23]; F = fear (video 1 "The Shining") [23]; F' = fear (video 2 "The Silence of the Lambs") [23]; H'' = Happy (autobiographical recall); F'' = fear (autobiographic recall); S = sad (video *"The Champ"*) [23]; **Manipulation Checks:** PX = PANAS-X [32]; ER = Microsoft Emotional Recognition; FR = Noldus FaceReader [6]; **DVs:** PBI = Privacy Behavioral Intention [34]; IUIPC = Internet users' information privacy concerns [18].

*Informed Consent and Opt-Out.* During the recruitment process, participants were informed about the duration and requirements for the user studies. Participants were given an information sheet and a consent form which contained details about information that will be collected during the user studies. On the consent sheet they were presented with an opportunity to opt out at any stage without any penalties. All participants were given the opportunity to exercise informed consent.

*Deception.* The true purpose of the user studies was not disclosed to the participants; rather they were informed that the aim of the user studies was to assess their opinions about online information management. They were presented with questions on privacy concerns, personality traits, privacy behavioral intentions and demographics. At the end of the user study, the real aim of the user study was explained during the debriefing session.

*Compensation.* All participants who completed either one or both parts of the user studies were duly compensated either with Amazon vouchers in person or cash using the provided payment platform.

*Data Protection.* We followed the institution's data protection policy. Participants' personal information were anonymized and stored on an encrypted hard drive.

### 5.4  Procedure

We offer a comparison of the three studies conducted in Appendix B. The overall procedure for the within-subjects experiment is as follows:

First the participants indicated their interest in a registration (pre task) form containing questions on privacy concerns, personality traits. The study was spread over two days; in the first day, the participants carried out the following steps, i.e. 2–3. On the second day, the participants were first induced to a neutral state and then they completed steps 4 and 5. The reason for this was to minimize the carryover effects of the video stimuli and effect of questionnaire fatigue.

The procedure consists of the following steps, where Fig. 2 illustrates the key elements of the experiment design:

*a)* Completion of pre-task questionnaire on demographics, alcohol/recreational drug use, IUIPC and CFIP surveys.
*b)* Neutral state.
   (a) Induction of a neutral baseline affect state,
   (b) DV questionnaires on privacy behavioral intentions,
   (c) Manipulation check with PANAS-X,
   (d) (Offline only) Manipulation check: Emotional Recognition (ER) and Facereader (FR) from video recording of the participant's face geometry.
*c)* Affect State 1: Either happy or fear, determined by random assignment.
   (a) Show video stimulus to induce affect.
   (b) DV questionnaire on privacy behavioral intentions,
   (c) Manipulation check with PANAS-X.
   (d) (Offline only) Manipulation check: Emotional Recognition (ER) and Facereader (FR) from video recording of the participant's face geometry.
*d)* Affect State 2: Complement of Affect State 1.
   (a) Show video stimulus to induce affect.
   (b) DV questionnaire on privacy behavioral intentions,
   (c) Manipulation check with PANAS-X.

(d) (Offline only) Manipulation check: Emotional Recognition (ER) and Facereader (FR) from video recording of the participant's face geometry.

e) A debriefing questionnaire, used to check for missed or misreported information, subjective thoughts during study session.

## 5.5 PBI Measurement

We used the self-report PBI scale by Yang and Wang [34] to measure the participants' privacy behavioral intentions. The reason for choosing this tool is because it considers privacy behavioral intention as a multi-dimensional construct, providing an all compassing assessment of PBI. This tool is made up of 14 questions which assess sub-scales: information disclosure intention (IDI), protection intention (PI) and transaction intention (TI). We have previously validated this tool in comparison with IUIPC [18] considering dimensions of the Theory of Planned Behavior (TPB) [1]. In our evaluation, we found that the privacy concern measured in IUIPC [18] has characteristics of a long-term subjective norm. PBI on the other hand seemed more aligned with a short-term behavioral intention.

## 5.6 Manipulation

In the three studies, all participants were required to watch standardized stimulus videos that induce neutral, fear and happy affect states. The three stimulus videos were selected from a list of stimulus videos recorded in the *Handbook of emotion elicitation and assessment* [2]. As recommended in the Handbook, participants were asked to watch a scene from *Alaska's Wild Denali*, to elicit a neutral affect state. To elicit happy, and fear affect states, participants were exposed to specified scenes from *When Harry met Sally* and *The Shining* respectively. These stimuli have been precisely defined and validated as standard measures to induce affect, as documented by Ray and Gross [23].

## 5.7 Manipulation Check

We used a 15-item Positive and Negative Affect Schedule (PANAS-X) self-report questionnaire with a designated time horizon "at this moment") as main instrument to assess the manipulation success. For PANAS-X, we select the sub-scales fear and joviality to assess the affect states fear and happiness, respectively. According to Watson and Clark [32], the joviality scale is "the longest and the most reliable of the lower order scales, with a median internal consistency estimate of $\alpha_{jov} = .93$." The fear lower order scale is reported a median consistency of $\alpha_{fear} = .87$.

While we also used psycho-physiological tools (Microsoft Emotional Recognition (ER) and Noldus FaceReader [6]) in the lab, we report only the PANAS-X results in this paper as all the participants were assessed with this instrument.

# 6    Results

We describe the different samples in Appendix B and offer their descriptives in Appendix C.

## 6.1    Manipulation Check: PANAS-X

*Assumptions.* Both the differences between happy and fearful conditions on PANAS-X joviality and fear were not normally distributed, $W = 0.94, p < .001$ and $W = 0.83, p < .001$ respectively. We thereby choose to use a Wilcoxon Signed-Rank test.

*Success of the Fear/Happy Manipulations.* The fear reported by participants was statically significantly greather in the fearful condition $(M = 1.57, SD = 0.77)$ than in the happy condition $(M = 1.26, SD = 0.49)$, $V = 18286, p < .001$,
    The joviality of participants was statistically significantly less in the fearful condition $(M = 2.24, SD = 1.1)$ than in the happy condition $(M = 2.54, SD = 1.17)$, $V = 10398.5, p < .001$, Hedges' $g_{av} = -0.26$, 95% CI $[-0.36, -0.17]$.
    Hence, we reject the null hypotheses $H_{MC,fear,0}$ and $H_{MC,jov,0}$ and, thereby, consider the affect manipulation with the chosen video stimuli successful.
    Figure 3 contains a trigraph overview of all effects between all conditions, for joviality and fear respectfully.

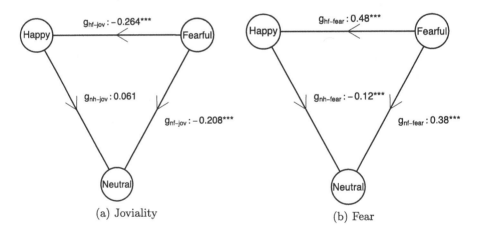

(a) Joviality                    (b) Fear

**Fig. 3.** Comparison of Hedges $g$ of manipulation checks wrt. joviality and fear.

## 6.2   Privacy Behavioral Intention

*Assumptions.* The differences between happy and fearful conditions on Privacy Behavioral Intention (PBI) were not normally distributed, $W = 0.94, p < .001$. We made the same observation for affect-neutral comparisons as well as sub-scales. We will use a Wilcoxon Signed-Rank test for the comparisons between conditions.

*Differences Between Conditions.* The PBI of the fearful condition ($M = 4.18$, $SD = 0.9$) was significantly greater than in the neutral condition ($M = 4.1$, $SD = 0.85$), $V = 28284.5, p_{MC(12)} < .001$, Hedges' $g_{av} = 0.1$, 95% CI $[0.04, 0.16]$.

Similarly, the PBI of the happy condition ($M = 4.18$, $SD = 0.9$) was significantly greater than in the neutral condition ($M = 4.1$, $SD = 0.85$), $V = 29363.5, p_{MC(12)} < .001$, Hedges' $g_{av} = 0.09$, 95% CI $[0.03, 0.16]$.

*However*, PBI was *not* statistically significantly different between fearful condition ($M = 4.18$, $SD = 0.9$) and happy condition ($M = 4.18$, $SD = 0.9$), $V = 23314.5, p_{MC(12)} = 1.000$, Hedges' $g_{av} = 0.01$, 95% CI $[-0.05, 0.06]$.

Consequently, we reject the null hypotheses $H_{nf,PBI,0}$ and $H_{nh,PBI,0}$. However, we were not able to reject the null hypothesis $H_{hf,PBI,0}$.

We report the difference between conditions first in the trigraph plot of Fig. 4 on PBI and its subscales. Then we offer a traditional forest plot on the same data, with effect sizes grouped by DV scale (Fig. 5).

## 6.3   PBI Sub-scales

We focus our attention on the PBI sub-scale comparisons that are likely statistically significant based on the effect sizes and confidence intervals reported in Fig. 5.

The protection intention (PI) of the fearful condition ($M = 4.28$, $SD = 1$) was significantly greater than of the neutral condition ($M = 4.15$, $SD = 0.92$), $V = 26202.5, p_{MC(12)} < .001$, Hedges' $g_{av} = 0.13$, 95% CI $[0.06, 0.2]$.

PI of the happy condition ($M = 4.27$, $SD = 1$) was significantly greater than of the neutral condition ($M = 4.15$, $SD = 0.92$), $V = 25749.5, p_{MC(12)} < .001$, Hedges' $g_{av} = 0.12$, 95% CI $[0.05, 0.19]$.

Hence, we reject the null hypotheses $H_{nf,PI,0}$ and $H_{nh,PI,0}$, but failed to reject the null hypothesis $H_{hf,PI,0}$.

Finally, the significance of the IDI difference between neutral and fearful condition is in question (especially after MCC). And, indeed, we did not find a statistically significant difference between the IDI scores of these conditions, $V = 9504.5, p_{MC(12)} = .975$, $g_{av} = -0.08$, 95% CI $[-0.16, 0]$.

For null hypothesis $H_{nf,IDI,0}$ as well as the remaining sub-scale null hypotheses, we consider them as not rejected.

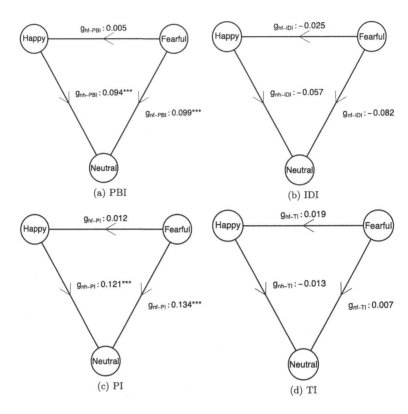

**Fig. 4.** Comparison of Hedges $g$ of PBI and its sub-scales Information Disclosure Intention (IDI), Protection Intention (PI), and Transaction Intention (TI).

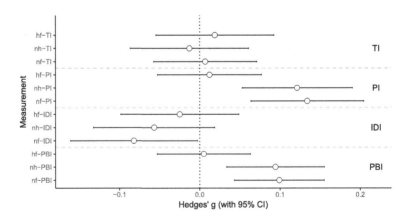

**Fig. 5.** Forest plot on PBI and its sub-scales for the combined dataset.

## 6.4   Interactions

It deserves closer attention why the main condition (happy-fear) has shown a lower effect size than comparisons between the neutral and affect-induced states. To shed light on this situation we compute interaction plots on dichotomized PX fear and happy scores (high/low).

*PBI Interactions.* Figure 6 considers the interactions for the main DV pbi. Sub-Figure 6a clearly shows the cross-over interaction between happy and fear conditions on the experienced fear in high or low levels of PX fear. Joviality (Fig. 6b) does not show any interaction.

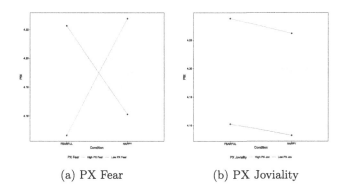

(a) PX Fear                     (b) PX Joviality

**Fig. 6.** Interaction plots of PBI on PX affects and condition.

Whereas participants with high fear in the fear condition exhibit a lower PBI score, participants with high fear in the happy condition show a higher PBI score. Vice versa, participants with low fear show a higher PBI score in the fear condition and show a lower PBI score in the happy condition.

*Sub-scale Interactions.* We face a complex situation in the interactions on sub-scales, displayed in Fig. 7. There are varying degrees of interactions.

Information Disclosure Intention (IDI) is impacted by interactions in opposing directions, yet not crossing over (Fig. 7a and Fig. 7d).

Fear yields a cross-over interaction on Protection Intention (PI) (Fig. 7b). The impact of joviality on PI yield no interation (Fig. 7e). This sub-scale shows the clearest difference between impact of fear and joviality on sub-scale.

Fear has a cross-over interaction on Transaction Intention (TI) (Fig. 7c). Joviality shows a milder interaction on TI in the same direction (Fig. 7f).

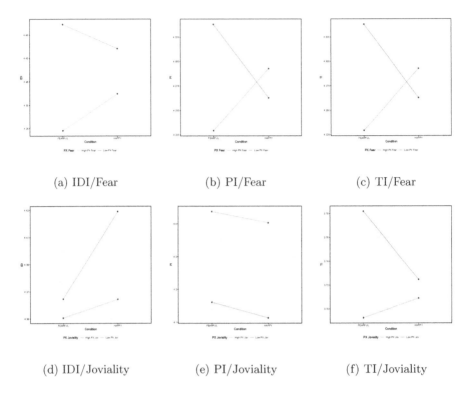

(a) IDI/Fear          (b) PI/Fear          (c) TI/Fear

(d) IDI/Joviality     (e) PI/Joviality     (f) TI/Joviality

**Fig. 7.** Interaction plots of PBI subscales (IDI, PI, TI) on PX affects and condition.

## 6.5    Regression

We conducted four of mixed-methods multiple linear regressions with the R package nlme. We selected the PANAS-X variables joviality and fear as predictors, abbreviated as pxjov and pxfear. We included the factor of study dataset as co-variate to account for differences between sampling platforms. The subject ID is considered a random effect. The response variable was either overall Privacy Behavioral Intention (pbi) or the sub-scale score for Information Disclosure Intention (idi), Protection Intention (pi) or Transaction Intention (ti). In general, we fix the predictors in advance and check the overall models with a Likelihood-Ratio test.

*PBI.* The pbi model incl. the dataset co-variate was statistically significant, $\chi^2(5) = 441.094, p < .001$. The predictors pxfear and pxjov are not statistically significant, indicating a marginal increase of about a 0.05 of pbi per point increase of both corresponding affective predictor variables. The dataset factor is statistically significant. Both the Prolific and the MTurk platforms imply an increase of pbi level by 0.27 and 0.36, respectively. Figure 8a contains the forest-plot of the coefficients as effect sizes.

*IDI.* The idi model was statistically significant, $\chi^2(5) = 309.774, p < .001$. The predictor pxfear is statistically significant, each point of pxfear accounting for a decrease of Information Disclosure Intention idi of $-0.21$. The other predictors (incl. dataset) were not significant. Figure 8b depicts the effect sizes with their confidence intervals.

*PI.* The pi model was statistically significant, $\chi^2(5) = 381.306, p < .001$. The predictor pxjov is statistically significant, each point of pxjov accounting for an increase of Protection Intention pi of 0.09. The dataset made a statistically significant difference in Prolific and MTurk implying an increase of pi of 0.36 and 0.46, respectively. We display the effect sizes in Fig. 8c.

*TI.* The ti model was statistically significant, $\chi^2(5) = 298.244, p < .001$. However, none of the predictors showed a significant impact on Transaction Intention ti (cf. Fig. 8d).

## 7 Discussion

### 7.1 Incidental Affect Impacts PBI and Protection Intention

We found that both fear and happy affect states caused an increase of Privacy Behavioral Intention as well as the sub-construct Protection Intention. The magnitude of the effect of fear and happy states is roughly equal.

In the comparison between fear and happy affect states themselves, we did *not* find a significant effect. More to the point, we found that the effects between

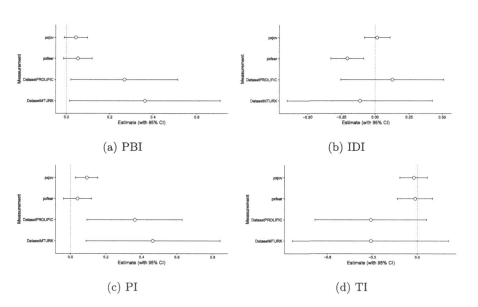

(a) PBI                                  (b) IDI

(c) PI                                   (d) TI

**Fig. 8.** Regression coefficient forest plots for PBI and its sub-scales.

neutral and the fear/happy were 20-fold the size of the effects between fear and happy condition. Similarly, Coopamootoo [4] and Fordyce et al. [8] observed non-significant effects of happy and fear on privacy behavioral intentions and password choice, respectively, without having provided a plausible explanation.

Furthermore, we observed a cross-over interaction in the fear measurements, but not in the joviality measurements, shedding further light on the low effect between fear and happy conditions.

## 7.2  PBI Sub-constructs Are Affected Differently

While Protection Intention was significantly affected by fear as well as happy conditions, we found much smaller and, then, non-significant effects on Information Disclosure Intention and Transaction Intention. That these emotions act on the Protection Intention, but not on IDI or TI yields further evidence for the complex influence of incidental affect on PBI. These observations are again substantiated by observed interactions on sub-constructs. Musingly, we could say: "It's complicated."

The situation certainly calls for further investigation to ascertain how affect states impact security-relevant intentions and behaviors. From our analysis so far we conclude that simple comparisons of just two affects while ignoring the neutral state do not cut the mustard.

## 7.3  Consulting the Circumplex Model for a Hypothetical Explanation: Arousal

We consider Russel's circumplex model of affect (cf. Fig. 1, [24]), acknowledging that it is not without contention [12]. We find fear classified as negative-valence/high-arousal and happiness classified as positive-valence/high-arousal. Both emotions have the high arousal in common. We have not anticipated this effect before this study and can only offer a declared *post-hoc* hypothesis: "Arousal itself has a positive impact on Protection Intention and, hence, on Privacy Behavioral Intention."

Is this hypothesis plausible? Groß et al. [10] proposed Selye's arousal curve as an alternative explanation for the impact of cognitive effort and depletion on password choice they observed. Hence, arousal was considered a plausible explanation in affective-cognitive effects on security and privacy before. While Fordyce et al. [8] explicitly investigated this problem by analyzing the impact of stress on password choice, the question of arousal itself was not settled. To the best of our knowledge, there has been no such investigation in online privacy, yet. However, given the results of this study we opine that arousal can no longer be ignored in similar studies and needs to be considered as a possible confounding variable.

## 7.4  Limitations

*Sampling.* Our participants were recruited from different crowdsourcing platforms, AMT and Prolific Academic, as well as through flyers and e-mails for the lab experiment. The sampling method employed to recruit our participants was based on self-selection or availability, and not random. The participants involved in our user studies were mainly from the US, possibly a norm based effect may have had an effect on the study results.

*PBI Instrument Properties.* The questions for PBI sub-scales were not evenly distributed with two questions assessing information disclosure intentions, nine questions assessing protection intentions and four for transaction intentions [34].

*Affect Induction Properties.* Though we used standard self reporting tools to measure affect states as well as standardized tools for affect induction, the affect induction could have been more robust and consistent if further affect induction techniques were employed to reinforce the induced affect states.

The standardized stimulus videos used were produced more than 10 years ago. As a result some participants were familiar with the film scenes and knew what to expect. This raises the question if an increased effect on affect states could have been observed if the films were not known.

Contrary to our expectations, we obtained reports from a small percentage of participants, who indicated that they enjoyed the fear stimulus film and reported high happiness scores after watching it. We imagine that this effect is rooted in the pop-culture co-notation of the films and personal preferences of users for certain genres.

# 8 Conclusion

We are first to offer an analysis of incidental affect on privacy behavioral intention (PBI) and its sub-constructs. Incidental affect refers to affect present in a user independent of the current task. Hence, our analysis is more general than earlier preliminary work on integral affect, that is, affect induced by the task at hand.

For the first time, our analysis contributes a systematic fine-grained comparison of neutral, happy and fear states of PBI and its sub-constructs as well as observed interactions. Our analysis offers a compelling explanation for low effect sizes observed between happy and fear states: Compared to neutral states, *both* affect states cause an increased PBI as well as an increased Protection Intention of similar magnitude. Consequently, earlier analyses that only compared fear and happy states ended up with only registering tiny non-significant effects.

Our research raises further questions on a wider range of user studies with affect induction and binary comparisons between affect conditions, incl. work-in-progress papers on integral affect [4] and contributions on the impact of fear on password choice [8].

**Acknowledgments.** This study benefited from Newcastle University's psycho-physiological eye tracking lab. We are indebted to the Newcastle University's School of Computing for the offering the funds for the participant compensation. Thomas Groß was supported by the ERC Starting Grant CASCAde (GA n°716980).

# A    Within-Subjects Study Variants

In the offline study, participants were invited to complete the user study in a lab environment. All participants were exposed to the two treatment conditions, using a constrained random assignment across - happy and fearful. This assignment assured that the order of stimuli exposed to the participants was fairly balanced. All three studies consist of four parts:

*a)* participant registration (including demographics and personality/privacy trait questionnaires),
*b)* a control PBI session with a neutral video,
*c)* first PBI session with a randomly chosen stimulus video (happy/fearful),
*d)* second PBI session with the complementary stimulus video (fearful/happy).

All the three studies were within-subject randomized controlled trials with a random assignment of participants to an order either (1. happy, 2. fearful) or (1. fearful, 2. happy).

*Differences.* The difference between the studies are:

*a)* online participants completed a combination of the pre-task survey and the first phase of the study on the same day while in the offline study the participants completed the registration before stating the main study.
*b)* The second difference is no video recording was conducted with the online participants while we video recorded the facial expressions of the offline participants.
*c)* The online study uses as assignment a simple uniform random assignment.
*d)* The offline study uses a constrained random assignment maintaining a balance between stimulus orders.

# B    Sample

The sample was combined from three studies with different properties but same methodology: (i) Offline, (ii) AMT, and (iii) Prolific.

*Study 1: Offline Lab study.* The participants were recruited through flyers and emailing lists within the faculties of Social Sciences, Medical Sciences and Computer Science at the host university. 95 participants from Newcastle University registered online to participate in the study. Of those 95 participants, $N_L = 60$ participants completed the study by physically visiting the lab twice. In terms of ethnicity, 54% of the participants were Caucasian, 26% Asian and 20% were African. In terms of classification of studies, 56.7% of the participants were studying for a postgraduate degree, 37.7% were studying for an undergraduate degree, 3.3% of the participants had secondary school education and the remainder did not report their education background. Table 3 summarizes the descriptive statistics of this sub-sample.

*Study 2: Online AMT study.* The study was conducted in a series of sessions on Amazon Mechanical Turk. Out of 100 registrations, a total of 70 AMT workers completed both sessions of our study. However, 31 responses were found to be unsuitable, by which retained a sub-sample of $N_M = 39$ observations, described in Table 4.

*Study 3: Prolific Academic study.* The same experiment was conducted on Prolific with a considerably greater completion rate than in the AMT Study. In the first session of affect study we conducted on Prolific 50 submissions were made; out of which 39 completed the study. A second batch requesting for 200 participants was conducted. 217 completed the first part of the study; 211 returned and completed the study. 15 incorrectly completed surveys were excluded. 235 observations were included in this sub-sample, its descriptives being summarized in Table 5. Table 2 shows the demographics distribution in this sub-sample.

**Table 2.** Demographics of study 3 on Prolific

| Age | |
| --- | --- |
| 18–23 | 46.4% |
| 24–29 | 28.1% |
| 30–35 | 12.8% |
| 36–41 | 6.4% |
| 42–47 | 2.9% |
| 48–53 | 1.3% |
| 54+ | 2.1% |

| Gender | |
| --- | --- |
| Female | 39.1% |
| Male | 60.9% |

# C    Descriptives

We offer the descriptive statistics for the conditions happy and fearful across the three samples (Lab, MTurk, and Prolific) in Tables 3, 4, and 5, respectively.

**Table 3.** Descriptives of the lab experiment ($N_L = 60$)

| | Condition fear | | | Condition happiness | | |
| --- | --- | --- | --- | --- | --- | --- |
| | Fear | Joviality | PBI | Fear | Joviality | PBI |
| $M$ | 1.55 | 2.71 | 3.94 | 1.13 | 3.27 | 4.01 |
| $SD$ | 0.84 | 1.23 | 0.93 | 0.26 | 1.18 | 0.89 |

**Table 4.** Descriptives of the MTurk experiment ($N_M = 39$)

|       | Condition fear | | | Condition happiness | | |
|-------|------|----------|------|------|----------|------|
|       | Fear | Joviality | PBI | Fear | Joviality | PBI |
| $M$   | 1.43 | 2.37     | 4.32 | 1.53 | 2.23     | 4.31 |
| $SD$  | 0.80 | 1.16     | 1.08 | 0.78 | 1.28     | 1.10 |

**Table 5.** Descriptives of the Prolific experiment ($N_M = 226$)

|       | Condition fear | | | Condition happiness | | |
|-------|------|----------|------|------|----------|------|
|       | Fear | Joviality | PBI | Fear | Joviality | PBI |
| $M$   | 1.59 | 2.09     | 4.23 | 1.25 | 2.40     | 4.20 |
| $SD$  | 0.75 | 1.02     | 0.85 | 0.46 | 1.07     | 0.86 |

# References

1. Ajzen, I.: Theory of planned behavior. Handb. Theor. Soc. Psychol. **1**(2011), 438 (2011)
2. Coan, J.A., Allen, J.J.: Handbook of Emotion Elicitation and Assessment. Oxford University Press, Oxford (2007)
3. Coopamootoo, K.P., Groß, T.: Why privacy is all but forgotten: an empirical study of privacy & sharing attitude. Proc. Priv. Enhanc. Technol. **2017**(4), 97–118 (2017)
4. Coopamootoo, K.: WIP: fearful users' privacy intentions-an empirical investigation. In: 7th Workshop in Socio-Technical Aspects in Security and Trust. Newcastle University (2017)
5. Crawford, J.R., Henry, J.D.: The positive and negative affect schedule (PANAS): construct validity, measurement properties and normative data in a large non-clinical sample. Br. J. Clin. Psychol. **43**(3), 245–265 (2004)
6. Den Uyl, M., Van Kuilenburg, H.: The FaceReader: online facial expression recognition. In: Proceedings of Measuring Behavior, vol. 30, pp. 589–590 (2005)
7. Ekkekakis, P.: The Measurement of Affect, Mood, and Emotion: A Guide for Health-Behavioral Research. Cambridge University Press, Cambridge (2013)
8. Fordyce, T., Green, S., Groß, T.: Investigation of the effect of fear and stress on password choice. In: Proceedings of the 7th Workshop on Socio-Technical Aspects in Security and Trust, pp. 3–15. ACM (2018)
9. Gerber, N., Gerber, P., Volkamer, M.: Explaining the privacy paradox-a systematic review of literature investigating privacy attitude and behavior. Comput. Secur. **77**, 226–261 (2018)
10. Groß, T., Coopamootoo, K., Al-Jabri, A.: Effect of cognitive depletion on password choice. In: Peisert, S. (ed.) Learning from Authoritative Security Experiment Results (LASER 2016), July 2016
11. Han, S., Lerner, J.S., Keltner, D.: Feelings and consumer decision making: the appraisal-tendency framework. J. Consum. Psychol. **17**(3), 158–168 (2007)
12. Larsen, R.J., Diener, E.: Promises and problems with the circumplex model of emotion. In: Emotion: Review of Personality and Social Psychology, No. 13, pp. 25–59 (1992)

13. Lazarus, R.S., Lazarus, R.S.: Emotion and Adaptation. Oxford University Press on Demand, Oxford (1991)
14. Lerner, J.S., Keltner, D.: Beyond valence: toward a model of emotion-specific influences on judgement and choice. Cogn. Emot. **14**(4), 473–493 (2000)
15. Li, H., Luo, X.R., Zhang, J., Xu, H.: Resolving the privacy paradox: toward a cognitive appraisal and emotion approach to online privacy behaviors. Inf. Manag. **54**(8), 1012–1022 (2017)
16. Li, H., Sarathy, R., Xu, H.: The role of affect and cognition on online consumers' decision to disclose personal information to unfamiliar online vendors. Decis. Support Syst. **51**(3), 434–445 (2011)
17. Loewenstein, G.: Emotions in economic theory and economic behavior. Am. Econ. Rev. **90**(2), 426–432 (2000)
18. Malhotra, N.K., Kim, S.S., Agarwal, J.: Internet users' information privacy concerns (IUIPC): the construct, the scale, and a causal model. Inf. Syst. Res. **15**(4), 336–355 (2004)
19. Marci, C.D., Glick, D.M., Loh, R., Dougherty, D.D.: Autonomic and prefrontal cortex responses to autobiographical recall of emotions. Cogn. Affect. Behav. Neurosci. **7**(3), 243–250 (2007). https://doi.org/10.3758/CABN.7.3.243
20. McGuinness, D., Simon, A.: Information disclosure, privacy behaviours, and attitudes regarding employer surveillance of social networking sites. IFLA J. **44**(3), 203–222 (2018)
21. Nwadike, U., Groß, T., Coopamootoo, K.P.L.: Evaluating users' affect states: towards a study on privacy concerns. In: Lehmann, A., Whitehouse, D., Fischer-Hübner, S., Fritsch, L., Raab, C. (eds.) Privacy and Identity 2016. IAICT, vol. 498, pp. 248–262. Springer, Cham (2016). https://doi.org/10.1007/978-3-319-55783-0_17
22. Qiao-Tasserit, E., Quesada, M.G., Antico, L., Bavelier, D., Vuilleumier, P., Pichon, S.: Transient emotional events and individual affective traits affect emotion recognition in a perceptual decision-making task. PLoS ONE **12**(2), e0171375 (2017)
23. Ray, R.D.: Emotion elicitation using films. In: Handbook of Emotion Elicitation and Assessment, pp. 9–28 (2007)
24. Russell, J.A.: A circumplex model of affect. J. Pers. Soc. Psychol. **39**(6), 1161 (1980)
25. Russell, J.A.: Core affect and the psychological construction of emotion. Psychol. Rev. **110**(1), 145 (2003)
26. Russell, J.A., Barrett, L.F.: Core affect, prototypical emotional episodes, and other things called emotion: dissecting the elephant. J. Pers. Soc. Psychol. **76**(5), 805 (1999)
27. Scherer, K.R., et al.: On the nature and function of emotion: a component process approach. Approaches Emot. **2293**(317), 31 (1984)
28. Siedlecka, E., Denson, T.F.: Experimental methods for inducing basic emotions: a qualitative review. Emot. Rev. (2018). https://doi.org/10.1177/1754073917749016
29. Slovic, P., Peters, E., Finucane, M.L., MacGregor, D.G.: Affect, risk, and decision making. Health Psychol. **24**(4S), S35 (2005)
30. Västfjäll, D., et al.: The arithmetic of emotion: integration of incidental and integral affect in judgments and decisions. Front. Psychol. **7**, 325 (2016)
31. Wakefield, R.: The influence of user affect in online information disclosure. J. Strateg. Inf. Syst. **22**(2), 157–174 (2013)
32. Watson, D., Clark, L.A.: The PANAS-X: manual for the positive and negative affect schedule - expanded form. Technical report, University of Iowa, Department of Psychology (1999)

33. Watson, D., Clark, L.A., Tellegen, A.: Development and validation of brief measures of positive and negative affect: the PANAS scales. J. Pers. Soc. Psychol. **54**(6), 1063 (1988)
34. Yang, S., Wang, K.: The influence of information sensitivity compensation on privacy concern and behavioral intention. ACM SIGMIS Database DATABASE Adv. Inf. Syst. **40**(1), 38–51 (2009)

# Which Properties Has an Icon? A Critical Discussion on Data Protection Iconography

Arianna Rossi[(✉)] and Gabriele Lenzini

SnT, University of Luxembourg, Esch-sur-Alzette, Luxembourg
{arianna.rossi,gabriele.lenzini}@uni.lu

**Abstract.** Following GDPR's Article12.7's proposal to use standardized icons to inform data subject in "an easily visible, intelligible and clearly legible manner," several icon sets have been developed. In this paper, we firstly critically review some of those proposals. We then examine the properties that icons and icon sets should arguably fulfill according to Art.12's transparency provisions. Lastly, we discuss metrics and evaluation procedures to measure compliance with the Article.

**Keywords:** Icons · Graphical symbols · Pictograms · Evaluation · Data protection · Privacy · Standardization · Security · GDPR · ISO · Compliance

## 1 Introduction

The General Data Protection Regulation (GDPR) obliges data controllers to inform data subjects about how their personal data is processed (Artt. 13 and 14). It requires that such communication is performed "in a concise, transparent, intelligible and easily accessible form, using clear and plain language" (Art.12.1). It also states that "information [..] may be provided in combination with standardised icons in order to give in an easily visible, intelligible and clearly legible manner a meaningful overview of the intended processing" (Art. 12.7).

Such an endorsement has motivated many organizations (private companies, research groups and public authorities) to develop and use icons[1] to improve the aspect, and allegedly the intelligibility, of their on-line and off-line legal documents. Moreover, we believe that there is a feeling of pressure to propose a set of icons for data protection in the hope that others will adopt it and, eventually, standardize it—not necessarily in this order.

However, it is still unclear what makes an icon and an icon set "effective" in the sense intended by the GDPR, *i.e.*, helpful to achieve conciseness, transparency, and intelligibility. There is no doubt that a sheer use of icons is not sufficient to reach the goal. Icons can be as ambiguous as text, while the simplistic explanation 'one picture is worth a thousand words', with an appeal to the

---

[1] In this article, the terms "icons" is used interchangeably with graphical symbols and pictograms.

© Springer Nature Switzerland AG 2021
T. Groß and T. Tryfonas (Eds.): STAST 2019, LNCS 11739, pp. 211–229, 2021.
https://doi.org/10.1007/978-3-030-55958-8_12

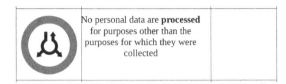

**Fig. 1.** An icon from a highly criticized code of icons included in an amendment to the GDPR draft [1]

'picture superiority effect', is not necessarily a compelling argument. The first is a popular saying[2], whereas picture superiority does not refer to the clarity of communication, but rather explains why images are recognized more immediately [24] and memorized more efficiently [25] than their linguistic counterparts.

Thus, even though icons can overcome communication barriers due to different languages and literacy levels [7,26] and are thus used to deliver crucial information in public, emergency or dangerous situations [35], one should be aware that the use of icons *per se* is not always the key. Without a systematic understanding of how pictograms are interpreted, of the message they intend to convey, of the context where that message is dispatched, icons can hardly serve GDPR's Art. 12. Indeed, bad examples exist: *e.g.*, one of the amendments to the GDPR included a code of icons that was criticized for its lack of intelligibility and later abandoned (see Fig. 1). Besides, it should be clarified which *properties* contribute to reach the aims of visibility, intelligibility, and legibility envisaged by the GDPR's transparency principle, and how to measure them.

One question remains pending: how can the use of icons realize, if at all, the provision of GDPR's Art. 12? Discussing possible answers to such question is, in part, the goal of this paper. As we will argue in the remainder of this article, the ease of interpretation of an icon depends on several factors [23] like concreteness, familiarity and legibility of its single elements. When included in an icon set, its understandability also derives from established conventions, efforts of standardization, and widespread adoption. Neglecting such facts may lead to sloppy and misleading visualizations, which in turn can cause mistaken interpretations [9] and achieve obscurity *in lieu* of transparency. Confusing and badly used icons can even lead to ill decisions [29] and unintentionally lure users into privacy-invasive or security-adverse practices in direct violation of the GDPR's *raison d'être*.

## 2   An Overview of Projects on Data Protection Icons

The intention of Article 12.7 is to foster the development of a regulated pictographic system which, if consistently used, would help controllers to "effectively"

---

[2] Apparently, its origin can be rooted back to Leonardo da Vinci, who wrote: "poet [..] the painter betters you, because your pen will be consumed before you can describe fully what the painter represents immediately with its art" (translation from [44]).

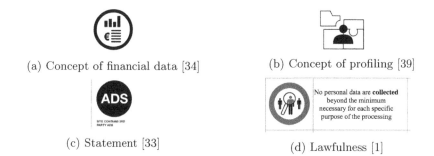

(a) Concept of financial data [34]      (b) Concept of profiling [39]

(c) Statement [33]                      (d) Lawfulness [1]

**Fig. 2.** Various examples of data protection icons

(*i.e.*, more effectively than lengthy, dense, verbose documents) inform data subjects of their data processing. Information duties (Artt. 13–14) provide for the communication of *e.g.*, the identity of the data controller; if data is shared, with whom and if it is transferred outside the EU; the data retention period; the purpose and the legal bases for the processing; as well as recalling the rights of the data subjects.

There are already many attempts to visualize this information. Some pre-exist the GDPR and were reviewed in [38]. Other initiatives, incentivized by Art. 12.7, have followed (*e.g.*, [34,39,41]), while others are currently under development[3] (*e.g.*, [6,11]). This inventory integrates our previous work on data protection icons [37,39,40] and a literature review made by other scholars[4]. The kind of information visualized by all these icon sets shows extreme variation: individual concepts (*e.g.*, financial data, profiling, see Fig. 2a, 2b); statements about the presence of a data practice (*e.g.*, "The site contains 3rd party ads", see Fig. 2c); and indications on the lawfulness or riskiness of data processing (*e.g.*, "No personal data are collected beyond the minimum necessary for each specific purpose of the processing" see Fig. 2d). Such iconographic richness is not necessarily negative. In icon design, it is envisaged to create at first many variants for the same referent and then select the best one through user studies. Besides, since the European Commission is expected to regulate on the topic, no authoritative indication exists on the modality of conception, realization and implementation of an icon set. However, in agreement with both the GDPR (Recital 166) and its interpretation by the WP29 [5], which emphasize the need for an evidence-based approach to study how icons can promote transparency, we expect that a selection should be based on the assessment of specific "effectiveness qualities". Yet, a comprehensive evaluation methodology for GDPR icons has been only marginally discussed in the literature.

---

[3] We are even aware of additional initiatives, that are not public yet.
[4] I.e. the Research group 'Data as a Means of Payment', Weizenbaum Institute for Networked Society (see https://www.weizenbaum-institut.de/en/research/rg4/).

*Critical Discussion of GDPR Icon Evaluation and Design Methodologies.* The vast majority of icon projects that we have reviewed focuses on producing a graphical system, without however gauging the outcomes towards the fulfillment of the GDPR's Article 12. Only a minority of the previously cited attempts have been evaluated [1,17,19,39]. Moreover, in such experiments, we observed that the focus is placed on the immediate comprehensibility of the icons, but disregards what makes them understandable, like the legibility of the elements of the graphical symbol, familiarity with the corresponding concept or learnability of the graphical language (see Sect. 4). This approach has brought researchers to cursorily discard the majority (or even the totality) of the elements of an icon set, for instance in [17,32]. Rossi and Palmirani [39], assessed legibility and comprehensibility and, albeit their testing outcomes admittedly constitute a first indication of good or bad design choices, the research did not reach definitive and generalizable results. Other relevant qualities, that will be defined in Sect. 4, have been simply disregarded. None of the above initiatives proposed an holistic approach for the evaluation of icons' effectiveness.

Moreover, none of the above works has considered the intended context of use to shape the goal and function of the icons: should they simply attract attention? Or are they expected to facilitate comprehension, thus fulfilling transparency goals? Or should they rather help to browse through a text quicker? In addition, even when the function was specified, it remained unclear whether the selected icons were a good fit for that function: for instance, if icons are meant to help search for specific items in long textual privacy policies, it should be assessed whether they efficiently support that task.

The research that we reviewed has also methodological limitations: the respondents' number is generally low (10–20), selected from a population of high school or university students (thus indicating a rather young and well-educated population, arguably even tech-savvier) and mostly mono-national. Thus, the outcomes of such studies cannot be generalized to the EU population to which the GDPR applies.

## 3   Methods and Tools

We aim to develop an evaluation scheme for "effectiveness" that might serve several icons initiatives to answer the following questions:

(i)  *Which properties characterize an "effective" icon?*
(ii) *Which methods are commonly used to evaluate such properties?*

We focus on properties that can be evaluated and on methods that can be followed in the evaluation because the use of icons as a means to implement transparency in data protection has legal consequences on individuals. Therefore, gathering evidence to motivate whether a graphical solution is effective according to the GDPR's intended purpose is a fundamental and necessary matter. In this perspective, providing tools to assess an icon's effectiveness is a task that completes and assists the icon design process, as it will also be discussed in Sect. 8.

In order to define properties and methods, we followed a workflow that consists of 5 steps: **step 1 - literature review**: collect the different properties usually discussed in relation to icons from the literature about ergonomics of graphical symbols (Sect. 4); **step 2 - completion**: *complete* the collection with some properties of our own (Sect. 4), and determine the intended efficacy of an icon in specific contexts of use (Sect. 5); **step 3 - selection**: *select* among those properties that fulfill GDPR's requirements (Sect. 6); **step 4 - measures and metrics**: determine and discuss measures and metrics to gauge such dimensions (Sect. 7); **step 5 - assessment procedures**: discuss such properties and measures for the framework of data protection (Sect. 8).

The first step, literature review, has been conducted orderly. We looked for (i) previous studies on privacy icons; (ii) works on Google Scholar digital library using the following terms, searched anywhere in text (in brackets the term in disjunction):

$$\left\{ \begin{array}{c} properties, \\ qualities, \\ characteristics \end{array} \right\} \textbf{ and } \left\{ \begin{array}{c} icons, signs \\ graphical\ symbols, \end{array} \right\}$$

$$\left\{ \begin{array}{c} evaluation, \\ assessment \end{array} \right\} \textbf{ and } \left\{ \begin{array}{c} icons, signs \\ graphical\ symbols, \end{array} \right\}$$

(iii) previous reviews or summaries of icons' characteristics and evaluation methods, namely [8,23,27,43,46,47,49]; (iv) item reference lists from the above articles; (v) inquiry on International Organization for Standardization (ISO) library with the following combination of terms:

$$\{evaluation\} \textbf{ and } \{graphical\ symbols\}.$$

We read titles and abstracts and browsed the articles, and retained studies and standards about public information signs, warning signs, and GUIs. We excluded studies on medical pictograms and road signs.

Our literature research is limited by the criteria we used, the data sources we queried, and by when we performed our research (till July 2019): projects on data protection icons are blooming, therefore more works will likely be published. Additional digital libraries can be considered in the future (*e.g.*, ScienceDirect and its Applied Ergonomics Journal). Our queries can also be expanded with additional combinations of terms and synonyms. Finally, documents from other domains can be included in the search (*e.g.*, medicine, bio/chemical-hazards, code of the road).

## 4   Icon Properties

To propose a categorization of the properties found in the literature on ergonomics of graphical symbols, we recur to the notion of semiotic triangle that defines the sign [31] (as shown in Fig. 3): some characteristics only concern the graphical symbol (Sect. 4.1); some others concern the referent, *i.e.*, the concept to which the symbol refers (Sect. 4.2); others concern the interpretant, *i.e.*, the process of interpretation (Sect. 4.3). A few dimensions do not concern individual pictograms, but the

216     A. Rossi and G. Lenzini

icon set as a batch (Sect. 4.4). Lastly, a few characteristics (marked with an asterisk *) have been derived from others and do not find an explicit definition in the
literature. These constitute our own addition to the set of properties.

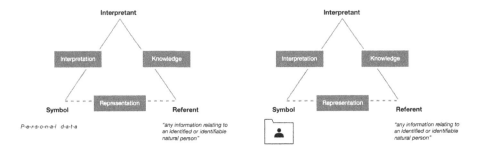

**Fig. 3.** Two semiotic triangles showing the relation between symbol, referent and interpretant. The concept of personal data is represented with two different symbols, i.e. a
written, linguistic utterance in the left triangle and an icon in the right one, that can
originate different interpretations.

### 4.1   Properties of Graphical Symbols

These are the characteristics pertaining to the graphical and perceptual aspect
of the icon, i.e. the graphical symbol (Table 1).

**Table 1.** Properties of the symbol

| | |
|---|---|
| Visibility | Capacity to stand out from other stimuli in the immediate environment [47] |
| Legibility | Ease of identification of the shapes composing the icon [15] |
| Complexity | Amount of details and their intricacy [23]. Affects *legibility* [14] and *ease of recognition* [47], but leads to more precise interpretations [50], thus impacting *comprehensibility* |
| Concreteness | Extent to which a symbol depicts objects or people [23]. Determines faster learning and more accurate *comprehensibility* for new exposures compared to abstract icons [47] |
| Familiarity | Frequency of using a symbol. Impacts ease of access to memory and time of recognition [23], related to *comprehensibility* |
| Distinctiveness | Ease of discriminability of one icon w.r.t. others [43]. Can impact *comprehensibility* |
| Style | The way an icon is designed (e.g. filled-in or solid, color, outline). Can influence ease of recognition [3], i.e. *comprehensibility* |
| Quality | How professional an icon looks. Relates to *legibility* [47,49] |
| Hazard | How specifically an icon displays a threatening or harmful condition [49]. Relevant for warning signs |

## 4.2   Properties of the Referent

These are the properties that characterize the concept represented by the graphical symbol (Table 2).

**Table 2.** Properties of the referent

| | |
|---|---|
| Visualizability | Ease of creating a mental image of the concept. Impacts ease of depiction and thus *comprehensibility* at first exposures [47] |
| Concreteness | Reference to objects and people, as opposed to abstract concepts (e.g. feelings) [23]. Relates to *visualizability* and thereby impacts *comprehensibility* |
| Complexity | Amount of details of the concept [23]. Can influence icon design, therefore impacting *legibility* and *comprehensibility* |
| Familiarity | Extent to which the concept is known to the interpreter [23]. Determines *comprehensibility* at first exposures |

## 4.3   Properties of the Interpretant

The following properties concern the process of interpretation, *i.e.*, the thought that originates from the sign [28] (Table 3).

**Table 3.** Properties of the interpretation process. The ones marked with an asterisk have been derived from other properties

| | |
|---|---|
| Comprehensibility | Ease of understanding of an icon's meaning. Depends on *legibility, familiarity,* and *semantic distance* |
| Semantic distance | Closeness of relationship btw. symbol and function [23], also defined as arbitrariness or meaningfulness [27]. Determines *learnability* and *comprehensibility* [47] |
| Learnability* | Ease of learning of a symbol. Determines ease of *comprehensibility* |
| Culture-independence* | Extent to which an icon is comprehensible to more than one culture or linguistic community. Thus affects *comprehensibility* |
| Text-independence* | Ease of icon interpretation without verbal label. Relates to *comprehensibility, concreteness,* and *familiarity* |

### 4.4   Properties of an Icon Set

These properties concern the icons as a set, rather than an individual icon (Table 4).

**Table 4.** Properties of an icon set, that are marked with an asterisk because they have been derived from other properties

| Amount* | Number of icons composing the set. If excessive, can cause cognitive overload |
|---|---|
| Completeness* | Capacity of representing all the items of information the icon set is meant to represent |

### 4.5   Interdependencies Among Properties

We conclude this section by highlighting which qualities determine other qualities. For instance, *legibility* depends on *complexity* and *quality* of the icon design. In turn, legibility is a reliable indicator of *comprehensibility* - indeed, as it will be illustrated in Sect. 7, these are the classical qualities considered in standardized evaluation methods. However, comprehensibility is affected by a complex mix of dimensions: *complexity* (of symbol and referent), *concreteness* of symbol, *familiarity* (of symbol and referent), *distinctiveness*, *style*, *visualizability* (in turn influenced by concreteness of the referent), *semantic distance*, *culture-independence*, *text-independence* (affected by concreteness and familiarity) and *learnability*. It is fundamental to consider these relations not only to define relevant measures to determine if an icon 'works', but also to develop useful guidelines for icon design.

## 5   Icons in Context

Three types of context should be considered for the analysis of pictograms [51]:

1. 'immediate', i.e., referring to the various symbols within one icon that interact to compose its meaning. It is therefore related to *legibility* and *complexity*.
2. 'proximate', i.e., intended as the field of interaction of one icon within a system of icons to construct meaning. It is therefore related to *distinctiveness*, *account*, and *completeness*.
3. 'environmental' (or context of use), i.e., referring to the place and actual conditions under which the icon is meaningful. It determines *comprehension*.

Section 2 has shown that the environmental context has not been properly considered in many privacy icons projects. Yet, previous research has emphasized the necessity of providing context to disambiguate a pictogram's intended meaning [43]: without contextual cues, low comprehension rates would falsely suggest that further design and testing are necessary [48]. Such consideration must be included in the evaluation procedures (see Sect. 7) to achieve a reliable indication of the effectiveness of an icon, by reproducing actual usage conditions, instead of asking individuals to speculate about the meaning of icons in a vacuum.

However, most of the data protection icon sets were developed as standalone elements and were assessed as such, even when their function and context of use had been envisaged, i.e. headline function in privacy policies [17,40]; in combination with text in a tabular format [32]; as specification of privacy preferences on social networks [19]. As discussed in Sect. 2, this limitation determined high discard rates of the evaluated icons.

Therefore, specifications about the environmental context must be taken into account to design a holistic evaluation methodology that realistically determines the efficacy of data protection icons. For exemplifying purposes, we propose three specific environmental contexts and usages, sketched in Fig. 4. Icons representing aspects of data processing activities can give salience to relevant information contained in a privacy policy that would otherwise be lost in undifferentiated text. If a privacy policy has a layered architecture, the function should be similar for both the first layer that summarizes the main points and the extended version. Previous research on the usability of legal documents, e.g., [30], has focused on 'companion icons' [18, p. 26], i.e. icons that represent the meaning of the text they accompany and that facilitate quick finding of relevant information. Alternatively, 'alert icons' [45, p. 23] can draw attention to risky practices (e.g. automated decision-making). Even consent management tools can benefit from pictograms: clickable icons can signify a data subject's explicit consent to certain practices or the withdrawal of such consent[5] [4]. Icons can also be conceived as elements of an identity management dashboard [42] where the data subject can adjust her privacy preferences and exercise her rights (e.g. access, erase or transfer her personal data). By conceiving icons within their intended environmental context, the selection of appropriate measures to evaluate if an icon 'works' in that context logically follows.

# 6    Mapping Properties to GDPR's Requirements

Among the properties described in Sect. 4, in the following we select those that correspond to the requirements set forth by the GDPR. Article 12.7 states that the information disclosed to data subjects "may be provided *in combination* with *standardised* icons in order to give in an easily *visible, intelligible* and clearly *legible* manner, a *meaningful overview* of the intended processing. Where the icons are presented electronically, they shall be *machine-readable*." Although the GDPR recitals do not provide any clarification, the principle of transparency was partially interpreted by the advisory body Article 29 Data Protection Working Party [5]: we integrate this partial interpretation with our own interpretation to map icon properties with the legal provisions (see Fig. 5).

---

[5] This practice is already established on smartphones, e.g. when users press on the pin icon to activate or deactivate geolocalization.

**1. Privacy policy**          **2. Consent request**    **3. Dashboard**

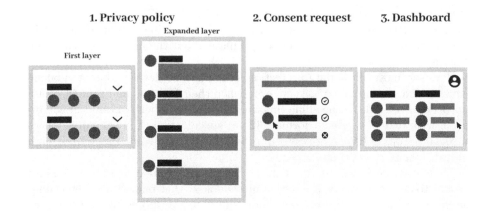

**Fig. 4.** A sketch exemplifying three possible contexts of use: 1. layered privacy policy; 2. consent management; 3. privacy dashboard. The blue circles represent placeholders for the icons

**In combination:** icons are meant to accompany, rather than replace text, thus excluding text-independence.

**Standardised:** polysemous term. 1. Standardized evaluation procedures [12,20, 21] envisage testing for *legibility, comprehensibility* and *culture-independence*; 2. widespread and homogeneous usage across applications enhances familiarity, oftentimes stimulated by large corporations (*e.g.*, padlock symbolizing secure connection). Thus *style* and *quality* seem also relevant.

**Visible:** capability of being readily noticed (i.e. salience) or easily found (i.e. accessibility) [5]. Corresponds to *visibility*.

**Legible:** corresponds to icon's *legibility*.

**Intelligible:** property of "being understood by an average member of the intended audience" [5, p. 7]. Corresponds to *comprehensibility*.

**Meaningful:** polysemous term[6]: 1. effective at conveying the intended meaning[7] (in a specific context), i.e. *comprehensible*; 2. useful[8]; 3. not misleading. For some authors, icon meaningfulness corresponds to *semantic transparency* [27].

**Overview:** ability to represent a summary of the processing practices. Overlaps with *completeness* of the icon set.

**Machine-readability:** ability to be read or interpreted by software applications [5].

---

[6] GDPR's translations in other languages do not disambiguate the term, *e.g.*, Italian: none; French: *bon* (i.e. good); German: *aussagekräftig* (i.e. meaningful/informative); Spanish: *adequato* (i.e. appropriate).

[7] American Heritage Roget's Thesaurus.

[8] Collins dictionary.

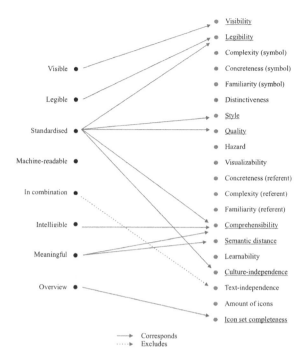

**Fig. 5.** Correspondences: GDPR's requirements (left) icon properties (right)

# 7   Methods of Icons' Evaluation

This section summarizes the main evaluation methods that were found in the literature.

**Visibility.** Visibility has a twofold nature: salience and accessibility. *Salience* is classically defined as the fixation points the viewer is most immediately drawn to and can be observed through eye-tracking software. The ease of finding of a target can reflect *accessibility* and can be indirectly determined through speed of recognition in a specific environmental context.

**Legibility.** Legibility consists in the correct identification of the icons' elements and can be operationalised by two measures: one assessing the accuracy of responses (i.e. if one icon object is correctly recognized) and one assessing their completeness (i.e. if all the objects depicted in the icon are recognized). To correctly evaluate this dimension, it is important to reproduce real-world interpretation conditions [49]: as the example in Fig. 6 shows, the icon size (like screen resolution and contrast) can affect legibility and, thereby, *comprehensibility*. Since *complexity* reliably indicates icon's legibility, during icon development, simple designs should be preferred.

(a) Icon as conceived

(b) Icon as possibly implemented

**Fig. 6.** Examples showing the impact of icon size on legibility. Source: [34]

**Comprehensibility.** Comprehensibility is the most important index of icon effectiveness [10]. This is why much research has been devoted to the elaboration of relative measuring protocols. Accuracy of association between graphical symbol and intended meaning is a typical assessment of icon comprehensibility: the ISO method [21] combines hit rate (i.e. the number of correct associations) with missing values and error rates (i.e. number of wrong associations) indicating possible flaws. The European Telecommunications Standards Institute (ETSI) [12] also adds subjective certainty about the association and subjective suitability, *i.e.*, a personal estimation of a pictogram's ability to represent its referent.

Multiple choice recognition tests, where respondents choose the meaning of an icon from a pool of possible candidates, are acceptedly discarded because they do not reflect realistic interpretation conditions [48]. Open-ended questionnaires where participants formulate hypotheses about the expected meaning of a pictogram are thus preferred, even though determining if an answer is correct or wrong can ultimately depend on subjective judgments. The latest published ISO testing procedure [21] elects the most comprehensible icon among three variants for the same referent, by calculating the highest mean percentage of correct interpretations. Acceptance criteria have been set to 66% of correct answers to declare a public sign understandable and 86% for safety signs. In other methods [12,14], participants simply choose the best symbol among multiple candidates for a specific referent.

Some test procedures [21] require to provide a verbal or visual description of the proximate or the environmental context where the symbol is expected to be used (e.g. Fig. 7), thus restricting the number of possible interpretations. This would reflect real-world understandability and enhance the ecological validity of the test [48]. Otherwise, as anticipated earlier, low comprehension rates would wrongly indicate that an icon is not understandable.

As shown at the end of Sect. 6, comprehensibility is impacted by other dimensions: faster and more accurate comprehension at first exposures directly depends on the icon's *concreteness*, the *semantic distance* between icon and referent, and the interpreter's *familiarity* with both pictogram and meaning. It is not strictly necessary to assess such dimensions (although this can be done through *e.g.*, subjective ratings [27]). However, should such properties not be at least considered in a comprehensibility test, its outcomes might indicate that some icons

(a) Padlock symbol

(b) Padlock symbol's context

**Fig. 7.** In a test, the provision of the intended context of use must not be misleading nor revelatory of the intended meaning [21]

must be discarded because their meaning is not immediately evident. Yet, when icons are abstract, arbitrary, or unfamiliar, meaning must be learned rather than deduced [47]. To obviate such problems, another ISO standard [22] introduces two consequent phases of testing. The first part consists in a familiarity training: test participants learn a list of concepts and their definitions. The second part tests the comprehensibility of graphical symbols as an association test between one symbol and six learned definitions.

**Learnability.** For the reasons explained above, it can be meaningful to measure ease of learning of an icon set [10]. For instance, longitudinal studies quantify speed of learning over a period of time, by monitoring number and frequency of exposure to the symbol before it is retained, and the evolution of accuracy of answers.

**Culture-Independence.** Unless symbols are made for a specific national audience, it is recommended that the testing is carried out in more than one nation and with more than one linguistic community. This ultimately impacts the number of participants: e.g. ISO standard for legibility [20] provides for 25 participants from one country, while ISO standard for comprehensibility requires 50 participants for each variant in each country [21].

**Discriminability.** Determining how easily one icon is discerned from another can be assessed through an association test between one or more icons and one or more referents. Not only the number of correct interpretations, but also the consistency of wrong associations can reveal which pictograms resemble too much for being used in the same context. As Fig. 8 shows, a low level of discriminability can also reflect similarity of the underlying concepts. This dimension is pivotal because it ultimately impacts *comprehensibility*.

**Evaluation of Icons' Function in the Context of Use.** According to the function they assume in a specific context (see Sect. 5), it should be determined if the icons are able to convey their intended meaning and enable the task they were designed for. For instance, if the icons are used as information markers in

(a) Right to object to processing           (b) Right to restrict the processing

**Fig. 8.** These two icons from [39] might be easily confused because of the similarity of their design and concept

privacy policies to enhance information finding, than classical usability tests can determine whether participants can find specific pieces of information faster, with more accuracy and with more satisfaction (and other relevant UX dimensions) [30], with respect to a pure-text document. If the icons are rather used as alert icons, than evaluation should focus on their ability to convey a sense of *hazard* and to stand out from the rest of the information (*i.e.*, *visibility*). Comparing the comprehensibility of a document enriched by icons with a pure textual document can indicate if they do improve understanding - or if their function is rather that of attracting attention, supporting memory, etc. This point is key to determine whether the data protection icons can achieve the transparency goals envisaged by the law-makers.

## 8    Discussion

At the end of this preliminary exploration of icons' evaluation methods, it becomes evident that there are a number of dimensions that should be embedded during icon design and a number of issues with established practices that are commented in the following.

The lack of objectivity in assessing answers to open questions concerning comprehensibility constitutes a first obstacle to the development of a reliable methodology. It can be however counterbalanced with inter-evaluator agreement measures and with the *a priori* establishment of a rigid set of acceptable answers, *e.g.*, through a pilot test. Yet, since it is hard to foresee the entire set of potential answers, a solid policy for such cases should also be set up. Interpretation tests can also be complemented with cognitive interviews to elicit further responding and thus attain higher comprehension rates [47]. Moreover, given the great quantity of privacy icon sets, electing the best alternative is also viable, provided that style uniformity is ensured to avoid choices based on aesthetic judgments rather than perceived efficacy.

Acceptance rates proposed by ISO also pose a dilemma: the established percentages are arbitrary and shall be rather adjusted to the gravity of the consequences of misinterpretation [7]. Since wrong understanding of an icon related to data processing has legal consequences for the data subject, it can be arguably proposed to adopt strict criteria of acceptance.

Users' characteristics also play an important role. In the view of international standardization, test participants should ideally be representative of the

European population of data subjects. Whether tests should be carried out in every single Member State is open to discussion. Yet, given the pivotal role of familiarity, different levels of education, technology expertise, age, and even privacy awareness should be represented. Moreover, the meaningfulness of the icon set mostly depends on individual preferences and concerns. Although comprehensibility tests should be ideally carried out both on paper and on screen, the second option can reach a higher and more diverse number of participants. One first step in this direction has been the recent creation of the Privacy Icons Forum[9], a platform that promotes best practices and the exchange of results among projects and institutions that research, develop and design privacy icons worldwide.

As seen earlier, a specific methodology for testing symbols with unfamiliar referents exists [22]. However, it is unclear how such tests can be carried out for longer lists of referents without causing user fatigue, which would compromise the soundness of test results. Indeed, it is recommended [20] to show no more than 15 symbols per respondent. Moreover, the familiarization procedure does not mirror realistic conditions: the majority of data subjects are not explicitly educated about the privacy, protection and security of data. To overcome the familiarity issue, one might resort to data protection experts—however, this would not mirror the intended audience of the icon set. For such reasons, longitudinal studies where ease of learning in context is observed should be preferred. Indeed, by drawing a parallel with familiarization processes with new GUIs, it is through repeated experience that people improve comprehension accuracy and speed on task. There is no reason why this should not apply to interfaces to the law, like legal documents, consent requests or privacy dashboards.

Finally, observations on concreteness, complexity, familiarity and style should influence icon design rather than icon evaluation, in order to avoid effortful testing that ultimately discovers obvious limitations of the icon set. For example, [50] found that adding complexity to an icon can lead to more precise interpretations. However, in realistic conditions of exposure, where an icon is quickly perceived rather than attentively observed, visual complexity might actually hamper legibility and recognition [14]. Besides, this result is not generalizable to symbols that must be recognized even if displayed at small size, e.g., few pixels of al screen. In the context of digital privacy, this concern is of utmost importance. Therefore, whereas it is self-evident that adding details sharpens comprehension, the real conundrum is the opposite, namely the extent to which an icon can be simplified without losing the ability to convey its meaning. Depending on the type of support and the icon function, the same symbol must be adapted to different sizes (see e.g. Google's or Apple's design guidelines on iconography [2,16]). Moreover, it should be possible to adjust the symbols to a specific graphical house style without altering their recognizability: the icons should be adopted by services with strong brand identity to ensure widespread adoption

---

[9] https://www.privacyiconsforum.eu/. The authors of this article are among the founding members.

and ultimately international standardization. This controversial point still needs to be carefully addressed and discussed with relevant stakeholders.

## 9    Conclusions and Future Work

This article has been motivated by the will of understanding under which conditions icons can support transparency of communication about data processing in an "easily visible, intelligible and clearly legible" manner, as envisaged by the GDPR's Art. 12. Thus, we collected and defined several properties that are relevant to evaluate icons and icon sets in correspondence with GDPR's requirements. Our list can be expanded and modified as the research progresses.

We presented several evaluation measures and critically discussed their appropriateness for the context of data protection. The properties we presented are not yet organized in a taxonomy with relations and dependencies, nor have we defined precise metrics for each of them: this constitutes future work. In the view of EU standardization and in support of the European Commission preparatory work, future research will tentatively provide a holistic evaluation methodology with precise metrics to assess the efficacy of icons as standalone elements and as functional elements in determined contexts of use. Ideally, such methodology will help the many entities that have designed, or are designing, data protection icon sets to empirically validate their work. Indeed, the necessary condition for indicators of on-line privacy and transparency to gain traction is, according to Reidenberg *et al.* [36], the development of evaluation criteria, the production of objective and demonstrable output, and the reliable proof of intelligibility and accessibility.

The research outlined in these pages has scientific and practical relevance even beyond the GDPR's scope. Both the current proposal for an ePrivacy Regulation and the US Federal Trade Commission recommend the use of icons to increase transparency [13]. Requirements on standardised templates and visual indicators to enhance information transparency have been advanced in consumer protection (*i.e.*, Consumers' Rights Directive) and in the insurance sector (*i.e.*, Directive on Insurance Distribution). The definition of design and evaluation guidelines for icons can also be usefully applied to other domains, *e.g.*, in the communication of security and privacy risks.

## References

1. Albrecht, J.P.: REPORT - on the proposal for a regulation of the European parliament and of the council on the protection of individuals with regard to the processing of personal data and on the free movement of such data (General Data Protection Regulation). Technical report. A7–0402/2013, European Parliament. Committee on Civil Liberties, Justice and Home Affairs (2013)
2. Apple: Human Interface Guidelines. https://developer.apple.com/design/human-interface-guidelines/

3. Arledge, C.P.: Filled-in vs. outline icons: the impact of icon style on usability. Ph.D. thesis, School of Information and Library Science of the University of North Carolina at Chapel Hill (2014)
4. Article 29 Data Protection Working Party: Opinion 15/2011 on the Definition of Consent WP187 (2011)
5. Article 29 Data Protection Working Party: Guidelines on transparency under regulation 2016/679, 17/EN WP260 rev.01 (2018)
6. Berlin Open Lab: privacy icons workshops (13 Mai und 15 Mai 2019). https://www.privacy-icons.info/
7. Boersema, T., Adams, A.S.: Does My Symbol Sign Work? Information Design: Research and Practice, p. 303. Taylor & Francis Group, Routledege (2017)
8. Boersema, T., Adams, A.S.: International standards for designing and testing graphical symbols. In: Information Design: Research and Practice (2017)
9. Bresciani, S., Eppler, M.J.: The pitfalls of visual representations: a review and classification of common errors made while designing and interpreting visualizations. SAGE Open 5(4), 1–14 (2015)
10. Dewar, R.: Design and evaluation of public information symbols. In: Zwaga, H., Boersema, T., Hoonhout, H. (eds.) Visual Information for Everyday Use: Design and Research Perspectives, Ch. 23, pp. 285–303. Taylor and Francis, London (1999)
11. Efroni, Z., Metzger, J., Mischau, L., Schirmbeck, M.: Privacy icons: a risk-based approach to visualisation of data processing. Euro. Data Prot. Law Rev. 3, 352 (2019)
12. ETSI (European Telecommunications Standards Institute): Human Factors (HF); Framework for the Development, Evaluation and Selection of Graphical Symbols EG 201 379 V1.1.1 (1998-12) (1998)
13. Federal Trade Commission: Mobile privacy disclosures: building trust through transparency. Technical report, Federal Trade Commission - Staff Report (2013)
14. Fontaine, L., Fernandes, O., McCormick, K., Middleton, D.: Universal symbols in health care - phase 2: symbol design research report. Technical report, Hablamos Juntos/SEGD (2010)
15. Ghayas, S., Sulaiman, S., Khan, M., Jaafar, J.: The effects of icon characteristics on users' perception. In: Zaman, H.B., Robinson, P., Olivier, P., Shih, T.K., Velastin, S. (eds.) IVIC 2013. LNCS, vol. 8237, pp. 652–663. Springer, Cham (2013). https://doi.org/10.1007/978-3-319-02958-0_59
16. Google: Material design. https://material.io/design/
17. Graf, C., Hochleitner, C., Wolkerstorfer, P., Angulo, J., Fischer-Hübner, S., Wästlund, E.: Final HCI research project. Technical report, PrimeLife Consortium (2011)
18. Haapio, H., Passera, S.: Contracts as interfaces: exploring visual representation patterns in contract design. In: Legal Informatics. Cambridge University Press, Cambridge (2017)
19. Iannella, R., Finden, A.: Privacy awareness: icons and expression for social networks. In: Proceedings of the 8th Virtual Goods Workshop and the 6th ODRL Workshop, pp. 1–15 (2010)
20. International Organization for Standardization: ISO 9186.2008:2. Graphical symbols - Test methods - Methods for Testing Perceptual Quality (2008)
21. International Organization for Standardization: ISO 9186–1:2014. Graphical symbols - Test methods - Part 1: Method for testing comprehensibility (2014)
22. International Organization for Standardization: ISO 9186–3:2014. Graphical symbols – Test methods Part 3: Method for testing symbol referent association (2014)

23. Isherwood, S.J., McDougall, S.J., Curry, M.B.: Icon identification in context: the changing role of icon characteristics with user experience. Hum. Factors J. Hum. Factors Ergon. Soc. **49**(3), 465–476 (2007)
24. Madigan, S.: Picture memory. Imagery, memory and cognition, pp. 65–89 (2014)
25. Malamed, C.: Visual Language for Designers: Principles for Creating Graphics that People Understand. Rockport Publishers, Beverly (2009)
26. Marom-Tock, Y., Goldschmidt, G.: Design for safety: symbol genre in safety signs. In: Proceedings of IASDR2011, the 4th World Conference on Design Research (2011)
27. Mcdougall, S.J., Curry, M.B., de Bruijn, O.: Measuring symbol and icon characteristics: norms for concreteness, complexity, meaningfulness, familiarity, and semantic distance for 239 symbols. Behav. Res. Methods Instrum. Comput. **31**(3), 487–519 (1999)
28. Moriarty, S.E.: The symbiotics of semiotics and visual communication. J. Vis. Literacy **22**(1), 19–28 (2002)
29. Nurse, J.R., Creese, S., Goldsmith, M., Lamberts, K.: Guidelines for usable cybersecurity: past and present. In: 2011 Third International Workshop on Cyberspace Safety and Security (CSS), pp. 21–26. IEEE (2011)
30. Passera, S.: Beyond the wall of text: how information design can make contracts user-friendly. In: Marcus, A. (ed.) DUXU 2015. LNCS, vol. 9187, pp. 341–352. Springer, Cham (2015). https://doi.org/10.1007/978-3-319-20898-5_33
31. Peirce, C.S.: Logic as semiotic: the theory of signs. Philosophical Writings (1902)
32. Pettersson, J.S.: A brief evaluation of icons in the first reading of the European parliament on COM (2012) 0011. In: Camenisch, J., Fischer-Hübner, S., Hansen, M. (eds.) Privacy and Identity 2014. IAICT, vol. 457, pp. 125–135. Springer, Cham (2015). https://doi.org/10.1007/978-3-319-18621-4_9
33. Popova, M.: Mozilla's privacy icons: a Visual language for privacy data rights (2011). http://bigthink.com/design-for-good/mozillas-privacy-icons-a-visual-language-for-data-rights
34. Privacy Tech: Privacy icons. https://www.privacytech.fr/privacy-icons/
35. Ramírez, R.: Reviewing open-access icons for emergency: a case study testing meaning performance in Guemil. Visible Lang. **52**(2), 32–55 (2018)
36. Reidenberg, J.R., Russell, N.C., Herta, V., Sierra-Rocafort, W., Norton, T.: Trustworthy privacy indicators: grades, labels, certifications and dashboards. Wash. Univ. Law Rev. **96**(6), 1409 (2019)
37. Rossi, A.: Legal design for the general data protection regulation. A methodology for the visualization and communication of legal concepts, Dissertation thesis (2019). http://amsdottorato.unibo.it/9060/
38. Rossi, A., Palmirani, M.: A visualization approach for adaptive consent in the European data protection framework. In: Parycek, P., Edelmann, N. (eds.) Proceedings of the 7th International Conference for E-Democracy and Open Government, CeDEM 2017, pp. 159–170. Edition Donau-Universität Krems, Krems (2017)
39. Rossi, A., Palmirani, M.: DaPIS: an ontology-based data protection icon set. In: Peruginelli, G., Faro, S. (eds.) Knowledge of the Law in the Big Data Age. Frontiers in Artificial Intelligence and Applications, vol. 317. IOS Press (2019)
40. Rossi, A., Palmirani, M.: What's in an icon? Promises and pitfalls of data protection iconography. In: Leenes, R., Hallinan, D., Gutwirth, S., Hert, P.D. (eds.) Data Protection and Privacy: Data Protection and Democracy. Hart Publishing (2020)

41. Specht, L.u.B.: Handbuch Datenrecht in der Digitalisierung, chap. Informationsvermittlung durch standardisierte Bildsymbole - Ein Weg aus dem Privacy Paradox? Erich Schmidt Verlag (2020). https://esv.info/lp/datenrecht/
42. Tesfay, W.B., Hofmann, P., Nakamura, T., Kiyomoto, S., Serna, J.: PrivacyGuide: towards an implementation of the EU GDPR on internet privacy policy evaluation. In: Proceedings of the Fourth ACM International Workshop on Security and Privacy Analytics, pp. 15–21. ACM (2018)
43. Tijus, C., Barcenilla, J., De Lavalette, B.C., Meunier, J.G.: The design, understanding and usage of pictograms. In: Written Documents in the Workplace, pp. 17–31. Brill (2007)
44. da Vinci, L.: Trattato della pittura (1540), from Leonardo da Vinci's Paragone: a critical interpretation with a new edition of the text in the Codex Urbinas, Farago C. J. (1992)
45. Waller, R., Waller, J., Haapio, H., Crag, G., Morrisseau, S.: Cooperation through clarity: designing simplified contracts. J. Strateg. Contracting Negot. 2(1–2), 48–68 (2016)
46. Wogalter, M.S.: Factors influencing the effectiveness of warnings. In: Visual Information for Everyday Use, pp. 127–144. CRC Press (2014)
47. Wogalter, M.S., Silver, N.C., Leonard, S.D., Zaikina, H.: Handbook of warnings, chap. Warning symbols, pp. 159–176. Lawrence Erlbaum Associates, Mahwah (2006)
48. Wolff, J.S., Wogalter, M.S.: Comprehension of pictorial symbols: effects of context and test method. Human Fact. 40(2), 173–186 (1998)
49. Young, S.L., Wogalter, M.S.: Predictors of pictorial symbol comprehension. Inf. Des. J. 10(2), 124–132 (2000)
50. Zender, M.: Advancing icon design for global nonverbal communication: or what does the wordbow' mean? Visible Lang. 40(2), 177 (2006)
51. Zender, M., Mejia, M.: Improving icon design: through focus on the role of individual symbols in the construction of meaning. Visible Lang. 47(1), 66–89 (2013)

# Author Index

.

Printed in the United States
by Baker & Taylor Publisher Services